Data for Decisions

INFORMATION STRATEGIES FOR POLICYMAKERS

Data for Decisions

INFORMATION STRATEGIES FOR POLICYMAKERS

DAVID C. HOAGLIN

RICHARD J. LIGHT

BUCKNAM McPEEK

FREDERICK MOSTELLER

MICHAEL A. STOTO

Abt Books

CAMBRIDGE, MASSACHUSETTS

Library of Congress Cataloging in Publication Data
Main entry under title:

Data for decisions.

Includes bibliographies and index.
1. Policy sciences—Research. 2. Social sciences—
Research. I. Hoaglin, D. C.
H97.D37   001.4'2   82-1629
ISBN 0-89011-567-2   AACR2

© Abt Associates Inc., 1982

Printed in the United States of America

To the memory of John P. Gilbert

Contents

Examples of Data Collection
and Application

Preface

Policymakers translate information into action. Sometimes they must commission others to gather and summarize data on an issue. Often they must act in the face of conflicting information. To gauge the quality and relevance of the information, they need to know the properties of the various data-gathering methods. In a nontechnical but policy-oriented way, this book summarizes the different methods of acquiring information for policy and presents their strengths and weaknesses.

For each method, we provide a checklist of critical questions. The answers will give a feeling about the quality of a study and its appropriateness for the problem at hand. Policymakers care about the quality of a study, not only because they want to make wise decisions, but also because they have to defend decisions supported or opposed by the study.

This book is intended for professional policymakers and their supporting staffs and for others who commission and interpret information-gathering activities. It is also directed toward those who supply information—research agencies and workers in the field—that they may better serve policy needs. In addition, students of policy and management should find the book helpful.

Our purpose is to provide a basis for a reasoned assessment of the value of data gathered for a policy study, using criteria that can be applied to a completed study or to one being planned. We provide concrete examples for illustration but do not tell how to carry out each type of study in technical detail. This is primarily a "what is it" and a "what could best answer the question" book, not a "how to do it" book. We offer methods of gathering information rather than methods of analysis.

Policymakers gather information from many sources in a variety of ways. Obviously, they choose methods that enlighten them about the problem under study, whether welfare, defense, education, or tax reform. Beyond this, the methods have differing abilities to answer three key questions: "How does it work?", "What is the state of the world?", and "What will happen?". Without turning policymakers into experts in carrying out these methods, this book indicates which methods solve what problems. Ordinarily, several information-gathering methods can be used to answer a key question, and a good choice depends on knowing their strengths and weaknesses.

Because each information-gathering method points primarily at answering one of the above three key questions, the book has three main parts:

√ cause and effect (Chapters 2 through 4),

√ measuring the status quo (Chapters 5 through 10),

√ predicting the future (Chapters 11 through 14).

Answering the question "What will happen?" requires us to combine ideas of cause and effect with information about the status quo and then to apply forecasting methods.

Each chapter addresses a single method of data collection. We have tried to make the chapters self-contained so that they can be consulted separately; however, some material overlaps. For example, experiments and observational studies share common features. In the checklists, although most questions deal with a specific data-gathering method, some questions may apply to several methods. Usually one will need to evaluate several alternatives rather than just a single type of study design. In the front of the book a list of examples together with their position in the book may help the reader rediscover an illustration.

By and large, the methods chapters can be read in any order, but it is helpful to read the experiments chapter first. The short chapters on economic experiments (an especially technical chapter), panel and longitudinal studies, computerized information sources, and mathematical models are extensions of the chapters that immediately precede them. The discussion of management records relies on the observational studies chapter.

Within the first three parts of the book, the chapters deal with specific methods. The primary methods chapters (2, 4, 5, 7, 8, 11, 12, and 14) have a special organization. After a brief introduction, most discuss the following:

√ examples of use,

√ features,

√ what the method is not,

√ strengthening devices,

√ merits,

√ weaknesses,

√ checklist for assessing the quality of a study,

√ policy implications,

√ conclusions.

For some methods, the merits turn out to be the mirror images of the weaknesses, and then these two sections are combined.

Short chapters deal with special issues and important themes in information policy—checking for mistakes and frauds, privacy and confidentiality, questions common to all data-gathering methods, and strengthening our information system.

Acknowledgments

Our coworker, John P. Gilbert, participated in planning and in writing early drafts of some of these chapters before his death in January 1980. Dedicating this book to him cannot adequately reflect how much we miss his wit, wisdom, and good fellowship. Since we all had worked with him in a variety of projects, and had planned many more, his loss was not only a setback to this book but also a terrible blow to a collection of research programs in which John played key roles.

We owe a special debt to Laurence Lynn because his work for the National Academy of Sciences–National Research Council on knowledge acquisition for policy suggested to us the need for this book.

Lincoln Moses advised us about the sections dealing with policy issues. Dorothy Rice gave us a great boost by reorienting our plan for the chapter on official statistics. Donald Feeney prepared several valuable examples. Allen Hammond gave us organizational and stylistic advice. Robert Boruch's periodic letters on random topics kept us abreast of materials that have contributed in several places. Howard Raiffa suggested the Benjamin Franklin letter.

Anne Bigelow did the research leading to the chapter on data bases and helped prepare the bibliography and the manuscript.

Donald Searls, Nancy Burton, and Wayne Martin of National Assessment of Educational Progress supplied us with materials.

In addition to managing the preparation of the manuscript and dealing with so many authors, Marjorie Olson contributed special studies in the chapters on case studies and on introspection and advice. Cleo Youtz helped with the bibliographic work. Mary Naus, Connie Tuton, and Gertrude Shaw assisted in preparing the manuscript.

The Surgery Group of the Faculty Seminar at the Harvard School of Public Health offered criticism and advice on some chapters, and so special thanks go to John Bailar, Benjamin Barnes, Gregg Dinse, David Dorer, John Hedley-Whyte, Ellen Hertzmark, Harmon Jordan, Philip Lavori, Robert Lew, Alan Lisbon, Thomas Louis, Kay Patterson, Jane Teas, and Grace Wyshak.

Miriam Green Hurley, Helen McPeek, and Miles McPeek kindly reviewed the final draft of the manuscript.

The cartoons and graphics were supervised by Linda Clement at Abt Associates. The cartoons concerning representative sampling were drawn by Martha Cain and appear here by permission of the editors of the *International Statistical Review*. We appreciate the advice on artwork given by Clark Abt, Robert Erwin, and David Napior.

Support for the project came in part from the National Science Foundation through grant SES75-15702 to Harvard University.

David C. Hoaglin
Richard J. Light
Bucknam McPeek
Frederick Mosteller
Michael A. Stoto

Cambridge, Massachusetts
January 1982

CHAPTER 1

Overview

On March 5, 1975, Russell Train, administrator of the Environmental Protection Agency (EPA), had to make a final decision on the automobile industry's request to postpone the imposition of emission standards (Lynn 1980). In 1970, under the leadership of Senator Edmund Muskie, Congress had amended the Clean Air Act of 1963 to speed up the timetable for the imposition of strict automobile emissions standards for hydrocarbons, carbon monoxide, and nitrogen oxides to the 1975 model year. After an initial refusal, EPA administrator William Ruckelshaus granted a one-year extension in 1973. Congress extended the deadline again in 1974, in response to the Arab oil boycott. In the meantime, H. L. Misch, Ford Motor Company Vice-President for Environmental and Safety Engineering, told the EPA that catalytic converters, the main technology chosen by the auto industry to reduce emissions, could themselves indirectly produce sulphates, another form of pollutant. In 1975 Ford, Chrysler, and General Motors asked the EPA to extend the deadlines for one more year.

After a final meeting with Roger Strelow, Assistant Administrator for Air and Waste Management, and other advisers, Train considered the pros and cons of another postponement. Were the health effects of sulphates serious enough to warrant a further delay in the standards? Could alternative technologies be developed? Could he enforce the standards without the cooperation of the auto industry? How should his decision fit in with the economic and energy policies of President Ford and not anger Senator Muskie or other EPA congressional allies?

The technical aspects of the problem—the relative risks and benefits of catalytic converters, and the possibility of alternatives—
strongly influenced Train's final decision. He cared not only about
making the "right" decision, but also about justifying this move to
Congress, the public, environmentalists, and the auto industry. A few
months earlier, Dr. John Moran of the EPA's research facility in Dur-
ham, North Carolina, had produced an issue paper summarizing the
technical information available at the time of Train's decision. The information was obtained in diverse ways from many sources. This en-
semble of information, which used most of the techniques discussed in
this book, helped Train make his final decision. Let us examine what
was available to the EPA administrator.

The chemistry of catalytic converters and the production of sulphates were not well understood. *Experiments* on prototype automobiles had shed some light on how the type of catalyst and the sulphur
content of gasoline influenced the amount of sulphates emitted. Later
experiments on production automobiles told more about emissions
under actual operating conditions.

Health effects depend on the exposure of humans to sulphates.
Two basic approaches assessed how the amount of human exposure
depends on the amount of sulphates produced. Physical activity models use computers and *mathematical models* to simulate the dispersal
of sulphates in the atmosphere near roads and freeways. These *simulations*, of course, depend on assumptions about the amount of traffic,
on the configuration of roads and surrounding buildings and land, and
on wind conditions. The calculations lead to exposure estimates for
drivers under certain conditions. Surrogate models rely on estimates
of exposure to chemicals that are dispersed in a manner similar to sulphates. Environmental scientists essentially use *sampling methods* to
determine atmospheric concentrations of various pollutants near different types of roads under various traffic and weather conditions.

Estimates of the health effects of exposure to sulphates come from
both *experiments* and *observational studies.* Many studies have documented the effect of sulphates on animals and human volunteers. For
instance, the EPA's Community Health and Environmental Surveil-
lance System (CHESS) relates health outcomes to environmental exposure in several urban areas.

Train's decision rested on estimates of the benefits of the catalytic
converter in reducing emissions of hydrocarbons, carbon monoxide,
and nitrogen oxides—the original aim of the Clean Air Act. Relatively
strict emissions standards had been in effect in California, so that this
state offered a *natural experiment.*

The decision to extend the deadlines also depended on such variables as the amount of driving and the relative number of old and new automobiles on the road in the years after the standards would go into effect. *Official statistics* provided historical and baseline levels of these variables, and *forecasting techniques* extended the trends into the future.

Finally, alternatives to the proposed catalytic converters had to be considered. They ranged from minor modification of the catalysts or the sulphur content of fuel to major modifications of the internal combustion engine. Train had to rely on the *advice of experts* to develop feasible alternatives.

Train's decision could not ignore the economic effects of a setback to the automobile industry; his decision came during the severe economic slump of 1975. Nor could he ignore the administration's policies and previous stands on energy and the environment. But Train's final decision—to extend the deadline—relied on information from experiments, simulation models, sampling methods, observational studies, natural experiments, official statistics, forecasts, and the advice of experts, each with its inherent benefits and shortcomings.

Policymakers navigate a course through a sea of decisions. They choose a strategy for action. A problem arises. After assessing it, they gather information to try to understand it, its causes, and contributing factors.

CAUSE AND EFFECT: HOW DOES IT WORK?

Causation is important because policymakers intervene, and they want to know the effect of their intervention. Beyond a description of a program and its outcome, policymakers want to know whether what was done produced the desired effect and, if so, how much effect it produced. (Policymakers have other important concerns too: the political climate, the motivation for the project as perceived by the public, and the administrative effectiveness of the program staff.)

As Hume and other philosophers have unkindly pointed out, we can never prove the existence of a causal connection between two events in the strict, logical way we can prove a mathematical theorem. In practical work we also know that folk wisdom about causes may be mistaken. We can, nevertheless, adduce many different kinds of evidence to help nail causes down.

Policymakers try to link interventions and outcomes. Did an intervention lead to a change in outcome? For example, did changing the national speed limit from an average of 70 miles per hour to 55 miles per hour, just after the 1974 OPEC oil embargo, reduce highway traffic fatalities? Fatalities decreased; was this due to the lower speed limit?

Sometimes people regard innovations as similar to plumbing projects. Plumbers know the properties of pipes, how water runs, and so on. They design a system, try it out, and if it works, fine. They never think of doing a trial of different techniques because they know the dynamics of the system. Unfortunately, the dynamics in a social policy situation are rarely so clear. We cannot be as confident as plumbers.

Before we can establish causation, we have to know whether the program can be put in place. Demonstrations are new activities or programs, usually viewed as prototypes of larger scale activities to follow. They are undertaken first to see if a new program can be implemented. For example, in Massachusetts the Brookline Early Education Project, sponsored by the Carnegie Corporation and the Robert Wood Johnson Foundation, proposed to improve school performance of young children by offering families comprehensive diagnostic and educational services from the birth of their child onward. No one knew whether public school staff could organize themselves to deliver such services, and whether families would participate. The services were introduced, and about 40 percent of the eligible families agreed to take part. This indicated that such a program could take hold in the pilot community. Without guaranteeing that the services would work elsewhere, the pilot program demonstrated that it is possible, under the right set of circumstances, to mount such an effort.

Once we know that a program can be installed, we may have questions about its consequences. We address these questions in the cause-and-effect chapters on controlled experiments and comparative observational studies.

Controlled Experiments

If two or more programs are to be compared, we may try them out by applying them to different groups of people or institutions. We call the programs "treatments"; some are innovations, like food stamps or the negative income tax.

When the investigator controls the assignment of competing treatments to experimental groups drawn from a larger population, the investigation is called a controlled trial. If well executed, such a trial provides the strongest evidence available for evaluating the relative effectiveness of the treatments or interventions tested.

To understand the effects of a change in a program or other treatment, it is necessary to make the change and observe the effects in a controlled, systematic way. Even our language shows it: "The proof of the pudding is in the eating."

As an example, in a national experiment to see whether the Salk vaccine was effective in preventing poliomyelitis (Meier 1972), children were randomly selected to receive an injection of either the vaccine or a harmless saline solution. Without such field trials, the effectiveness of new therapies is usually difficult to appraise. The saline solution was used so that a group of children just like those who received the vaccine underwent a treatment process but did not receive the vaccine. The physicians did not know which children were actually receiving the vaccine. If they had known, they would have been more likely to report bad side effects for those vaccinated and to attribute these effects to the vaccine, even if they occurred equally often in unvaccinated children. Similarly, if only volunteers had been injected, the groups might not have been comparable, because better educated groups are known to volunteer more and also are more likely to get polio than less educated groups.

Over the last fifty years, systematic, controlled experiments have become increasingly common in medicine, law, government, education, and social welfare programs. In this period we have learned much about avoiding pitfalls in their execution. Of course, trials are as old as history. The Bible records a nutritional experiment in the story of Daniel and the eunuch at the Court of Nebuchadnezzar.

Experimentation may be expensive, difficult, and occasionally not feasible. Perhaps ethical constraints intervene, or perhaps time or financial limitations make it impractical. A variety of other strategies give information about what happens after a treatment is applied. Each strategy may say something about the effectiveness of a policy. Nonetheless, the controlled experiment remains our primary means of linking cause with effect, and its reliability rests mainly on the strength of the control. Only to the extent that the experimental group is similar to the control group will differences in outcome illustrate the role of the causal factor. On rare occasions, natural groups may be found which seem to be similar in all respects except for degree of exposure to a policy or treatment. This situation is called a "natural experiment," and a study of these natural groups may establish causal association. The strength of this association rests on the similarity between the natural groups.

Comparative Observational Studies

When a government reform introduces an innovation to a whole population, we often ask how present results compare with former ones. We call this situation a quasi-experiment. To return to the example used earlier, when a new highway speed law is introduced, we compare past and present fatality rates. This form of investigation lacks background control, because the times when the new law and the old law operate are not identical—the weather may have been different, the population may have changed, or the highways themselves may have changed. In many areas of policy research, the year-to-year variation in outcome or performance is large. Thus, the quasi-experiment has the strength that the new treatment is deliberately installed, but the weakness that the circumstances to be compared, before and after, are not identical in other respects.

Observational studies can sometimes supply information about causation, as well as about levels of performance, outcome, and the natural history of a process. An example occurs when the causal link is short and direct. When we have a well-verified theory that can be applied, or when the effect is immediate and substantial in the absence of other reasonable explanations, observational studies may provide

DANIEL'S NUTRITION EXPERIMENT

My topic here is innovation and evaluation. I begin with an early experiment in nutrition. It was designed by Daniel of the Lions' Den, but for humans rather than lions. Daniel was held hostage in Nebuchadnezzar's court and, possibly for religious reasons, disapproved of the rich food, wine, and meat served there. The eunuch in charge feared for his own head if he were to give Daniel and his three friends merely the simple Judean vegetable fare called pulse (such as peas and beans). Daniel asked for a 10-day trial and promised to turn to the court's diet if the Judean hostages weren't then as healthy as the others. To turn to a translation of the original article, Daniel I:12–15 (*The Holy Bible*, King James Version):

"Prove thy servants, I beseech thee, ten days; and let them give us pulse to eat, and water to drink.

Then let our countenances be looked upon before thee, and the countenance of the children that eat of the portion of the king's meat: and as thou seest, deal with thy servants.

So he [the eunuch] consented to them in this matter, and proved them ten days.

And at the end of ten days, their countenances appeared fairer and fatter in flesh than all the children which did eat the portion of the king's meat."

Had this study been submitted as a report to *Science*, the reviewer might make the following remarks. First, there is no sampling problem because Daniel needed only to prove that he and his three friends were better off with the diet. He did not have to make the generalization to, say, the entire population of Judea or the human race. This is unusual because ordinarily we *are* trying to make such generalizations. For Daniel it was fortunate as well, because with such a small sample—Daniel, Shadrach, Meshach, and Abednego—the eunuch would have had to insist on using Student's t-test, and this would not be invented for another 2500 years, almost exactly.

Second, the length of the trial, 10 days, seems short for a nutrition experiment.

Third, the end point "fairer and fatter in flesh" seems not well defined. Other translations speak of "sleeker," which also is vague.

From the eunuch's point of view, the diet of pulse was an innovation, while the court's regular diet was the standard. And so Daniel designed a comparative experiment, an early evaluation of an innovation.

From F. Mosteller, Innovation and Evaluation, *Science* 211: 881–886, 1981, p. 881. Copyright 1981 by the American Association for the Advancement of Science. Reprinted with permission.

causal explanations. For example, when a previously rare event occurs frequently following the introduction of a new policy, such as deformities of limbs in babies whose mothers took the drug thalidomide during pregnancy, the unusual outcome compels us to accept a causal argument.

MEASURING THE STATUS QUO: WHAT IS THE STATE OF THE WORLD?

Not all policy information concerns effectiveness, causation, or the future. Frequently the question is, what exists today? Policy formulation depends a great deal on background information. What is the population of the Northeast? How much did welfare cost the Commonwealth of Massachusetts in 1981? How many additional people would be eligible if the requirements for entering a program were changed? How many of the potentially eligible would participate? These questions and many like them are largely answered by a knowledge of the present situation. Some important mechanisms for gathering current data are censuses, sample surveys, case studies, official statistics, and management records.

Censuses

A census examines every member of a population. Sometimes this may mean simply counting the members. In other instances we ask more elaborate questions. Since the late 1800s, the cost and complexity of conducting a census of large groups have led to investigations covering only parts of the population and, in the last fifty years, to extensive use of modern sample surveys, especially when considerable information is required from each individual or institution. The major strength of the census is its ability to produce information for small subpopulations.

Sample Surveys

In sample surveys, some individuals from a population are chosen to be in the sample and some are not. If a perfect census would not answer the questions being addressed, then neither will a sample survey. The decision maker wants to know the responses (properties) of all individuals in the population or those in subgroups of the population. The purpose is not to determine the treatment effect of inclusion in the sample, but usually to see what the whole population is like or how groups in the population differ. For example, we might compare age groups with respect to the percentage owning homes.

Censuses and sample surveys sometimes reveal situations in which nature seems to have performed an experiment for us. Do the people exposed to more sunshine get more skin cancer? We may be able to investigate the question by conducting a survey, but this is not a comparative experiment. We can learn a great deal about the prevalence or distribution of cancer and of sunshine, but because we cannot control the assignment of individuals to the treatment (exposure to the sun), we must worry about many other effects that confuse the picture. Perhaps the diet, the dress, or the ethnicity of people in different parts of the world is the primary cause of skin cancer, rather than the amount of exposure to sunshine, or perhaps the equatorial races have become genetically less susceptible to the carcinogenic effects of sunshine.

If we want to know about the present, we can look at a single point in time, as in the simplest census or sample survey. In other situations we want several looks. Much of the value of the U.S. census in 1980 comes from the fact that the government has taken a census every ten years since 1790. While the questions vary slightly from year to year, the continuity is sufficient to compare the results of the 1980 census with those of some previous censuses. For example, the 1980 census gives us the population of the state of New York in 1980, but the fact that we can also compare this figure with data for New York in 1960 and 1970 makes the 1980 census even more useful. A repeated census can be thought of as a time series: the same questions are asked repeatedly, and responses can be compared across time. Repeated sample surveys offer the same advantage. In election campaigns we understand the present preferences for political candidates in part by following their performance in election polls conducted in previous months and years.

Panel and Longitudinal Studies

The panel or longitudinal study asks the same questions of the same group of people, and is thus a refinement of repeated surveys. The Department of Agriculture has elaborate methods of estimating the production and future availability of agricultural products, based in part on repeated surveys of a panel of farmers and agricultural commodity dealers. The Consumer Product Safety Commission repeatedly surveys a panel of hospital emergency rooms, looking at the incidence and distribution of accidents involving products. In longitudinal studies investigators follow the same individuals for long periods of time. As in the Framingham Heart Study (Dawber 1980), the emphasis is usually on what happens to a group as it ages.

Case Studies

If we want to examine a process, an institution, or an event as a whole, the case study has been the traditional method of choice—John Hersey (1946) on the bombing of Hiroshima, for example. Usually the writing is lengthy, the sources have great variety, and the material is journalistically appealing. Generalizing the results to a new situation continues to be the main problem with the case study.

Official Statistics

Vast amounts of data are gathered, analyzed, and published each year by government, business, and quasi-public agencies. Whether specially collected or the by-product of day-to-day operations, this information is an important source of knowledge.

Although individual records are sometimes available, official statistics most often appear in aggregate form, such as the total amount of electricity produced by a state or the number of new army enlistments last month. Such numbers often help to define the magnitude of a policy problem.

Official indices offer special timely information. Millions of Americans watch closely each month for changes in the cost of living, an index derived from a time series maintained by the Bureau of Labor Statistics. Economists and bankers watch changes in the prevailing prime lending rate of the nation's large banks.

It is important to understand the definitions of official statistics and indices. The amount of petroleum products imported into the United States in the month of March, for example, can mean many things.* There are many ways to define "petroleum products"; the "United States" may or may not include U.S. territories. Oil can be counted as imported when the ship arrives at the dock, when papers are filed, when the oil actually arrives at its intended destination, or at numerous other points along the way. One definition of March —called the statistical month—includes all data on imports not previously reported but arriving by April 15; it may include import reports a year or two old if they have been delayed. Often a definition reflects

---

*Lincoln Moses, personal communication.

bureaucratic convenience rather than the most appropriate concept, and what seems most appropriate for one intended use may not be satisfactory for another.

Management Records

In their normal course of work, governments, businesses, and institutions generate and record vast amounts of data. Even though they have been collected for the purpose of management, such records provide potentially useful information for policymakers. Society has always generated management records, and computerization is making these data more easily available for further analysis. If the relevant management data can be found, they often save the policymaker an expensive and time-consuming special study. For example, school attendance records might be used to measure the local intensity and course of a flu epidemic.

PREDICTION: WHAT WILL HAPPEN?

Understanding the mechanisms of cause and effect and measuring the status quo prepare the policymaker to answer an important question: what will happen if the government does (or does not) intervene? Policy decisions concern changes in the system. Their effects always occur in the future, some sooner than others. A basic concern of the policymaker is to predict the consequences of proposed policies.

One aspect of prediction is planning. For example, sensible strategies for road building and power plant construction rely on estimates of future demand. Many aspects of future demand are the result of present trends, which can be more or less adequately predicted.

Policymakers frequently deal with exceptionally complicated situations. For instance, the EPA sets emission standards for automobiles and manufacturing plants. The agreed-upon goal is to reduce the exposure of humans to harmful pollutants and to improve their health. Although much is known about individual steps in the processes of production and diffusion of pollutants and the role they play in causing disease, it is difficult to pull this material together to understand the costs and benefits of a proposed emissions standard. Models organize the various bits and pieces of knowledge so that policymakers can compare and evaluate alternatives.

Predicting helps policymakers anticipate future problems. The future is largely a consequence of what we do and what happens today. For example, the future availability of energy depends both on the size of our renewable resources today and on our long-range capital construction decisions. Forecasts serve both to warn us of difficulties and to evaluate the efficacy of present interventions as remedies. Decision makers have more than enough problems to deal with; it is hard to focus attention on something that will happen many years from now. Yet forecasts connect the future consequences with current policies and thus provide a way to get problems on today's policy agenda.

Simulation and Modeling

Because of potential disruption or the multiplicity of alternatives, it will occasionally seem practical to simulate the action of a policy before deciding whether to implement it. Sometimes the simulation is physical. For example, the Corps of Engineers has constructed an elaborate scale model of the Mississippi River Basin to assess the effects of changes in levees, flood spillways, and channel dredging.

As a method of gathering data simulation provides information about the outcomes of a policy without actually instituting it. Simulation requires both relevant existing data, and a model for the behavior of the system. This model can be simple or complex, physical or mathematical, but we must know something about how the system works. Simulation is likely to be most effective for issues that can be analyzed within the structure of an existing system. If the policy to be investigated represents a major modification of the present system, simulation may not be appropriate, because our model for the behavior of the system may no longer be adequate.

The relative ease of simulating a variety of proposed policies makes it possible to consider a broader range of alternatives than would be feasible if it were necessary to implement actual treatments, even in a series of pilot programs. On the other hand, because a simulation may need substantial existing data, as well as some sort of model, it requires sophistication to construct. It is much less expensive, however, to build a model waterway than a real one.

Computerization has increased the use of mathematical modeling and simulation. These methods have wide use in business, economics, and the physical sciences. They are becoming more common in medicine, regulation, and law.

Forecasting

One need not know every detail of how a system works to understand its behavior. A careful examination of historical trends often reveals regularities that we can assume will continue into the future. Population is a key factor in determining future demand for hospital services. Overall demand depends on the total population in the area served by the hospital, but the demand for more specialized services, such as maternity wards and chronic care facilities, depends on the age composition of the population. The overall population change may be quite complex, but it can be studied as the product of an aging current population plus in- and out-migrants. Often the component processes are quite regular, and when put together, they clearly indicate future demands.

Introspection and Advice

Sometimes the process we wish to make predictions about is so complex, or we know so little about its workings, that we turn to other strategies for prediction. We may ask an expert to consider the matter. An individual who has worked in the field a long time can often make an intuitive prediction based on a wealth of experience, even if the process cannot be laid out in sufficient detail to make a useful model. Sometimes it is useful to consult a panel of experts or a planning staff.

Delphi Method

The Delphi Method can be used to poll the opinions of experts in a fashion that achieves many of the advantages of a group working together and sharing ideas. At the same time, the views of the panel members can be insulated from the potentially disruptive influences of reputation, personality, and rhetorical skill.

In seeking to use expert advice or the Delphi method, it is important to ask first if an expert's views on the issue under study can be expected to be more valid or useful than those of an ordinary citizen. Is the expert likely to know something special, or would a thoughtful lay adviser be just as helpful?

REASONS FOR COMMISSIONING SPECIAL STUDIES

Policymakers may have special reasons for gathering information: laying a foundation for a study, forestalling debate, resolving a conflict, choosing among several policies, or justifying a decision that has already been made.

Laying a Foundation

In the opening stages of an investigation, we may gather data just to get a general idea of the important elements of the problem. For example, to study science education, we may start by gathering data almost indiscriminately to see how much time and effort go into this field in the United States, Canada, Japan, the two Germanies, Great Britain, and Russia in precollege, college, and graduate school. We ask about expenditures, about the training of scientists and engineers, and about the scientific education of citizens. Then we ask what special programs would cost to achieve various goals.

Delaying Tactic

Often the time is not ripe for resolving an issue. Instead of tabling it, one method of putting off debate and decision is to call for more data. The cynic may think of this as merely a delaying tactic, which it often is, but the opportunity to gather data that can be timely later should not be lightly dismissed.

Conflict Resolution

Occasionally a political conflict can be avoided or resolved by gathering data if they reveal either overwhelming evidence in favor of one policy choice or no evidence in favor of any of the choices. Either outcome, however unlikely, might take the heat off the policymaker. Of course, no one expects either extreme outcome to be the situation, but it can occur.

Optimizing

When various policies are under consideration, information gathering may be oriented to choosing the best or at least a very good policy. For example, a system of dams can be designed in any of several ways to produce power, irrigation, and recreational facilities, and to prevent flooding. A study may quickly reduce the large number of design possibilities to a few that offer similar outstanding benefits, as occurred in a Water Resources Seminar at Harvard University some years ago.

Justifying Decisions Already Made

Having decided on a course of action, the policymaker may want to commission a study to justify the position taken. (Closely related to this purpose is that of political advocacy—gathering data to support a position and suppressing information that contradicts it.) However biased this approach may be, we should recognize that decisions already made often have been reversed, either because some new fact was revealed or because of checks and balances in the political system. Nevertheless, conducting a study of an issue that has already been resolved is a depressing task for the conscientious researcher.

The long-run effect of conducting studies to justify decisions already made is to destroy the credibility of the investigators. If they try to provide the answers the policymaker wants instead of simply presenting the data, their reputation as honest data gatherers goes out the window, their advice becomes a liability, and the policymaker's clout from authoritative information is lost.

It is remarkable that in modern times the major political figures in this country and a few others have understood and respected the need for credible information. They not only have kept their hands off the process, but also have acquiesced in methods for insulation. For example, reports of U.S. unemployment and cost-of-living figures are scheduled long in advance and are not released early, even though such statistics clearly affect the popularity of the political party in power.

CONCLUSION

This book describes methods of collecting data to learn about cause and effect, to measure the status quo, and to predict the future. Usually more than one method is available for each purpose, and in special circumstances methods used for one purpose may also be useful for another. The final four chapters deal with special issues and important themes in information policy.

Rather than instructing the reader in the various methods of collecting data for policy decisions, we provide a basis for evaluating the quality of information gathered by these methods. We discuss the features, strengths, weaknesses, and possible applications of each, and offer a quality checklist.

REFERENCES

Dawber, T. R. 1980. *The Framingham Study: The Epidemiology of Athero-sclerotic Disease.* Cambridge, Mass.: Harvard University Press.

Hersey, J. R. 1946. *Hiroshima.* New York: Knopf.

Lynn, L. E. 1980. Automobile Emissions Control: The Sulfates Problem (A, B, and sequel). In *Designing Public Policy.* Santa Monica, Calif.: Goodyear Publishing Company. (Cases copyrighted by the President and Fellows of Harvard College.)

Meier, P. 1972. The Biggest Public Health Experiment Ever: The 1954 Field Trial of the Salk Poliomyelitis Vaccine. In *Statistics: A Guide to the Unknown,* Judith Tanur et al., eds. San Francisco: Holden-Day.

PART I

Cause and Effect

CHAPTER 2

Experiments

For identifying causal relationships between interventions and observed outcomes, the controlled trial offers great strength. We discuss the rationale underlying the experiment and also some methods for improving its reliability and implications for new situations.

HISTORICAL EXAMPLES

The early experimental data on scurvy come from two experiments. One dealt with prevention, the other with treatment.

Prevention of Scurvy

Four British ships sailed in 1601 from England to India under the leadership of Captain James Lancaster (Purchas 1625). Sailors on the largest of these, the flagship, received three teaspoons of citrus juice every day, and those on the other ships received none. The 202 flagship sailors did not get scurvy, whereas almost all of those on the smaller ships (108, 88, and 82) did. Men from the flagship had to move to the other three ships in order to rig them, because so many sailors on the small ships became sick or died.

LIND'S SCURVY DIETS

Six Diets in James Lind's Experiment on Curing Scurvy Begun May 20, 1747 on H.M.S. Salisbury.

Basic diet: water gruel and sugar, fresh mutton broth, puddings, boiled biscuit with sugar, etc., barley and raisins, rice and currants, sago and wine, barley water acidulated with tamarinds plus *cremor tartar.*

Experimental treatments added to the basic diet, two sailors to each:

Diet 1: Two spoonsful vinegar three times per day on an empty stomach and gargle.
Diet 2: Sea water, half pint per day, more or less (given to the two worst patients).
Diet 3: One quart of cider a day.
Diet 4: Twenty-five gutta of elixir vitriol three times daily on an empty stomach plus gargle.
Diet 5: Two oranges and one lemon every day on an empty stomach (six days exhausted the supply). One sailor became fit for duty in six days and the other in less than four weeks while still at sea.
Diet 6: Bigness of a nutmeg three times a day, of an electuary of garlic, mustard seed, rad.raphan., balsam of Peru, and gum myrrh.

From J. Lind, *A Treatise of the Scurvy*, Edinburgh: Sands, Murray, and Cochran, 1753, reprinted 1953, Edinburgh: The University Press, p. 145.

Treatment of Scurvy

About 150 years later, in 1747, physician James Lind gave each of six pairs of sailors with scurvy a different treatment (Lind 1753). The two sailors who ate citrus fruit recovered and returned to work, the rest did not. Actually, those who drank cider seemed slightly better or no worse. Lind's experiment comes closer than Lancaster's to the ones we discuss in this chapter.

Several related observational studies are described in historical records. Certain sailors with scurvy, on landing at a port, ate many onions and recovered right away. The Dutch sailors were known to eat sauerkraut and to be less susceptible to scurvy, but other nations paid no attention.

Lind persuaded the British Navy to send one fleet fresh fruit and vegetable provisions when it was on a long sea mission—a blockade—and scurvy was avoided in spite of the long time at sea. When vitamin C was not included in their diets, sailors on long voyages contracted scurvy at a great rate and died from it by the thousands.

It was another forty-eight years after Lind's six-pair experiment before the British Navy introduced lime juice (actually lemon juice usually, though sometimes the cheaper but less effective limes were used) as a matter of policy on long sea voyages. In 1865 maritime laws were passed requiring that citrus be provided on long sea voyages, thus finally ending the British problem with scurvy.

FEATURES OF THE COMPARATIVE EXPERIMENT

In a comparative experiment the investigator imposes two or more treatments on members of a population to see how well the treatments achieve one or more prestated goals. The results are usually also reviewed for effects not included in the original plan. The main features of the comparative experiment are described below.

Treatments

Treatments are two or more actions or policies whose effects are to be compared. In the Lind experiment the six diets are the treatments.

Target Population

The group of individuals who could receive any of the treatments to be compared is the target population. Members of the target population can be persons, families, neighborhoods, towns, hospitals, stores, classrooms, or schools. In the Lind experiment all British sailors were the target population, not just his dozen.

Samples

Samples are subgroups of the target population receiving the experimental treatments. The investigator wishes to generalize the results observed in these samples to all the individuals in the population. Lind had six samples of two sailors each.

Control

The investigator determines the allocation of treatments to the individuals in the samples. The sick sailors took what Lind gave them.

Outcome Measure

An outcome measure is a result, thought to be due to the treatment, that can be measured or evaluated, or whose presence or absence can be noted for each individual in the samples. Lind's outcome measure was cure or no cure of scurvy.

Secondary Observations

These are observations of additional outcomes, sometimes called side effects, some of which may not have been anticipated as primary observations. For example, some medications cause nausea or vomiting. A job program for youth may train them to work but encourage them to leave school before graduating. Sometimes these variables could have been incorporated into the primary observations, but because they may be suggested after the experiment is underway and even by the results, it is convenient to discuss them separately. Lind did not report side effects.

Background Variables

In most experimental investigations the individuals in the target population and in the sample differ from each other in ways that may affect the conclusions. When these characteristics are recorded as part of the study, they are referred to as background variables. They include such facts as age and severity of disease in medical studies, sex and socioeconomic status in studies of social policies, and age and grade in educational investigations.

BROOM-HILDA   By Russell Myers

Analysis

The data analysis estimates the effects of the treatments on the outcome measures and assesses the accuracy of these estimates. The analysis may also estimate the effects of other factors related to the outcomes observed. Lind did not need to make a formal analysis because of the small sample size and simplicity of his design, plus the slam-bang effect of citrus juice and the total failure of the other diets.

Inference

Through inference, the investigator generalizes the experimental results to the population as a whole and to the policy issues being considered by the decision makers. Lind used the oft-observed fact that once scurvy set in, patients continued to deteriorate, and he reasoned that an improvement offered compelling proof of the merits of the juice. Lind's inference assumes that sailors will respond alike to the citrus juice.

An idealized and simplified version of the rationale for the inference based upon a comparative experiment assumes that:

1. The individuals in the samples treated react to the treatments in the same way as the rest of the population.
2. The difference in their treatments is the only factor affecting the outcomes of the different groups.

According to this logic, because the only difference is in the treatment, it must have caused any differences in outcome observed in the samples. Because the samples react like the rest of the population, applying a treatment to the entire population will have the same effect as it did on the sample. For Lind's experiment, the inference was borne out by later experience.

Decision making itself is not part of the experiment. The individual making a decision considers economics, politics, feasibility, timeliness, and information about other treatments or goals that may not have been studied in the experiment. To return to Lind, convincing the British Admiralty that citrus juice prevents and cures scurvy, choosing the citrus fruits to use, setting standards for their procurement and storage aboard ship, and developing regulations for dosage and responsibility for administration at sea, although part of the management process, fall outside the scope of the experiment and our discussion. Nevertheless, experiments can also help in making decisions about such matters.

The comparative experimental method is used to conduct a causal analysis. We want to answer the question: What is the effect of the treatment? or Which treatment produces the more favorable change? If we believe that the treatments change the state of the individuals, then we can compare the performance of the groups after treatment. The key assumption is that the treatment caused the change in performance.

The results of controlled trials can relate to policy at different levels. Sometimes the formal experiment is carried out only after considerable development work. The treatments have been invented and tried out in pilot studies, but the program itself is not yet in place. What can be found out from censuses, surveys, data banks, or observational studies will already have been discovered, and we need a direct confrontation between some defined alternative policies. After a successful experimental finding, we would expect direct implementation of the treatment (subject, of course, to the usual political, economic, and time constraints).

In other situations the trial is primarily designed not to test the relative efficacy of two or more competing policies, but to test for the presence or absence of a suspected causal connection that has policy implications. An example is the testing for carcinogenic effects of food additives. When such an additive is found to cause cancer, the Delaney Amendment requires that it be taken off the market. The legal status of other factors related to cancer in the environment is not so clear, and the policymaker is often faced with conflicting priorities that must be resolved. Thus, while the investigator, working in the narrow context of the experimental situation, often feels that the policy implications are direct, the decision maker, working in a larger context, sees the causal inference as only one facet of the situation.

WHAT THE COMPARATIVE EXPERIMENT IS NOT

How does the comparative experiment differ from other methods that seem to be similar in structure or intent? Actively imposing different treatments on the individuals on the basis of decisions controlled by the investigators is the primary feature. For the purpose of our discussion, if the investigator does not control the choice of treatments for individuals, the investigation is not a comparative experiment. It may, of course, still be a valuable investigation with causal implications; we are merely trying to clarify our use of language.

Observational studies, which compare individuals who have received different treatments historically, are easy to confuse with experiments. The observation that children of the well-to-do receive more years of education than those of the poor concerns the population as it stands; it does not tell us whether increasing the income of the poor will result in more education for their children. We had no control in assigning the income.

The everyday use of the word "experiment" to mean any introduction of an innovation is, for our purpose, an unfortunate source of confusion. If some individuals are chosen to receive an innovative treatment, others are chosen not to receive it, and the outcomes are compared, we have a comparative experiment in which the treatments are "innovation" and "no innovation."

Though the assumptions underlying the controlled trial seem simple enough in the abstract, experimenters and policymakers have found that in actual experimental and field situations it is often difficult to maintain the validity of the rationale. The devices that we discuss next increase the reliance that can be placed on the inference from a controlled trial.

STRENGTHENING CONTROLLED EXPERIMENTS

Several devices strengthen the evidence produced by controlled trials. They primarily strengthen the evidence for a causal link between treatments and observed outcomes in controlled trials. Because the controlled experiment depends on an argument by exclusion (no other causes or differences affected the experimental groups), we can strengthen its inference by taking steps to exclude any such differences. It is important to establish that the experimental groups were comparable at the outset, that the treatments were actually applied, and that the outcomes were evaluated in a uniform manner for all participants. Some of the strengthening devices noted below are hallmarks of good design, and a policymaker considering a comparative experiment, whether prospective or completed, will do well to ask which devices have been used.

Randomization

Using tables of random numbers to assign individuals to treatments approximately equates the treatment groups on variables not being controlled by stratification. For two groups, both get approximately equal numbers of men and women, if that is the intention. Randomization will produce about the same average age in the two groups and, more important, about the same distribution of ages. Randomization even produces such approximate balance for variables we do not know about. Thus randomization averts bias in the assignment of types of individuals to the treatments. The investigator should describe the method of randomization.

Stratification

If the population varies on important characteristics, we can divide the sample of experimental individuals into more homogeneous strata and then randomize treatment assignments so that the sizes of the treatment groups are balanced—have about the same number of individuals—within each stratum. For example, sex is an obvious variable for stratification when studying the effect of medications on hormones. Because the cross-classification of only a few variables generates a large number of strata, we are soon limited as to the number of stratifying factors. (The total number of strata is the product of the numbers of levels for the individual variables. For example, two sexes, three ages, four regions, and two treatments make $2 \times 3 \times 4 \times 2 = 48$ strata.)

Blindness

By concealing the identity of the treatment from the various actors in the experiment, we improve objectivity and prevent bias in the evaluation of treatment effects. Sometimes this information can be withheld from the treated individual, from the person who appraises the outcome, and even from those applying the treatment. In other instances, blindness is not practical. For example, surgical amputations cannot be concealed. The method of teaching spelling cannot be concealed from the teacher, though it might not be recognized by the pupil.

Sample Size

Large sample sizes, within reason, tend to give more reliable results than small ones. Increasing the size does not reduce the effects of biases in executing the study, if they exist. On the other hand, samples that are small may not offer much chance of detecting a difference, even if it is large enough to be important for policy decisions. These factors, as well as expense, need to be considered in planning the size of a study.

In statistical language, the probability of detecting an effect of a given size is called the *power*, a number between 0 and 1, preferably near 1. Several features of a comparative experiment combine to determine its power: the study design; the techniques of analysis; the significance level (the probability of claiming an effect when there is none: a number often chosen is 0.05; thus 5 times per 100 an effect would be claimed when none was present); the size of the sample; and the size the effect. A larger effect can be detected with greater power, and a larger sample size provides greater power for a given size of effect. Thus, in designing an experiment, the investigator should decide how small an effect might still be important for policy and then plan for a sample size large enough to give adequate power in detecting such an effect (say .8, meaning that in 80 investigations out of 100 an effect of the given size would be detected).

This step does not always receive adequate attention. Freiman et al. (1978) reviewed 71 clinical trials in which *no* statistically significant difference was reported between treatments. In each trial they looked at the reliability to see whether a substantial effect could have been missed. They found that these investigations could have a potential 25 percent improvement in 57 comparisons and a potential 50 percent improvement in 34 comparisons. Thus, many of the trials ran a serious risk of missing substantial improvements because their power was low. It is often possible to avoid this defect by planning for a large enough sample size. If one cannot do so, it may be preferable not to muddy the waters with a weak, inconclusive investigation.

Experimental Protocol

A document should define the exact nature of the study being undertaken. This plan defines the treatments and how they are to be applied—dosage, hours of instruction, advice to the judge—the criteria for including individuals in the sample, the background and outcome variables to be recorded and how they are to be measured, and a plan for analyzing the data.

MERITS OF THE EXPERIMENTAL METHOD

Comparative experiments usually perform best in answering narrow questions. Which of two well-defined treatments performs better on well-specified populations? The merits come from specifying the treatment, making sure it is administered, treating comparable individuals, having sufficiently large samples to make reliable estimates, making careful observations, using unbiased measurements, and conducting objective analyses with inferences to well-defined populations.

An important feature that adds power is the independence of individuals. If individuals can be selected and treated without producing effects on other individuals, this simplifies the inferences. Sometimes independence is not possible. Pupils taught in the same classroom cannot be regarded as independent, so the analysis ordinarily must move to the level of classrooms. Similarly, fluoridation applies to communities, not individuals, so we must analyze at the level of towns.

A federal or state agency that wants information about an ongoing program often makes it impossible or at least difficult for the investigator to obtain useful management data. Two brief examples suggest some lessons for research sponsors on how to organize the work that they contract out.

Head Start Evaluation

In 1969, after Head Start had been in operation for about three years, a group of investigators was hired to assess the program's effectiveness and to recommend management changes (Cicirelli et al. 1969). The research design was entirely post hoc; the investigators carried out an observational study that compared performance of children in Head Start with seemingly similar children not enrolled in Head Start. When the study was over, few differences between the two groups were found, but for five years policymakers in education argued about what the findings really meant (Bissell 1973). In the introduction to the actual research report, the principal author points out that because the buyer (the U.S. Office of Education) forced him, contractually, to carry out a retrospective, observational study design, there was no way to draw useful policy comparisons. His point was that this outcome was predictable in advance and that a carefully controlled experiment was still needed.

Manpower Training

A second example comes from the field of job training. In 1965 Congress passed the Manpower Development and Training Act (MDTA), which provided training and job placement for young school dropouts, ages 18–26. When the Department of Labor (DOL) instituted a series of training programs nationally, it gave substantial autonomy to the local training centers in choosing the training curriculum. When pressed to analyze the effectiveness of the MDTA program, the DOL pointed to this autonomy and argued that local variations made an overall study impossible. According to the National Academy of Sciences (1974), the DOL spent $180 million from 1963 to 1974 on evaluation studies of these programs, yet the nature of the evaluations rendered them essentially useless, and fifteen years after this well-intentioned legislation, we still did not know if the nearly $10 billion appropriation led to constructive results in the job market.

Contrast these situations with a happier story. In 1970 the U.S. Office of Education sponsored the television program "Sesame Street" and commissioned Educational Testing Service to study its effects on young viewers. The result was twofold. First, children who watched the program more frequently learned more letter and number skills than those who watched less frequently. Second, because of the well-designed evaluation, "Sesame Street" was changed over time in order to accommodate the special needs and interests of the children of poor families. Thus, the evaluation documented a clear positive outcome and led to improvements in the content of the program. It is noteworthy that, in its request for proposals (RFP), the Office of Education *required* that a randomized field trial be conducted. The data from this experimental study, when combined with observational information, provided insight into the effects of a program that 12 million children watch daily (Ball and Bogatz 1970).

SOCIAL, ECONOMIC, AND MEDICAL EXPERIMENTATION

Until fairly recently, economists thought it infeasible to inform public policy by using controlled experiments with direct interventions and control groups instead of observational studies or theoretical analyses. But since 1960, some substantial attempts to use experiments and near-experiments to study areas such as aid to the working poor, educational programs, and national health insurance have brought these techniques before the public eye. Here we discuss some pitfalls of analytic methods as a substitute for experiments. Some readers may wish to skip this material and move on to the next section.

What do experiments tell us? The motivating idea, well expressed by George Box (1966), is that if we want to see what happens when we change something in a complicated system, we need to change it and observe what happens. In causal work policy analysts often use statis-

tical devices called regression methods for analyzing observational studies, and this leads to difficulties. We are all used to saying that correlation is not causation and illustrating by pointing to a high correlation between quantities that seem ridiculous to relate, for example the correlation across years between the number of Presbyterian ministers in New York and the amount of Scotch whiskey produced in Great Britain. Although such amusing illustrations make the point about spurious correlation, they do not illuminate the causative problem with observational studies as brightly as does the next example.

Consider height versus weight for U.S. male adults. We can certainly fit a regression line of height on weight and then use weight to predict height. In a sense, the regression line serves the two purposes of predicting and summarizing the relation between the two variables in the population *as it stands.*

The regression does not tell us what will happen to an individual's height when we change his weight. We know from many sad experiences that in adults changes in weight produce practically no change in height. Thus, the regression for predicting height from weight was misleading for predicting what would happen when weight changes.

A regression equation such as

$$\hat{h} = 28 + \frac{1}{4}w$$

where w is the weight in pounds and $\hat{h}$ the estimate of height in inches, invites confusion. The equation seems to say that, if we raise w by 4 pounds, we get an increase of 1 inch in the estimate of height. If the equation is derived from an observational study, changing w refers to choosing different individuals, for example, moving from those in the population who weigh 160 pounds to others in the population weighing 164 pounds. The reference is to the population as it stands. Increasing w means measuring heights for other individuals who are heavier; it does not mean changing the weights of the individuals. The silent equation cannot remind us of this distinction in meanings.

More generally, when we relate a predictor variable to an outcome variable, based only on an observational study, we cannot count on the fitted relation to tell what will happen to outcome when the predictor variable is changed. The problem is sometimes spoken of as the difficulty of drawing inferences about change from cross-sectional data.

In practical policy situations we may introduce innovations by changing the values of some of the variables and observing changes in outcome variables. For example, we change the industrial taxes in a city and then observe the change in the amount of industry. Essentially, we are carrying out part of an experiment. This activity is not the same as looking at the relation between taxes and amounts of industry across cities. Researchers applying regression analysis to the population as it stands may be tempted to use their results to make invalid policy predictions. For example, a large coefficient in a regression equation (income elasticity) for schooling does not imply that low-income families will substantially increase schooling for their children if they receive an income supplement. Instead, the elasticity shows that high-income families spend much larger amounts of their income on schooling than do low-income families. It might also be true that low-income families would spend more on education if they had more money. The point is that these data do not address the question.

To give another example, regressions that predict output based on the population as it stands do not suggest the size of an output change resulting from an input change unless special assumptions hold, notably, that the production function is stationary across time or is the same for all countries or firms in the sample. Instead, such production functions describe the relationship between inputs and outputs across time, countries, or other observational units.

When regression methods are applied to data arising from experiments, where the changes are actually made and the outcomes observed, the causation argument is more likely to hold. This, of course, is a major attraction of experiments: we may be able to assess the effect of a change in policy.

Causation

Philosophers find *causation* among the easiest ideas to talk about and the most difficult to make concrete or useful. In advanced scientific work—physics, say—the term rarely arises, and yet it seems a helpful concept for explaining how or why something happened. Since tome after indigestible tome has explained, enshrined, or dismissed causation, we can afford to be brief while appreciating the oversimplification we offer.

Three ideas usually go hand-in-hand with causation: consistency, responsiveness, and reasonable mechanism.

If the first variable causes the second, we look for consistency in their relation. For example, if economic status causes amount of education, then we expect in a variety of populations that low income goes with less education and high with more. This can be verified by observational studies.

Pursuing the same example, responsiveness would require that changing economic status (for a group) leads to a corresponding change in amount of education. This can be verified by experiments.

We require a mechanism some people can understand that makes the cause work. Astrology gives us trouble because most of us fail to understand how the position of distant stars and planets will change our behavior or fate, even if we admit that full moons do have behavioral consequences and that sunspots might affect crops and thence the business cycle. Returning to our example, advanced education requires more money both for tuition and living expenses. Thus, reducing income would make advanced education more difficult to purchase, while adding income would make the purchase easier.

Generally, verifying the possible effectiveness of the mechanism requires step-by-step checking. If safety helmets were said to be reducing injuries in motorcycle accidents, one would need to make sure that they were being worn before accepting the conclusion.

Finally, it also helps if one can show that the second variable cannot cause the first. In our income-education example, since advanced education follows rather than precedes family income, it cannot very well cause the income. (It might cause post-education income.)

Those who wish a more extensive discussion of causation will find Cook and Campbell (1979) helpful.

Innovations, Reforms, and Experiments

If innovations were always blessings, we would scarcely need to test them, and if they were always failures, the same would be true. What can we say about the track record of innovations and reforms? To illustrate what has happened when social reforms have been assessed by experiments, we review the results of Gilbert, Light, and Mosteller (1975). They assigned a value to each of twenty-eight reforms, using a five-point scale: very good ++, good +, neutral 0, bad −, very bad − −. The score measures how well the innovation performed compared with the standard treatment it replaced. The scoring assumed that the innovations were cost-free. If cost were included, the scores would drop somewhat.

These studies were classified into social, sociomedical, and medical innovations. The first group includes eight, of which four are: negative income tax, studies of bail, training of police, and attempts to reduce delinquency among girls. The second group includes eight, of which four are: experiments on probation for drunks, effects of broadening health insurance benefits, training mothers whose children have had tonsillectomies, and training physicians in comprehensive medical care. The third group includes twelve, of which four are: the Salk vaccine experiment for polio prevention, treatment of cancer of the bronchus, vagotomy, and gastric freezing for ulcer.

Table 2-1 shows that fewer than half of the innovations were considered improvements, though few seemed to have a negative effect. A neutral score (0) need not be bad if the innovation costs no more than the standard treatment. The social and sociomedical innovations usually did cost more; the medical ones were mixed.

The authors were concerned that their sample might not be satisfactory because they chose social and sociomedical experiments as known to them, and they had no systematic source. The medical innovations came, with two exceptions, from a systematic computer search of the medical literature. To consider what might happen with objective sampling from a larger medical literature, Gilbert, McPeek, and Mosteller (1977) studied surgical innovations that had been tested by experiments (randomized clinical trials). They made one change in

TABLE 2-1 *Summary of ratings of social, sociomedical, and medical innovations as compared with the standard treatment*

	Rating					
	−−	−	0	+	++	*Totals*
Social			3	2	3	8
Sociomedical		1	4	2	1	8
Medical	1	1	6	2	2	12
Totals	1	2	13	6	6	28

From J. P. Gilbert, R. J. Light, and F. Mosteller, Assessing Social Innovations: An Empirical Base for Policy. In *Evaluation and Experiment: Some Critical Issues in Assessing Social Programs*, C. A. Bennett and A. A. Lumsdaine, eds., New York: Academic Press, Inc., 1975, p. 114. Reprinted with permission.

the scoring system. Innovations receiving a neutral score were divided into two groups, those regarded as successful, because they provided a valuable alternative treatment for some patients, and those considered disappointing, because they were more troublesome, more expensive, or more dangerous than the standard treatment.

They also broke the innovations into two groups, those where the therapy for the disease was changed, called primary treatments, and those where the recovery from the therapy was to be improved (reduced infections, reduced thrombosis, reduced complications following surgery), called secondary treatments. Table 2-2 shows the results. Again, slightly fewer than half of the innovations improved on the standard treatments. Before the tests, the innovations were highly regarded, or they would not be likely to have been brought to expensive randomized trials. Thus, innovations do not automatically turn out to be improvements, even in the hands of the most careful people.

TABLE 2-2 *Ratings for surgical innovations: randomized controlled clinical trials*

	Disappointment			Success			
	−−	−	0	0	+	++	*Totals*
Primary	1	3	7	2	5	1	19
Secondary	3	3	3	2	2	4	17
Totals	4	6	10	4	7	5	36

From J. P. Gilbert, B. McPeek, and F. Mosteller, Progress in Surgery and Anesthesia: Benefits and Risks of Innovative Therapy. In *Costs, Risks, and Benefits of Surgery*, John P. Bunker, Benjamin A. Barnes and Frederick Mosteller, eds., New York: Oxford University Press, 1977, p. 128. Copyright © 1977 by Oxford University Press, Inc. Reprinted with permission.

Poorly Controlled Trials

What happens when less carefully controlled investigations have been carried out? It is difficult to compare policy studies, but surgical studies provide an analogy. Gilbert, McPeek, and Mosteller (1977) also reported scores for controlled nonrandomized trials in surgery, as shown in Table 2-3. Nearly half of the controlled trials without randomization received very positive scores (+ +), and more than half were considered an improvement.

An even more telling example is given by Chalmers (forthcoming), who reports on many separate studies of the same new operation to stop bleeding in the esophagus, portacaval shunt. Among these, seven were adequately controlled and eighty-eight were poorly controlled or uncontrolled. After each experiment, the investigators reported their degree of enthusiasm for the new operation. Table 2-4 shows the results of the 95 studies.

TABLE 2–3 *Ratings of controlled nonrandomized trials*

	Disappointment			Success			
	— —	—	0	0	+	+ +	*Totals*
Primary					1	2	3
Secondary	1	1	2		1	3	8
Totals	1	1	2	0	2	5	11

From J. P. Gilbert, B. McPeek, and F. Mosteller, Progress in Surgery and Anesthesia: Benefits and Risks of Innovative Therapy. In *Costs, Risks, and Benefits of Surgery*, John P. Bunker, Benjamin A. Barnes and Frederick Mosteller, eds., New York: Oxford University Press, 1977, p. 130. Copyright © 1977 by Oxford University Press, Inc. Reprinted with permission.

TABLE 2–4 *Ratings of therapeutic trials of portacaval shunt operations, 95 investigations*

	Degree of Enthusiasm			
Controls	*Marked*	*Moderate*	*None*	*Totals*
Adequate	0	3	4	7
Poor	18	2	1	21
None	50	14	3	67
Totals	68	19	8	95

Reprinted from T. C. Chalmers, The Randomized Controlled Trial as a Basis for Therapeutic Decisions, Chapter 2 in J. M. Lachin, N. Tygstrup, and E. Juhl, eds., *The Randomized Clinical Trial and Therapeutic Decisions*, New York: Marcel Dekker, Inc., to be published in 1982, by courtesy of Marcel Dekker, Inc.

HUGO MUENCH'S LAWS OF CLINICAL STUDIES

Law 1: No full-scale study confirms the lead provided by a pilot study.

Law 2: Results can always be improved by omitting controls.

Law 3: In order to be realistic, the number of cases promised in any clinical study must be divided by a factor of at least ten.

From J. E. Bearman, R. B. Loewenson, and W. H. Gullen, Muench's Postulates, Laws, and Corollaries, or Biometricians' Views on Clinical Studies, Biometrics Note No. 4, Bethesda, Md.: Office of Biometry and Epidemiology, National Eye Institute, National Institutes of Health, 1974.

In both examples, less well-controlled studies generate more enthusiasm for innovations than do well-controlled ones. (Note that well-controlled investigations are rarer in the Chalmers study.) These results all support Hugo Muench's "law" (Bearman et al. 1974), which essentially says that nothing improves the performance of an innovation more than lack of controls. We have here a fair amount of empirical evidence that when innovations are assessed without well-controlled experiments, they are likely to be overrated.

WEAKNESSES OF EXPERIMENTS

Comparative experiments are not useful as a primary method of generating original ideas for treatments. These usually come from insights, theory, or from collections of earlier investigations. The comparative experiment can be used for evolutionary development of an innovation, but it is not especially good for the original development of a treatment though, no doubt, exceptions exist. In evolutionary development we suppose a program is in place at many sites, such as manpower training programs, food stamp programs, or local post offices. At collections of such sites, experiments can be conducted to see how to improve the service or other enterprise being carried on.

Enforcing the Treatment

The inference to be drawn from experimental results is weak when the treatment cannot be enforced, though sometimes this scientific weakness may be satisfactory for practical work.

Vitamin C and Colds

To discover whether massive doses of vitamin C reduce the frequency of colds, we randomly assign half a group of patients to vitamin C pills and half to a placebo. For some reason, more of the patients taking vitamin C drop out of the experiment than do those taking the placebo. Now what? The remaining patients may no longer be well matched.

Or some people taste the contents of their pills and conclude that they are or are not receiving vitamin C. Now we have four treatments: receiving vitamin C and believing it is vitamin C, getting vitamin C and believing it is the placebo, and so on. In one investigation it turned out that what one believed seemed to have more effect than what one got. Now the investigator has lost control of the treatment, and correlations between health and attitudes toward effectiveness of medications confuse the evaluation of vitamin C.

We have already seen that experiments are difficult when individuals cannot be isolated. When experiments impinge on large organizations or regions, lack of control and lack of comparability can be stumbling blocks. We discuss this in Chapter 3.

National Health Insurance, School Systems

If the only way to handle a treatment is to apply it to a whole geographic region, and the treatment is relevant only to that region, the comparative experiment seems inappropriate unless one can try first one and then another treatment. But one can scarcely introduce one national health insurance program one day and an entirely different one the next. Similarly, it is hard to compare having a public school system with having a private school system, because the time and funding required to set up and stabilize the systems are so great that we would never get comparability.

Ethics

Ethical and political considerations may rule out many sorts of experiments.

Drug Availability

Some argue that we can handle the problems of drug addiction by making drugs freely available at a low price. This would allow addicts to maintain their habits without committing crimes to get funds, and it would avoid defining drug addiction as a crime. Opponents of this view say that taking drugs is a crime and that abetting this activity is immoral; moreover, the availability of low-cost drugs would almost certainly spread their use, and so this is undesirable. Thus, the experiments cannot be done. Instead, we have to do more constrained investigations, which are not entirely satisfactory.

Length

When experiments have to be lengthy, they may be of doubtful value. Technologies and conditions change, and what would have been useful at one time may not be useful at another. A twenty-year study of the horse for transportation starting in 1910 would have found itself obsolete before completion (though it might be useful again in 2000).

One must not be taken in too much by such arguments. Many of society's problems and properties stay the same for a long time. Large social problems, such as poverty, alcoholism, juvenile delinquency, crime and punishment, and unemployment, as well as social institutions (taxes, courts, armies, schools), seem to persist for long periods in much the same form.

QUALITY CHECKLIST

A policymaker should consider several characteristics in evaluating the quality of a comparative experiment. Not all of them are appropriate to every experiment, but when present, they help to strengthen the reliability of the inference.

1. *Are the treatments defined operationally and were they actually imposed on all the individuals? Has the latter been proved?* When comparing treatments, the investigator wants to be sure that the stated treatments are the ones imposed. For example, if we want to know whether more homework will improve achievement in cognitive studies, some distinctions need to be made between such treatments as "assigning more homework" and "doing more homework." If we wanted to know whether doing more homework improves performance, then comparing the behaviors of those who have and have not been assigned more homework may not be enough.

In a study of the use of outpatient medical facilities, some patients were given extra medical insurance benefits with no extra premium, and others were not given these extras. The intent was to study the effect upon use of hospital beds. It was later found that many of the patients in the group who had the extra benefits were not aware of them.

This raised the question, could changes in behavior be reliably attributed to the extra benefits? (In this example, it might not be important whether the patients understood about the extra benefits if the physicians in charge of their therapy did.)

One way around the issue of whether the treatment is the one imposed is to define the treatment as "being given the opportunity to have a particular treatment." This approach has merits, but the causal link seems weaker. Nevertheless, for policy considerations, the important point may be opportunity rather than execution.

2. *Has randomization been used?* In assigning units to different treatment groups, usually randomized studies can be regarded as improvements over nonrandomized studies. Randomization controls approximately for variables not directly controlled and especially for variables not being measured. Randomization also protects the investigation from claims of bias in allocating individual treatments. The policymaker will ask two questions. First, whether randomization was said to be used, and second, whether the actual randomization has been well described. Some investigators mistakenly believe that haphazard assignment is equivalent to randomization with genuine random numbers. Both the use of random numbers and the documentation reflect on the quality of the investigation. Although the assignment of treatments to subjects may seem a rather trivial detail of a large investigation, so many studies in the past have come to grief on this point that it cannot be ignored.

3. *What degree of blindness has been imposed?* In many investigations it may be difficult to maintain objectivity when one knows the treatment that has been imposed, especially if one has strong beliefs in the efficacy or lack of it for certain treatments. In treating individual persons, investigators have available several degrees of blindness to strengthen the inference and make surer that the outcomes are the results of the treatments rather than the results of the beliefs of the evaluators, treaters, and/or participants in the investigation.

Treatments can sometimes be masked so that subjects do not know which treatment they are receiving. If we are comparing recreations, such an approach may not be possible. However, if the treatments are pills, they can often be constructed to be indistinguishable to the patient, to the physician prescribing the medication, and to the person who evaluates the effect of the treatments on the patients. When none of these three actors can identify the treatments, the experiment is said to be triple-blind. Often only single- or double-blindness can be arranged.

Blindness, when feasible, is essential to careful experimentation. When blindness clearly cannot be provided, the experimenter needs to ask whether this and other devices for strengthening the investigation have been adequately considered and what the effects of knowing the treatments may be on the various actors. Blindness gives a level of assurance that the results were not affected by observer bias or by extraneous psychological factors that cannot be achieved by any other mechanism. Thus the use of both random assignment and blind evaluation insulates the experiment from this category of criticism.

Another form of blindness concerns the randomization. If someone can know what treatment the next person entering the investigation is to receive, then part of the objectivity is lost. If the subject has views about the merits of the treatments or prefers one of them (such as receiving additional income rather than not receiving it), such preferences are likely to spill over into the assignments. For example, if researchers studying the gains from giving additional milk to schoolchildren give milk to the smaller children and not to the larger ones, the observed gains from additional milk may be minimized.

4. *Were the samples stratified in an appropriate manner?* Stratification, when it can be used, strengthens the experiment's power to detect differences between the treatments because it makes the treatment groups more homogeneous and improves prior comparability.

5. *Were the samples checked for maldistribution on important variables?* It is possible for chance to play surprising tricks. When we deal with many variables, some are bound to be substantially out of balance, especially in small samples. When background variables are poorly balanced, sometimes the researcher can adjust for this by a method called covariance analysis. Checking for imbalances and reporting their possible effects are part of good analysis. Simply comparing the distribution of background variables for the different treatment groups is wise, but it does omit the important step of comparing the effects of imbalances and possibly making analytic adjustments for them.

6. *Were the data collection procedures checked for accuracy and reliability?* In large studies, particularly those that involve several different sites or institutions, the definitions and methods of measuring background and outcome measures must be kept comparable at the different sites and constant over the time span of the study. Forms and data handling procedures should be designed to minimize the chances of recording and transcription errors. Studies of accuracy of coding and punching and internal consistency checks add strength.

7. *Were standard methods of statistical analysis used?* In evaluating a report, it can often be revealing to ask whether a standard method of analysis has been used in the statistical treatment of the data. Use of elaborate nonstandard analyses may indicate that the author has searched diligently for a technique that yields some desired conclusion for the particular set of data but has not reported the conflicting results of customary analyses.

It is important, however, not to define "standard" too rigidly. In many problems any of several techniques, each based on certain technical assumptions, could justifiably be applied to the data. The report should describe the results of applying at least one of these standard techniques. It may also explain that a special feature of the data or an evident failure of some underlying assumption makes a particular nonstandard analysis desirable.

Thus, failure to discuss any of the standard analyses would be reasonable cause for suspicion, but careful attention should also be given to the validity of assumptions and to the particular features of the data, which may call for special analyses, in addition to the standard ones. New statistical techniques are always being developed.

8. *Are the assumptions valid?* Do the assumptions of the experimental design and analysis seem reasonable? Were important background variables controlled in the design or adjusted for in the analysis? Were the types of individuals selected appropriate for the treatments being investigated? Did the outcome *measures* used assess effectively the outcomes at issue in the plan of the study, that is, the result that one wishes to generalize to the population? For example, performance in spelling is the outcome measure we would want, though hours spent studying spelling may be some indication of the ultimate performance. Similarly, a gain in "liking" spelling lessons is nice, but if it does not produce better spellers, we have improved only attitudes, not performance.

9. *Are the results of the investigation reasonable?* The policymaker and other consumers of information will naturally be more confident of a study if its results can be understood or explained in terms of accepted theories, and if they fit in with the results of other similar studies. It is true that some of the most important studies are those that upset existing theories; however, they are also the ones that the policymakers will have to examine most carefully; often repetition will be necessary to verify the findings.

10. *Does the work discuss difficulties?* The course of true love never did run smooth, nor do experiments or any other kind of investiga-

tions. Careful investigators report their difficulties (the rabbits ate up half the crop). Less careful ones do not bother, thereby giving the impression of much simpler and cleaner outcomes. Be suspicious of any report that describes an apparently perfect study, especially in the social domain.

When reading an overview or summary of a study, we usually ask, "Did the treatment work?" and focus less on details of carrying out the study. But the details or difficulties can themselves be informative if a program is to be widely implemented. For example, suppose a program for parole supervision of prisoners on a work-release program is studied at several prisons. One question to be asked is whether the program reduced recidivism. Practical difficulties may also be revealed, and developing a list of questions during an initial evaluation may prove useful for implementation. Was the parole supervised similarly by several parole officers at each prison? In other words, is there a clearly identifiable treatment? Even if parole was supervised similarly by different parole officers at one prison, were there differences among prisons, for example, regional differences across the country or differences because of union agreements?

Several points emerge here. First, if treatment implementation varies across sites, it may not be wise to aggregate sets of dissimilar data. Second, even if these differences in treatment are acceptable, they should be noted as a feature of the new program. Finally, if we believe that these differences among treatments are part of social reality, and if the program is to be enlarged to serve a hundred times as many prisoners, it should be clearly understood that no single program is being generalized, but rather many variants, some of which will inevitably be more successful than others.

11. *Are the investigators competent?* What is the reputation of the investigators? Have their other studies stood the tests of time and criticism? Did they have a vested interest in a particular result? If so, how much could that have influenced the actual result reported? Were sufficient resources and expertise used to conduct the study?

12. *Are the effects real and important?* The policymaker always has to consider whether the result is genuine and important. In large studies small effects may prove to be real but of no consequence for policy, though small gains in a large population can be valuable. In small studies potentially important large effects may have little backing because of the uncertainty of the data. Also, effects that are large enough to affect policy may escape detection in small studies. Then the policymaker might (1) make a temporary decision and seek better (more) information, or (2) continue the old policy.

QUALITY CHECKLIST

1. Treatments defined and imposed?
2. Randomization?
3. Blindness?
4. Stratification?
5. Balance in variables?
6. Checks on data procedures?
7. Standard statistical analyses?
8. Assumptions?
9. Reasonable results?
10. Discussion of difficulties?
11. Competence?
12. Substantial effects?
13. Ethical investigation?
14. Feasible?

Most of the twelve points noted above are relevant to a study in the planning phase, because we want the finished study to fulfill as many of these criteria as possible. Two other points apply to proposed studies.

13. *Is the investigation ethical?* Before doing any experiment and many observational studies, one has to question whether the investigation is ethical. Generally, it is regarded as unethical to withhold from people one of a set of treatments that is known to be better than the others. It may also be unethical to act as if one treatment is known to be better when this knowledge has not been documented, though this idea has not been widely appreciated. Believing too much too soon has its own ethical consequences. Antoine de Saint-Exupéry says, "As for the Future, your task is not to foresee, but to enable it" (1950).

Some experiments use misinformation in their treatments. However, lying to people makes for awkward relationships in the short run and in the long run may defeat the experimental approach altogether, because it destroys the credibility of the investigators and of the whole experimental process. Fortunately, in recent years we have developed committees and procedures for considering the ethics of human experimentation.

Finally, more and more people are now convinced that experiments that cannot possibly resolve the issues they address—that is, poorly designed experiments—are also unethical.

14. *Is the investigation feasible?* Is the plan so big and complicated that it will fall of its own weight? However ethical or valuable the investigation, do political problems prevent its successful execution? To perform an investigation known in advance to be infeasible is itself unethical, because a poorly executed experiment wastes resources and may put people and institutions at risk for no profit to society. These are issues that the planner must face. Evaluation of performance contracting in education is probably an example of an investigation made infeasible by the political situation and timing. The contracts were hurriedly let and short-term, and the designs were not as tight as they should have been (Gramlich and Koshel 1975). Performing an investigation under these circumstances can be counterproductive because it can spoil a later opportunity to make the same investigation under more favorable circumstances.

POLICY IMPLICATIONS

Controlled experiments require support from policymakers if they are to be done and done well. Ordinarily these experiments take time to be created and run properly, and the policymaker should make sure that the time frame for the work is appropriate.

The policymaker must also consider whether a very long experiment would be appropriate. In some policy areas conditions change substantially over time, and one must consider whether the findings will still be useful when the study is completed.

Politics

The decision to conduct an experiment instead of an observational study, a case study, or a sample survey probably requires considerable political clout. Experiments require deliberate, differential changes, and prior beliefs about the benefits being examined can impinge on views of appropriateness. Moreover, since participants in an experiment are treated differently, the seeming inequities may invite political attack.

Organization

Experiments may require more organization than other data-gathering methods that interfere less with the situation as it stands.

Small Changes

A common difficulty with the controlled experiment is that changes in outcome observed in response to changes in the input variables are very modest, if favorable at all to the innovation. Although disappointing, such findings may go far to answer policy questions.

Evolutionary Improvements

Experiments can be used to examine evolutionary improvements in large-scale programs already in operation. Many standard programs have the key feature that makes experiments attractive: they are composed of essentially independent units that are almost identical in their purpose. Examples are school systems, state and municipal governments, post offices, highways, hospitals, stores, and farms. Such units form an attractive base for the comparison of potential improvements using experimental designs. They also have the advantage of performing the actual function in the ongoing program or system. When experiments are performed in isolation from the system, they have to be reevaluated after being introduced to that system. An operating system offers many opportunities for investigations of great potential value.

CONCLUSION

The well-conducted controlled trial is the most definitive method of investigating causal relationships both in the laboratory and in the field. It offers the best evidence for comparing the relative effectiveness of a limited number of programs, or program variants. Using the controlled trial, the researcher focuses on the target population; controls the allocation of individuals to the programs; measures outcomes, side effects, and background variables; and bases inferences on a careful comparative analysis of the data. Randomization, stratification, an explicit protocol, and, where feasible, blindness and adequate sample sizes strengthen the results of experiments. In less focused situations, evidence from controlled trials can often help estimate the cost-effectiveness of the various options available. In some cases time and funding constraints may make a comparative trial infeasible. Where feasible and practical, however, controlled trials in a policy area will tend in the long run to increase our knowledge and understanding of the effectiveness of various interventions, and hence the effectiveness of policies made on the basis of this knowledge.

REFERENCES

Ball, S., and Bogatz, G.A. 1970. *The First Year of Sesame Street: An Evaluation*. Princeton, N.J.: Educational Testing Service.

Bearman, J.E.; Loewenson, R.B.; and Gullen, W.H. 1974. Muench's Postulates, Laws, and Corollaries, or Biometricians' Views on Clinical Studies. Biometrics Note No. 4 (April). Bethesda, Md: Office of Biometry and Epidemiology, National Eye Institute, National Institutes of Health.

Bissell, J.S. 1973. Planned Variation in Head Start and Follow Through. In *Preschool Programs for the Disadvantaged*, Vol. 2, J. C. Stanley, ed. Baltimore: Johns Hopkins University Press.

Box, G.E.P. 1966. Use and Abuse of Regression. *Technometrics* 8:625–629.

Chalmers, T. C. To appear in 1982. The Randomized Controlled Trial as a Basis for Therapeutic Decisions. In *The Randomized Clinical Trial and Therapeutic Decisions*, J.M. Lachin, N. Tygstrup, and E. Juhl, eds. New York: Marcel Dekker, Inc.

Cicirelli, V.G.; Cooper, W.H.; and Granger, R.L. 1969. *The Impact of Head Start: An Evaluation of the Effects of Head Start on Children's Cognitive and Affective Development*. Athens, Ohio: Ohio University and Westinghouse Learning Corporation. (Distributed by the Clearinghouse for Federal Scientific and Technical Information, U.S. Department of Commerce, National Bureau of Standards, Institute for Applied Technology [PB 184 328]).

Freiman, J.A.; Chalmers, T.C.; Smith, H. Jr.; and Kuebler, R. R. 1978. The Importance of Beta, the Type II Error and Sample Size in the Design and Interpretation of the Randomized Control Trial. *New England Journal of Medicine* 299:690–694.

Gilbert, J.P.; Light, R. J.; and Mosteller, F. 1975. Assessing Social Innovations: An Empirical Base for Policy. In *Evaluation and Experiment: Some Critical Issues in Assessing Social Programs*, C.A. Bennett and A.A. Lumsdaine, eds. New York: Academic Press. pp. 39–193.

Gilbert, J.P.; McPeek, B.; and Mosteller, F. 1977. Progress in Surgery and Anesthesia: Benefits and Risks of Innovative Therapy. In *Costs, Risks, and Benefits of Surgery*, J.P. Bunker; B. A. Barnes; and F. Mosteller, eds. New York: Oxford University Press, pp. 124–169.

Gramlich, E.M. and Koshel, P.P. 1975. *Educational Performance Contracting*. Washington, D.C.: Brookings Institution.

Lind, J. 1753, reprinted 1953. *A Treatise of the Scurvy*. Edinburgh: The University Press.

National Academy of Sciences. 1974. *Final Report of the Panel on Manpower Training Evaluation. The Use of Social Security Earnings Data for Assessing the Impact of Manpower Training Programs*. Washington, D.C.: National Academy of Sciences.

Purchas, S. 1625, reprinted 1905. *Hakluytus Posthumus or Purchas His Pilgrimes*. Vol. II. Glasgow: James MacLehose and Sons.

Saint-Exupéry, A. 1950, reprinted 1979. *The Wisdom of the Sands*, translated by S. Gilbert. Chicago: University of Chicago Press.

FURTHER READING

Campbell, D.T., and Stanley, J.C. 1963. Experimental and Quasi-Experimental Designs for Research on Teaching. In *Handbook of Research on Teaching*, N. L. Gage, ed. Chicago: Rand McNally. Reprinted 1966 as *Experimental and Quasi-Experimental Designs for Research*. Chicago: Rand McNally.

Cook, T. D., and Campbell, D. T. 1979. *Quasi-Experimentation: Design and Analysis Issues for Field Settings*. Chicago: Rand McNally, pp. 10–36.

Gilbert, J.P.; Light, R. J.; and Mosteller, F. 1975. Assessing Social Innovations: An Empirical Base for Policy. In *Evaluation and Experiment: Some Critical Issues in Assessing Social Programs*, C.A. Bennett and A.A. Lumsdaine, eds. New York: Academic Press, pp. 39–193.

Gilbert, J.P.; McPeek, B.; and Mosteller, F. 1977. Statistics and Ethics in Surgery and Anesthesia. *Science* 198 (18 November):684–689.

Riecken, H.W., and Boruch, R.F., eds. 1974. *Social Experimentation: A Method for Planning and Evaluating Social Intervention*. New York: Academic Press.

CHAPTER 3

Special Considerations For Economic Experiments*

THE ECONOMIST'S VIEW OF EXPERIMENTS

Policies are often designed to influence behavior by modifying the associated economic incentives. Sometimes the policy goal is to alter the status of the economic factors themselves. Thus, for some readers, it may be instructive to view experiments from an economic perspective, as Alice Rivlin has done (Rivlin 1974). She divides policy experiments into four categories and discusses problems of execution and statistical inference. For convenience, we give these categories names: micro-experiments, macro-experiments, production experiments, and reorganization experiments.

MICRO-EXPERIMENTS

Micro-experiments can come close to the statistician's ideal. In these experiments, small *independent* demanders (or suppliers) respond to taxes, subsidies, or income supplements. By independent, we mean that the decision of one demander is not linked to those of other demanders and that each demander, by joining the market, raises the price of the good to all other demanders by a small, almost negligible, amount.

*This discussion is from F. Mosteller and G. Mosteller, "New Statistical Methods in Public Policy I: Experimentation," *Journal of Contemporary Business* 8, no. 3 (1979): 79–92. It is reproduced here with permission from the *Journal of Contemporary Business*.

For example, households or individuals chosen randomly from a large geographic area would decide how much of a subsidized good, such as physicians' services, to purchase independently of other households in the experiment. The total increase in the quantity demanded by all the households in the experiment would be small relative to the market, so that we could claim that the market demand and supply curves remain nearly constant. That is, the price charged by suppliers and paid by nonsubsidized buyers would not change, and neither would the prices for substitutes and complements. Thus, the micro-experiment gives us an estimate of the elasticity of demand in the region of the original market price and the subsidy price, holding constant all other prices.

Micro-experiments do not always involve subsidies. For example, the negative income tax experiment changes the "price" of leisure or income foregone. To simplify greatly, a negative income tax guarantees an individual a minimum income, and it taxes each dollar earned by a certain percent. Those who earn less than the minimum income receive a "negative tax," while those who earn more pay a "positive tax." By changing the marginal tax rate and the minimum income level for a sample of households, the investigator can measure the effect of different negative income taxes on hours worked and earnings, while scarcely shifting the labor supply curve.

Theoretically, micro-experiments could test the response of suppliers in an industry, but in many industries the suppliers have large market shares and their actions influence industrial activity. For example, large firms can raise the prices of inputs by expanding production. Unlike micro-experiments involving individual workers (the unorganized labor market) or families, those involving firms are likely to violate the independence assumption.

To repeat, micro-experiments have three distinctive features: the treatment is a change in price (tax or subsidy), income (voucher or income supplement), or both; the investigator controls the treatment, such as the magnitude of the price change; and the participants can be randomly chosen and independent.

MACRO-EXPERIMENTS

In macro-experiments the whole market responds to taxes or subsidies, which can be placed on either the demand or supply side of the market. To study the magnitude of response in the whole market, it must be saturated, and the experiment's participants need not be small or independent. Since the impact of the policy will be large, the market demand or supply curve or both will shift, and the investigator will not have control over the size of the price change.

The subsidy macro-experiment lowers the price paid by all demanders and thereby raises the quantity of services or goods that they demand. This marketwide expansion of demand (shift of the demand curve) raises the market price received by sellers and affects prices for substitutes, complements, and inputs. Thus, the subsidy macro-experiment increases the quantity that is demanded and sold, raises the market price, and changes prices in other markets. The subsidy macro-experiment gives an estimate of the elasticity of supply in the region of the original and the new market prices without holding constant other prices. Recall that the subsidy micro-experiment gave an estimate of the elasticity of demand, holding constant other prices. To get an estimate of the elasticity of demand without holding constant other prices, the macro-experiment would have to tax or subsidize the supply side of the market.

Macro-experiments give a more complete picture of the interaction between demand and supply curves that is lacking when we study the demand or supply curve alone. Also, macro-experiments affect markets for substitutes, complements, and inputs, revealing additional consequences of policy.

PRODUCTION EXPERIMENTS

Production experiments measure the relation between inputs and outputs for a product or service. Their purpose is to encourage the discovery and development of new methods of production rather than relying upon techniques currently employed in the market.

In many settings production experiments can also come close to the statistician's ideal. For example, an agricultural production experiment on pigs might study alternative diets that are low in cost and chemical additives. Because a great deal is known about appropriate foods for pigs, experiments can be developed without much difficulty. The treatments would be various measured combinations of foods, and the output would be total weight gained during a specific time period.

In other experiments the inputs and outputs seem harder to standardize. An education production experiment might study alternative programs to increase the vocabulary of fourth graders. Mechanical ways of studying vocabulary, such as flash cards, can be specified carefully, but more creative vocabulary games are harder to standardize.

REORGANIZATION EXPERIMENTS

Reorganization experiments strive to alter market and institutional structures and conditions to deliver different final outcomes. These experiments combine elements of macro-experiments and production experiments and depend on a chain of interrelations. By giving parents education vouchers and the opportunity to choose schools for their children, "schooling" acquires more of the characteristics of a traditional market. Parents who want particular kinds of training for their children can use their vouchers to select schools that offer the appropriate programs. To meet demands for a large variety of specialties, each studied by a few, a traditional school system must be well endowed. With the voucher system, schools compete for students, and parents choose schools that teach the desired specialties.

By changing the ground rules, reorganization experiments alter both the means of production and the final product. Since reorganization experiments rely on a chain of interrelations, the final product is likely to be much more difficult to achieve than the product of a direct input-output process. Moreover, reorganization experiments may require considerable time and investment, because creating a new kind of factory or a new kind of university may require a great deal of capital. For all these reasons such experiments are the most difficult to carry out.

PROBLEMS OF EXECUTION AND INFERENCE

Table 3-1 summarizes the many problems that can arise in planning and conducting the four kinds of experiments.

By political interference (item 4), we mean both opposition to performing the experiment and modification of the experimental conditions and treatments. Such interference prevents policy analysts from discovering the effects of treatments that they want to study by restricting the selection of subjects and by causing the analysts to test treatments different from the ones intended.

Participants in and administrators of experiments (items 5 and 6) also may interfere. Participants can undermine the goals of the experiment by altering their behavior during the experimental period. Family goals that conflict with those of the experimenter can be a powerful interfering force (item 5). The interference may be in the best interest of the family, but not of the experiment. For example, if a family member receives an "income supplement," such as a school lunch, the family may transfer some of the supplement to other family members, perhaps by changing eating schedules and serving sizes, and using the money saved to buy other things, such as clothing and heat. Micro-experiments and macro-experiments seem less prone to interference from participants because the treatment and the outcome are directly connected.

Administrators can foil experiments by modifying the treatments (item 6). In trying to "help" subjects in the control group, administrators may supplement the control treatment with additional resources. Such interference may be more likely in production and reorganization experiments involving long-range investment in future well-being and opportunities.

The Hawthorne effect (item 8) states that people may behave differently when they know that they are being observed. For example, they may work harder.

Table 3-1 argues that micro-experiments and production experiments are more feasible to carry out and easier to interpret than macro-experiments and reorganization experiments. The former kinds tend to be lower in cost and involve less interference from political institutions than the latter kinds. Micro-experiments and direct production experiments may also have less interference from participants.

These are strong reasons for pursuing micro-experiments and production experiments. But we must not overlook the contribution that macro-experiments and reorganization experiments make to the full assessment of policy. Though the results of repeated sampling in a market may look promising, the outcome of a new policy in the market as a whole can differ considerably because of interactions within as well as outside the market. Macro-experiments and reorganization experiments provide a more complete picture of the policy, even if we must place less confidence in the results because the controls are less effective and because the sample size may be one—that is, one group. For example, a housing supply study might be applied in one city with no application of treatment in another city. Even in the presence of political interference, large-scale experiments may suggest whether policies could be successfully implemented without distortion.

TABLE 3-1 *Summary of problems of execution and inference for four types of experiments*

Problem	Micro-Experiments	Macro-Experiments	Production Experiments	Reorganization Experiments
1. Specification and measurement of treatments and outcomes	Treatments can be carefully specified in the form of tax-subsidy or income supplement schedules. In labor and product markets outcomes can often be carefully specified, but in service markets they may be difficult to specify. Indivisible products or products with a spectrum of characteristics (such as houses) may also be difficult to measure.		Inputs and outputs can be easy or hard to specify, depending on the nature of the area studied and the extent of accumulated knowledge in the area.	These experiments involve all the specification and measurement problems of the first three experiment types.
2. Sample selection	These experiments may use randomized selection of the participants in the control and treatment groups.	These experiments require saturation of a region.	These experiments may use randomized selection of the participants in the control and treatment groups.	These experiments require saturation of a region.
3. Cost	These experiments may be low in cost.	These experiments tend to be expensive due to the high cost of saturating a region.	These experiments may be low in cost.	These experiments tend to be expensive due to the high cost of saturating a region and to the development of new economic and social organizations.

4. Interference from political institutions	These experiments may undergo little interference from political institutions.	These experiments are likely to undergo little interference from political institutions due to the saturation of a region.	These experiments may undergo little interference from political institutions.	These experiments are likely to undergo interference from political institutions due to the saturation of a region and to the conflict between political institutions and social reorganization.
5. Interference from participants	These experiments may undergo little interference from participants because of the direct connection between treatment and outcome.		These experiments are likely to undergo interference from participants because of the indirect connection between treatment and outcome.	
6. Interference from administrators	These experiments may undergo little interference from administrators.		These experiments are likely to undergo interference from administrators when areas such as health and education are studied.	
7. Temporary and permanent effects of the experiment	In all experiments that run for short periods of time, the results may reflect temporary rather than permanent effects. To develop assurance that policy effects are permanent, longer-term experiments must be run.			
8. Hawthorne effect	This confounding effect may be present in all of the experiment types.			

CONCLUSION

Economic experimentation is a strong tool for assessing changes in policy. Using data from the population as it stands is a dangerous substitute for testing the behavioral response of individuals and groups to policy changes.

Of the four types of experiments we discuss, micro-experiments and production experiments tend to be more feasible to carry out and to have more reliable interpretations than macro-experiments and reorganization experiments. Nevertheless, because they focus on the outcomes of interactions among individuals and institutions, macro-experiments and reorganization experiments give a fuller view of policies.

REFERENCES

Mosteller, F., and Mosteller, G. 1979. New Statistical Methods in Public Policy I: Experimentation. *Journal of Contemporary Business* 8, no. 3: 79–92.

Rivlin, A.M. 1974. Allocating Resources for Policy Research: How Can Experiments Be More Useful? *American Economic Review* 64, no. 2: 346–354. Reprinted 1977 in *Statistics and Public Policy*, W.B. Fairley and F. Mosteller, eds. Reading, Mass.: Addison-Wesley, pp. 243–254.

CHAPTER 4

Comparative Observational Studies

Comparative observational studies provide evidence frequently used by policymakers to:

√ compare the effectiveness of two or more treatments,

√ see how well a particular program works,

√ understand the cause of an event.

Such studies have much in common with comparative experiments, and this chapter complements the one on experiments. Here we emphasize the variety of methods that qualify as observational studies and discuss four categories of such studies, noting their strengths and weaknesses for policy.

Although our focus here is on the comparative study, we emphasize that other kinds of observational studies are covered in other chapters. For example, a one-time sample survey is a type of observational study; we discuss it in depth in Chapter 5 on surveys.

This chapter follows the standard outline that we have chosen for data-gathering methods. We begin with an illustration of a large comparative observational study carried out in a policy context.

EXAMPLE: PRESCHOOL PROGRAM EVALUATION

As long as tests have measured the relative performance of schoolchildren, those from poor families have done worse on almost all standardized tests than those from rich families. As part of the War on

Poverty in 1965, President Lyndon Johnson's administration developed several programs to close the educational performance gap. Title I of the Elementary and Secondary Education Act allocates money to school districts based on how many poor children attend school there. Head Start, a remedial program of education, nutrition, and day care, tries to prepare poor children for school.

These programs underwent many evaluations beginning in the late 1960s. Completed in 1969, the first major evaluation of Head Start was directed jointly by Victor Cicirelli, a psychologist at Purdue University, and by the Westinghouse Learning Corporation (1969). It illustrates the strengths and weaknesses of an evaluative observational study. We give a simplified description. The researchers sampled 200 Head Start centers from the full national list. Within each center, they drew a sample of eight children. Since Head Start had been active during the previous year, they collected information that might be called post-test data. For example, they collected data from the 1600 Head Start children on IQ, linguistic level, physical health, and emotional development.

But what should these data be compared to? To a comparison, or control group, which had to be assembled retrospectively. To create a comparison group, the evaluators decided to match subjects retrospectively, using what is called the *case-control method*. For each group of eight children in a Head Start center, they identified eight children living in the same town who were similar to the Head Start children in terms of age, race, family income, and sex. From this control group of 1600 children, the investigators collected the same information as for the Head Start children.

When all data from all 3200 children were in, the investigators examined the difference in average performance between Head Start pupils and control pupils for each of the major outcome variables. They reported clear findings of no difference between Head Start and control group children.

What was the upshot of this study? First, critics attacked its methodological flaws. The research design called for only one measurement in time—after the program had been operating—and no preprogram data were available. The researchers offered no convincing justification for their method of selecting the control group. The "matching" features—race, sex, age, and family income—seem reasonable on the surface, but critics suggested that other, and possibly more important, variables may have been overlooked.

The most serious flaw, however, is the classic one that plagues all observational studies: the policymaker cannot make a valid causal inference. To assess the effects of Head Start, an ideal design would randomly divide children into two groups: one group receiving Head Start and the other not. Then, any outcome differences could be causally attributed to the program, since the groups would be similar in all respects except treatment. An observational study, such as Cicirelli-Westinghouse, which retrospectively compares people who received a treatment to others who did not, always stands open to the criticism that the two groups were not initially comparable. For instance, parents of poor, white, male four-year-olds who enroll their children in Head Start may differ in some ways from parents of poor, white, male four-year-olds who do not enroll their children. Possibly these differences are even more substantial than the effect of the program. We return to this idea, sometimes called *selection effects*, later in this chapter. To summarize, heavy criticism followed the publication of the study. Statisticians find themselves perennially impressed at the sudden methodological expertness of critics immediately following an unpopular finding.

A second result of this observational study was that it put policy-makers in a better position to do further investigation; it helped them organize a new, more systematic inquiry in 1971. Based on the controversial findings of Cicirelli-Westinghouse and the methodological debate that followed, the U.S. Office of Education commissioned a prospective (rather than retrospective) study. Although controlled, this "Planned Variation" study was not randomized. The Office of Education funded ten sponsors to develop models of what they thought Head Start should be. Each sponsor implemented the same model in five sites. The planned variation aspect was that a few key features, such as curriculum structure and level of parent involvement, varied systematically across sponsors. A few sponsors intentionally built in highly structured curricula, while others built in more open classrooms. Similarly, some sponsors emphasized parent involvement; others discouraged it.

Notice this is not a randomized field trial, because (no one and) nothing was randomized: curricula were not randomly assigned to sites; children were not randomly assigned to different types of Head Start centers. But this study moved one step closer to investigating systematically how different features of the Head Start programs influence children. Marshall Smith, Herbert Weisberg, and Anthony Bryk (1973) conducted the analysis at the Huron Institute over a period of three years. They found that, while overall the program effects were marginal, programs using certain curricula had consistently better results than programs using other curricula. This information was used in later program development. The researchers also found a relationship between type of curriculum and type of child.

The least able children from the poorest backgrounds benefited from the highly structured curricula but gained little or nothing from the less structured curricula. The most able children, on the other hand, benefited equally from both types of curricula.

Third, the original observational study, together with the Planned Variation follow-up, spawned many other small observational studies at local program sites. Now, after fifteen years of program operation, we find dozens of small studies conducted within a single Head Start center or in a small group of centers. A recent summary of these studies, together with follow-up data on children who were in Head Start ten years ago and are now in high school, reports clear evidence that the program is an overall success (Darlington 1980). But we must remember that an aggregation of observational studies suffers from the same caveat as each individual study: causal inferences are risky. In the end, this aggregation of many studies may lead to two different policy inferences:

1. Since many small studies show a modest degree of program success, the overall evidence is that Head Start works.
2. Because of the availability of these observational studies, no randomized, controlled trial has been done, not even a small one. Perhaps these other studies are delaying the randomized trial.

One or only a few randomized trials producing the same finding of modest program success would strengthen enormously the arguments of Head Start proponents. Each observational study has the limitation that causal inference is risky; not even twenty such studies can eliminate the limitation. A decision maker should remember this important point when commissioning studies to acquire information.

As we mentioned in the chapter on experiments, when a program exists at many different sites, the opportunity to improve it through evolutionary experimentation should not be overlooked. It can pay big dividends. Although political considerations must weigh heavily in making the arrangements and choosing the design for a program evaluation, increasing pressure from economy-minded citizens will force government agencies to prove the value of the programs they sponsor. Data from observational studies are but a first step in this process.

FEATURES OF OBSERVATIONAL STUDIES

Observational studies take several forms. The key feature is lack of planned or controlled intervention or allocation of people and treatments. This feature distinguishes the observational study from a comparative controlled study, where the word "controlled" indicates that the investigator assigns people or other units to treatments. In conducting an observational study, the investigator takes the cards (intervention) as nature or circumstance deals them out.

Observational studies are similar to case studies to the extent that the investigator gathers data in the field as they are available, without initial intervention. Unlike case studies, observational studies have a systematic and planned collection of data over several persons, institutions, or groups, using common definitions of background and outcome variables.

Four different designs of observational studies are often used to evaluate programs by comparing the effects of two or more alternative treatments or conditions. The four designs can be applied to any comparable units, as well as to persons. They can be laid out in a simple table—see Table 4-1—where rows indicate the number of treatment groups being compared, columns indicate at what time measurements are taken, and the cell entries describe key features of the measurement process. Before illustrating the four designs, we briefly summarize their features.

Cell (1) defines "single-group, after-only" studies. These involve observing people all of whom have received a treatment or been exposed to some activity. Since data appear only after the treatment,

TABLE 4-1   *Classification of comparative observational studies*

		When are measurements taken?	
		After only	*Before and after*
	One	Absolute standard (1)	Observe change over time (2)
How many treatment groups?	Two or more	Observe differences between groups; remember to ask whether groups were initially comparable. (3)	Observe difference of changes; see how initially comparable groups were. If initially comparable, ask how they got that way. (4)

this design forces us to compare the findings from an observational study to an externally set standard, because we have no comparison group within the study.

Cell (2) defines "single-group, before-and-after" studies. Here, while again no comparison group is available, we collect data on the same people both before and after an intervention. By looking at changes over time, we can estimate the influence of the intervention. But the absence of a comparison group deprives us of the capacity to estimate what would have happened anyway, without the intervention.

Cell (3) defines "two-group, after-only" studies. In this type, we compare two or more groups, perhaps one group that received a treatment and one that did not, or perhaps several groups, each receiving different versions of a treatment. The only data available are "after" measurements, so while we can compare the outcomes for two or more groups, we need to inquire whether they were initially comparable before the treatments.

Cell (4) defines "two-group, before-and-after" studies. It is the most elaborate of the four designs. Two or more groups each have measurements taken both before and after an intervention. To assess the effects of treatments, we can compare "gain scores" over the course of time. Here we also have data about how comparable the groups were initially. But we must be particularly careful with these data. If the groups were not comparable before treatment, we must ask whether an appropriate statistical adjustment can help us to equate them. If the groups were comparable before treatment, we must ask how and why. Had the several groups been formed by randomly assigning people among different treatments, we would not be surprised to find the different groups comparable before treatment. But if no randomization was formally done, we must ask whether we are looking at the equivalent of a natural randomization, or whether some feature of how people were divided into groups caused the pre-treatment similarities. For example, maybe the participants in the observational study were matched on several background variables, as they were retrospectively in the Cicirelli-Westinghouse example. Then, if we examine the groups on the variables for which they were matched, we shouldn't be surprised to find that they indeed match. But matching differs from randomization, because the matching variables may not represent all of the important variables.

Some examples will illustrate the issues that frequently arise in observational studies.

Learning Algebra (One-Group, After-Only Design)

An evaluation of schools illustrates the first form of observational study. Is school effective? Does it teach simple algebra? We can learn something about a high school's effectiveness by looking at people who have attended it. Some of them seem to know algebra moderately well, so the school probably teaches algebra moderately well. We assume that because of the law, which specifies that all children must attend school, we have no satisfactory comparison group. The strength of our inference that school causes the learning comes from knowing two facts. First, individuals do not invent algebra for themselves; it takes entire civilizations to do this. Second, studies of education show that mathematics is rarely learned on an individual basis except by advanced scholars.

In the one-group, after-only study, exactly what is being compared? Essentially, we compare the effect of treatment with that of no treatment. Somehow we must come up with a standard that would be attained if the treatment were not applied. For example, if after a three-week training program in welding, the trainees have achieved a given level of competence, one can assume that without the program they would have learned nothing about welding. Another form of program tries to bring people to a certain level or duration of accomplishment. For example, a training program may be developed to maintain people in their jobs who historically have not been able to get and hold a job. Here, when we have no comparison group, length of employment can be compared with some externally developed criterion.

Changing the Speed Limit (One-Group, Before-and-After Design)

An example of the second form of observational study arises from the national 55-mile-per-hour speed limit. For many years, safety groups argued that speeding is a major cause of highway accidents. They urged that the speed limit on highways be lowered. At the beginning of 1974, in response to the oil embargo, Congress reduced speed limits nationally from 70 to 55 miles per hour to conserve fuel. The data on traffic deaths changed dramatically. From 54,633 in 1971, 56,100 in 1972, and 55,511 in 1973, traffic deaths sank to 46,402 in 1974 and 45,853 in 1975. The National Safety Council reported 49,200 deaths in 1977, 51,500 in 1978, 51,000 in 1979, and 51,900 in 1980.

Can we infer from this observational study that lowering speed limits reduces traffic fatalities? Not in a rigorous way. Other changes may have occurred over time that could explain the change, or at least be severely tangled up (statisticians say "confounded") with it. For example, since fuel prices are up, perhaps people drive less (as well as more slowly). This might lead to fewer traffic deaths because of reduced exposure.

We cannot stress too strongly how careful an analyst must be when faced with data from this sort of observational study. For example, analysts may feel that even if they don't know the exact magnitude of every confounding factor, they at least know its direction and therefore can set upper or lower bounds. This kind of thinking is sometimes helpful, but it can also lead to trouble. Take the traffic deaths example again. We might think that increased fuel prices caused people to drive fewer miles, as well as more slowly. Something other than the speed limit changed: the number of miles driven decreased. Both decreases could contribute to the drop in traffic fatalities.

But other factors may matter. For example, higher fuel prices may indeed lead to fewer miles driven, but they may also encourage people to buy smaller cars with better gas mileage, suggesting that miles driven could increase once again. Moreover, those miles would be driven in smaller and less safe cars. For a given number of traffic accidents, the fatality rate might be higher when small cars are involved. Notice that this argument cuts in the opposite direction from the original hypothesis of reduced driving.

Without a comparison group—ideally a comparison group that is equivalent to the treatment group in every respect except that it did not receive the treatment—causal inferences become hazardous. In any policy analysis, the analyst must judge what factors need to be adjusted (such as fuel price, miles driven, and car size and safety, in the above example). These judgments are difficult to make, and in the end usually become efforts to approximate with the findings from an inadequate observational study the better information that might have come from a careful experiment, if it could have been done.

Two Examples: Head Start and Air Quality (Two-Group, After-Only Design)

The Head Start study by Cicirelli-Westinghouse, described earlier, illustrates this design. Head Start children were compared with non–Head Start children, and the only data available were postprogram test scores. Another example of this design tries to assess the effect of air quality on health. Investigators collect information on both the general health of residents of several places and the level of air pollution at each place. They have no data on the health of each person ten years ago.

What might an analyst make of a finding from this air quality study? For example, suppose that people who live in high-pollution areas are no sicker, on average, than those in low-pollution areas. Does this lead to a conclusion of pollution being harmless? Based on the available data from a two-group, after-only study, we cannot draw firm conclusions. Many possible explanations, only one of which is that air pollution is harmless, could lead to a finding of no difference in illness.

Possibly people who were sick ten years ago and living in high-pollution areas moved to low-pollution areas because they guessed correctly that the pollution was making them sicker. If so, fewer sick people would be living in high-pollution areas, and more sick people

THE WALL STREET JOURNAL

**"Of course your group had 25% fewer cavities
—your group had 25% fewer teeth."**

would be living in clean areas. If we observed only this outcome, without knowing where these people lived and what their health was ten years ago, we would miss the causal link entirely.

A second possibility is that air pollution affects people either severely or scarcely at all. Those who are scarcely affected stay in high-pollution areas and remain well. Those who are severely affected are no longer on this earth, so they do not influence the average health level at the high-pollution sites. Thus, overall, pollution will not seem to matter much, even though it kills.

The point behind these examples is not that we believe we know the correct answers. Rather, they illustrate the extreme difficulty of making a causal inference about an observed difference between two groups if we do not know how the groups were formed in the first place. Although we can make some good guesses about what could explain an outcome, they will remain only guesses without a systematic investigation of each guess.

Day Care Regulations (Two-Group, Before-and-After Design)

In the mid-1970s the U.S. Department of Health, Education, and Welfare (HEW) realized that by 1979 it would have to formulate new Federal Interagency Day Care Regulations. It therefore decided to commission a large national study to see what features of such centers, if any, should be regulated. To begin the effort, they focused on three features that they suspected of influencing the quality of care that children receive: (1) staff-child ratio, (2) level of caregiver training, and (3) group size (number of children per classroom). HEW commissioned a three-year study costing $7 million (Ruopp 1979).

The largest component of this effort was a several-group before-and-after observational study of forty-eight centers. Each center was categorized as either high or low on each of the three key variables, resulting in eight ($= 2 \times 2 \times 2$) categories of treatment. Each day care center fell into one of the eight. Since children attended the center chosen by their parents, the study lacked randomization or controlled assignment. The investigators measured the children's cognitive, social, and emotional development before and after attendance at each center.

The researchers found that the staff-child ratio was not closely related to outcomes, except at unrealistic extremes; that staff training mattered a fair amount; and that group size was the most important factor in determining how well a center seemed to serve children. For example, children who attended a day care center with two staff and fifteen children showed greater gains than children attending a center wth four staff and thirty children. Even though both centers have the same staff-child ratio, the smaller group of children is preferable.

In this example, notice that the treatments were already in place; the investigators did not set them up. We have called these situations natural experiments. Since before and after measures were available on every child (over 800 children were studied), the comparative gain scores could be examined. Yet the children were affiliated with particular centers entirely on the basis of self-selection; their families chose where they should go. Did this threaten the validity of the findings?

The investigators decided that perhaps the validity was threatened. To investigate this hunch, they compared certain characteristics of the children in different day care centers with features of the centers and found clear relationships. For example, the poorest children tended to be enrolled in the most expensive, richest centers, because Title XX of the Social Security Act requires certain expenditures on poor children, while middle class families had to pay out of their pockets. So they discovered confounding of family background and level of day care center resources. A second complication was the confounding of race with certain kinds of centers; those centers located in primarily white areas had primarily white children attending and low staff-child ratios, while centers in primarily black neighborhoods had mainly black children enrolled and high staff-child ratios. Thus, race and economic level confound all findings from this study and are even confounded with each other.

Realizing that it would be risky to base national regulations on the causal inferences from such a study, HEW commissioned an additional small randomized study to be carried out in Atlanta. It was less than one-third as large as the big observational study. Yet the findings in this particular case turned out to be very similar for the two studies. Once again, group size was the important variable; staff-child ratio, the variable that most academic advisers had put their chips on originally, turned out to be surprisingly unimportant. (The lack of effect of this variable—teacher-student ratio—in schools is one of the best documented facts in the field of education, partly because it is hard to believe. Study after study gets the same result. What is new here is the finding that it also applies to day care centers.) In 1979 HEW used the congruent results of the two studies as the basis for a new set of Federal Interagency Regulations.

WHAT THE OBSERVATIONAL STUDY IS NOT

Observational studies lack the key feature of controlling the assignment of treatments. If the goal of a policy study is to attribute an outcome to a treatment, or program, or policy change, it is valuable for the investigator to be able to assign treatments. As we discuss in the chapter on experiments, randomization is one method of assignment that is particularly valuable for making causal inferences.

This fact leads us to note once again the crucial weakness of an observational study: trouble may arise when using it for causal inferences. It also suggests a goal for the design and analysis of an observational study: to make it as much like a randomized experiment as possible. Most of the methods of strengthening such studies aim at this goal. Ultimately, an investigator wants to be able to compare those who receive a treatment with others who do not but who are otherwise similar.

STRENGTHENING OBSERVATIONAL STUDIES

Comparative observational studies, though lacking randomization, can be strengthened by using the same devices used to strengthen comparative experiments, such as blindness, stratification, and random sampling (from a population). Certain additional devices, such as covariance analysis and standardization, are used especially for observational studies in which the control and treatment groups do not match well on important variables associated with the outcome. These devices do not change the treatments, but they take what steps are possible in the analysis to adjust for disparities in the groups to be compared. In this section we tell briefly how to apply these methods.

Adjustment of Background Variables (Covariance Analysis)

Use background or other variables related to outcome to estimate by regression methods how much difference these variables make to the outcome. Then adjust each group's performance according to the observed pattern of background variables to make the outcomes more nearly comparable. (The usual objections to regression analysis of observational data as a substitute for experimentation—actually changing the variables—apply. See Chapter 2.)

Standardization

Stratify the treated group and the control group according to background variables. The strata will have disproportionate numbers of cases in the treated and control groups, and so they will not be comparable. Choose weights for these strata and apply them to the outcomes (for example, death rates) observed in the strata to get a summary statistic for each group. Compare these statistics. The choice of weights is arbitrary. Ideally one would choose weights that are appropriate for the population where the treatment is to be applied.

Multiple Control Groups

Strengthen the inference by supplying more than one control group of ancillary observations. For example, in sociological studies a group of juveniles involved in a program intended to reduce delinquency might be compared with untreated groups in nearby neighborhoods or with school groups.

Matching (Case-Control Method)

Match individuals in the treated group with those in untreated groups to equate background variables directly instead of making analytical adjustments.

Dose Response

Find observational groups that have differing intensity of treatment. For example, exposure to lead may differ for office workers, printers, and lead smelter workers. When outcome differs in a rational manner according to intensity of exposure, the findings carry more conviction.

Modeling and Simulation

Use theory and background information to estimate the performance that would occur in the absence of treatment. When this can be done, the difference between the observed performance and the modeled performance can be instructive. In some areas we can bring a good deal of data to bear. For example, in a problem on how best to serve consumers, we may be able to detail the distribution of consumer arrival times, service times, costs of waiting, and costs of additional queues and servers. Operations analysts have a well-developed theory of queues and their behavior. We may be able to measure several kinds of costs and losses by comparing a computer simulation of the queuing process with the observed results.

Path-Analysis or Simultaneous-Equation Models

These special kinds of regression analyses assume that we know the directions of causation, when several variables are present, and then derive the impact of the variables that policy can change. (See Chapter 13 on modeling.) When we know that if nothing were done to correct a condition it would just get worse, we can take the conservative tack of assuming that the situation will remain constant if untreated and measure gains from treatment from this position. For example, if a person with a deteriorating bone condition needs two canes to walk now, and a treatment makes it possible to walk with one cane, then the treatment gets credit for relieving the patient of one cane, even though we recognize that, had the condition persisted, crutches would ultimately have been required. If we know the rate of degeneration, we can use that information in measuring gains.

Historical Controls (and Problems of Definitions)

Comparing observational data with data on other groups gathered at other times and places can help strengthen the results of an observational study. For example, to see whether cloud seeding increased rainfall during a summer of one year, we might compare precipitation that year with rainfall at the same place in earlier years. Usually such information is used only in the early stages of an investigation. Later, investigators become wary of it. Today historical evidence concerning cloud seeding would be disregarded by serious scholars, though commercial interests might use such evidence for advertising. Many processes and institutions change a lot from year to year and generation to generation. Even the definitions of things change—for example, in measuring rainfall, placement of the rain-measuring devices can alter the findings. In medicine, some diseases lose their names entirely, but because they are no longer diagnosed does not necessarily mean that health has improved.

In the years between 1932 and 1980 the size and geographic distribution of grocery stores changed from small neighborhood enterprises to enormous buildings in malls. The concept of neighborhood cannot be the same at the two periods if one is to include consumer behavior as part of the notion of a neighborhood.

The treatment of schoolchildren by their teachers, parents, and peers changes from generation to generation, to say nothing of differences in the time spent watching movies and television or listening to the radio. Thus, we are not comparing the same sorts of people when we compare 15-year-olds in 1980 with those in the good old depression days of 1932. Even the proportion of children attending school at age 15 has changed. Since the population has changed in so many ways, even those differences in the cognitive performance of 15-year-olds then and now that appear large would leave us wondering about the causes.

MERITS OF OBSERVATIONAL STUDIES

What are observational studies particularly good for? Their strength is pragmatic: they usually do not require an investigator to control the assignment of treatments. They enable us to study what happened when a new treatment was implemented in the natural course of events, such as the 55-mile-per-hour speed limit.

A second merit is that they *may* detect the existence of special interrelations between treatments and kinds of people, or between treatments and kinds of sites. To illustrate, let us return to the example of structured and unstructured Head Start curricula. Several observational studies have compared these two types of curricula, with conflicting conclusions about which is preferable. If we assume that all the studies were done reasonably well, what might explain these conflicting results? Possibly some studies were done on populations where one program is better, and some on populations where the other program is better. Thus, we might profit from trying to identify variables that might explain the conflicting results. Joan Bissell (1973) did precisely such a study of Head Start programs and found the source of conflict: by and large, highly structured programs were preferable for low-IQ children, while the reverse was true for high-IQ children. Thus, observational studies give us an opportunity to look for interrelations between background variables and treatment effects. Such effects are called *interactions*.

WEAKNESSES OF OBSERVATIONAL STUDIES

The weaknesses of observational studies are the same as those of experiments. Three additional difficulties deserve our attention.

Weak Inference

Observational studies of types 1 and 2 (see Table 4-1) have no control group. The 55-mile-per-hour speed limit is an example. Maybe people not only drove more slowly but also less, or differently, or took different roads, and that explains the lower fatality rate. Thus, we do not know that the change in speed limit was what reduced the death rate.

Unequated Groups

Control groups in observational studies may not be comparable initially. If the children who often watch "Sesame Street" on television score higher than the children who watch it infrequently, what does that imply about the instructional value of "Sesame Street"? Not very much; those who watch it often may be brighter or may watch more television overall. In any event, these possible selection effects generate a well-known difficulty in observational studies, and they pose serious barriers to deciding on causes.

Third-Variable Effects

If an interaction between subject and treatment does exist, the results of a policy study done by using observational data alone may depend heavily on the allocation of people to treatments, thus creating misinterpretations. Consider the following hypothetical example, which illustrates the kind of finding that would occur when different populations perform better under different treatments.

We want to choose one of two reading curricula, A and B. In the educational literature we find two observational studies: Jones (2000) found that A is better than B; Smith (2001) found the opposite. Which curriculum should we adopt?

We look into the matter more closely. Jones found that on a standardized reading test A beat B by 5 points: the 40 children who received curriculum A had an average score of 75, while the 40 who received curriculum B averaged 70 on the test. Using the same sample sizes, Smith found just the reverse: the 40 children who received curriculum A averaged 65, while the 40 who received curriculum B averaged 70.

Breaking down the data by sex (see Table 4-2), we find an explanation for the apparently conflicting results: their outcomes are *identical as to effects* but *different as to allocations*. The two studies found boys and girls performing at the same levels for each curriculum, but

TABLE 4–2   *Curriculum study outcomes*

	Average Scores (sample sizes in parentheses)		
Jones	*Boys*	*Girls*	*Overall*
Curriculum A	80 (30)	60 (10)	75 (40)
Curriculum B	60 (20)	80 (20)	70 (40)
Smith			
Curriculum A	80 (10)	60 (30)	65 (40)
Curriculum B	60 (20)	80 (20)	70 (40)

in Jones's observational study more boys than girls received curriculum A, while in Smith's observational study the reverse was true. The difference in allocation might have been the result of incidental administrative decisions in the schools, since the students had been assigned to classes before the observational studies were begun.

To the extent that allocation decisions can influence the results of a study, it is important that we be aware that such decisions were made and how they combine with the effects of different treatments to lead to overall results. In the hypothetical curriculum example it is easy to identify sex as a third influential variable. In actual studies, where such variables may be numerous, ill-defined, and difficult to measure, we may not be able to recognize them. Thus, it is hazardous to attribute cause to a specific third variable unless the field is well understood.

QUALITY CHECKLIST

1. *How many measurements over time are available?* If several are available for either a treatment or a comparison group, they may offer help in assessing whether a treatment effect exists.

2. *How were the pretreatment data used, if such data are available?* Information may be available on values of the outcome measure prior to the treatment. Also, background information on the participants before the treatment may shed light on why they chose to participate or be exposed to a treatment.

3. *How comparable were the treatment and comparison groups on background variables that seem important?* In Chapter 2 on experiments we pointed out the virtue of randomization—that it equates treatment and comparison groups in terms of their distributions for all

background variables. Without randomization, it becomes especially important to understand how treatment groups differ in terms of background variables. If clear differences exist, adjustments should be made to try to equate the groups, imperfect as this effort can be. If clear differences cannot be found, the investigator still cannot be sure that different groups are comparable, but the search can at least focus on selection effects as a threat to causal inference.

4. *How were people assigned to, or how did they become affiliated with, a particular group?* What was the assignment process? Did people choose the treatment or regimen they received? If so, the analyst must watch for differences in the types of people who chose different treatments. Perhaps people received different treatments not by choice but as members of naturally occurring groups, such as people in one city breathing more polluted air than people in another. These group differences can make the estimation of treatment effects very difficult.

5. *Did other external factors change during the course of the treatment in ways that might have affected the outcome?* This is especially important if no comparison group is available against which to assess treatment group changes. Sometimes people or institutions exposed to a treatment are also exposed to other, external influences. For example, at the same time that the 55-mile-per-hour speed limit was introduced, smaller cars were being marketed, confounding any effect that the changed speed limit alone would have on traffic fatalities.

POLICY IMPLICATIONS

Poorly controlled prospective experiments have many of the disadvantages of well-controlled experiments and do not have the advantage of firmness in the results. Retrospective observational studies ordinarily do have the advantages of speed, lack of interference with the system, and low cost; their difficulty is that intervening variables may prohibit a causal conclusion.

Quasi-experiments, such as occur when conditions following a policy change are compared with those before, ordinarily offer an opportunity for analysis, but the choice of conducting or not conducting them usually is not up to the policymaker. Natural experiments also suffer from the weaknesses created by intervening variables. Again, nature does these experiments, and we can only find them, not choose to do them.

QUALITY CHECKLIST

1. How many time measurements?
2. Pretreatment data used?
3. Comparability of treatment groups?
4. Process of assignment?
5. What else changed?

The feature that may distinguish a strong policy analysis from one that is less successful in observational studies is an investigator's perseverance in tracking down confounding factors that may lead to biased results. In discussing weaknesses, we presented an example where performance on different curricula depended upon a student's sex; girls did better on curriculum B, while boys did better on A. If that information were not presented in a clear way in the original studies, it would be up to an investigator to identify the background variables, such as sex, age, or family income, that might clarify the results. To do this, the investigator must have some understanding of the process or system being studied.

Sometimes observational studies offer the only alternative to having no data at all. Other times they may complement management records, which themselves are a form of observational study. Epidemiologists in particular have made remarkable use of these studies. People cannot be starved for a long time to see what happens to their hearts if they are pushed beyond certain limits. Carcinogenic treatments cannot be randomly assigned to humans. Here, comparative observational studies have provided useful estimates of treatment effects.

Remember, however, that although observational studies can be conducted quickly and relatively inexpensively and they are non-invasive, their evidence can be treacherous.

CONCLUSION

Observational studies have clear strengths and weaknesses as policy tools. Their overriding weakness is that a causal inference about a treatment's effect is always risky. This weakness is just as worrisome when several observational studies have similar outcomes and therefore lead to the postponement of a more carefully planned randomized experiment. On the other hand, as a relatively simple way to collect data, and as a preliminary step along the way to designing a randomized experiment, observational studies can be useful policy tools. Particularly if the investigator understands the system being studied, observational studies can be used to disentangle the background factors that differentiate groups receiving different treatments.

Comparative observational studies may offer the only means of ever collecting any data at all about a treatment. Some events, such as earthquakes, are impossible to deliver as designed treatments, and certain treatments are unethical, as in many medical and social investigations. In these extremes, investigators must do their best with data from observational studies. The intent is usually to adjust the evidence from an observational study to approximate as closely as possible what would have happened if a randomized experiment had been conducted.

REFERENCES

Bissell, J. S. 1973. Planned Variation in Head Start and Follow Through. In *Preschool Programs for the Disadvantaged*, Volume 2, J. C. Stanley, ed. Baltimore: Johns Hopkins University Press.

Cicirelli, V. G.; Cooper, W. H.; and Granger, R. L. June 1969. *The Impact of Head Start: An Evaluation of the Effects of Head Start on Children's Cognitive and Affective Development.* Athens, Ohio: Ohio University and Westinghouse Learning Corporation.

Darlington, R. B. et al. 1980. Preschool Programs and Later School Competence of Children from Low-Income Families. *Science* 208 (11 April):202–204.

Ruopp, R. 1979. *Children at the Center: Report of the National Day Care Study.* Cambridge, Mass.: Abt Books.

Smith, M. S.; Weisberg, H. I.; and Bryk, A. S. 1973. *Results of the Head Start Planned Variation Experiment.* Cambridge, Mass.: The Huron Institute.

FURTHER READING

Anderson, S. et al. 1980. *Statistical Methods for Comparative Studies.* New York: John Wiley and Sons.

Cook, T. D., and Campbell, D. T. 1979. *Quasi-Experimentation: Design and Analysis Issues for Field Settings.* Chicago: Rand McNally.

Campbell, D. T., and Stanley, J. C. 1966. *Experimental and Quasi-Experimental Designs for Research.* Chicago: Rand McNally.

Campbell, D. T., and Boruch, R. F. 1975. Making the Case for Randomized Assignment to Treatments by Considering the Alternatives: Six Ways in Which Quasi-Experimental Evaluations Tend to Underestimate Effects. In *Evaluation and Experiment*, C. A. Bennett and A. A. Lumsdaine, eds. New York: Academic Press.

Cochran, W. G. 1965. The Planning of Observational Studies of Human Populations (with discussion). *Journal of the Royal Statistical Society, Series A*, 128: 234–266.

PART II

Measuring the Status Quo

CHAPTER 5

Sample Surveys

Sample surveys usually assess the state of nature at a certain time. That state of nature may be a frequency of occurrence, such as the fraction of single-family homes that have more than one bathroom, or it may be the response to a more complex attitudinal question, such as why people favor or oppose federal funding for abortions. The key point is that sample surveys rarely reveal a causal relationship, such as whether changing policy leads to a change in outcome.

We begin with three examples. In the first a sample survey helped legislators shape a new federal agency. The second describes how survey data contributed to a policy decision made by a school board in a small city. The third shows how a sample survey helped small business owners to improve the state legislative climate and laws affecting their businesses.

EXAMPLES

Child Abuse

Horror stories abound in the popular press about child abuse, neglect, and molestation. Abuse has been defined for the medical profession by Henry Kempe as a situation "in which a child is suffering from serious physical injury inflicted upon him by other than accidental means; is suffering harm by reason of neglect, malnutrition, or sexual abuse; is going without necessary and basic physical care; or is growing up under conditions which threaten his basic physical and emotional survival" (1962, p. 17).

The problem is not new, largely because of the traditional view of children as chattel. Aristotle wrote, "The justice of a master or a father is a different thing from that of a citizen, for a son or slave is property, and there can be no injustice to one's own property." The *Patria Potestas* gave a Roman father the legal right to sell, abandon, kill, or offer in sacrifice all of his children. Colonial America gave a father the statutory right to put his child to death and, if necessary, to call upon the assistance of the colony's officers to do so.

The child's legal status has changed considerably during the past hundred years. Children are now viewed as belonging to themselves and in the care of their parents, although social enforcement of children's rights has lagged behind this change. State social service agencies have helped increase public awareness of the maltreatment suffered by many children. Still, in the 1970s the Society for Prevention of Cruelty to Animals in New York City had more contributors than the Society for Prevention of Cruelty to Children.

Primarily in the last two decades, government programs have begun to take form. All fifty states have passed laws either encouraging or requiring citizens to report incidents of child abuse. Hospitals, police, and social service agencies also must report. The U.S. Department of Health and Human Services has taken the lead by formulating a national policy to counter child abuse and neglect. Until the early 1970s, this was done mainly through Title IV-A (Aid for Dependent Children), Title IV-B (Child Welfare Services), and Title V (Maternal and Child Health Programs) of the Social Security Act.

In the early 1970s both the U.S. House and Senate considered bills to set up a new federal administrative agency to prevent or ameliorate child abuse and neglect.

The proposed legislation outlined activities for this agency, to be called the National Center for Child Abuse and Neglect (NCCAN). The most common activities were services and preventive programs for families. But one feature of both bills was politically controversial: a national screening of all preschool children to ferret out cases of unreported abuse. The idea behind this screening was that children too young to be in school may not be connected to any network of people who could detect abuse. There are approximately 15 million such children. The bill proposed that "national health visitors" go to the homes of families of young children to offer community services and do informal spot checks on the children's development. This is not a new idea; it is national policy in Scotland. Yet it understandably engendered great controversy in the U.S. Congress, where issues of violating family privacy were heatedly debated. Even beyond the political question of such visits, how effective would they be? Fortunately, data and evidence could be collected to answer this question.

How common is child abuse? Those committing the crime avoid reporting it. Therefore, in spite of official state-level reports on abuse cases, it was generally agreed that the number of reports underestimated the true incidence. Management records did not provide a good direct estimate, and this led to widely disparate guesses.

For example, the testimony offered to Congress in 1973, during hearings for the creation of NCCAN, indicates that state registries had reports of 25,000 cases of abuse annually in America. Dr. Kempe, a pediatrician working extensively in the field, estimated 60,000 incidents annually. A 1970 survey of physicians, hospitals, institutions, and police departments in Massachusetts produced a statewide rate of occurrence which, projected to the national level, would amount to approximately 200,000 incidents annually. Dr. Vincent J. Fontana, chairman of the New York City Task Force on Child Abuse and Neglect, estimated in 1973 at an American Medical Association meeting that there would be approximately 1.5 million incidents of child abuse in America that year.

The enormous variation in these estimates matters, because the value of a national screening program depends heavily on the frequency of the event. For example, if abuse is extraordinarily rare, such as one case per million children, it would cost a vast sum per abused child to search for the fifteen abused children.

What was done? A sample survey provided some information. With support from the U.S. Department of Health, Education, and Welfare, Professor David Gil at Brandeis University commissioned the National Opinion Research Center (NORC) to estimate the national incidence of child abuse. In a survey of 1,520 adults, NORC asked respondents whether they "personally knew families involved in incidents of child abuse resulting in physical injury during the twelve months preceding the interview." Since 45 respondents, or 3 percent, reported such knowledge, Gil (1973) estimated that approximately 3 percent of children are abused.

Further analysis of these survey data suggested a lower rate of incidence. The 3 percent estimate would be reasonable if each respondent to the NORC survey knew a grand total of only one child who might or might not have been abused. But that is unrealistic. So this survey estimate was revised by Light (1973), taking account of how many children a respondent was likely to know altogether, and also how likely a respondent was to know about abuse. The revised estimate of the incidence of child abuse was about one-tenth of the original, or 0.3 percent.

What effect did this adjusted information from the NORC sample survey have on policy? A substantial one. Using the revised estimate of incidence, together with estimates of how well pediatricians and nurses can detect abuse, the Senate and House committees considering the legislation decided that a national screening program would lead to far too many false positive diagnoses to be useful. That is, when a screening program is undertaken, everyone hopes that abused children will be correctly diagnosed as abused, and also that nonabused children will be correctly diagnosed as nonabused. With a relatively uncommon event, such as abuse, even good accuracy in diagnosing abuse and nonabuse will still lead to categorizing many nonabusing families as abusers. This happens because child abuse is relatively rare, and so even a small proportion of misclassification of nonabused children as abused in a large population means that most children diagnosed as abused will actually be nonabused (see Figure 5-1).

A critic may wonder why the same difficulty doesn't arise for other large-scale screenings of rare events, such as tuberculosis. It does. But a false positive diagnosis of tuberculosis is a private occurrence that, when rechecked and discovered as false, does a person little harm, whereas incorrectly accusing a family of child abuse can do considerable social harm. For the proposed screening, the committee estimated that approximately 85 percent of children diagnosed as abused would in fact not be abused. Viewing this as an intolerably

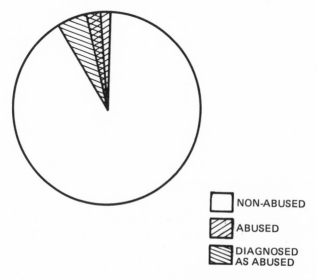

NON-ABUSED

ABUSED

DIAGNOSED AS ABUSED

FIGURE 5-1 *Detecting a rare event with imperfect diagnosis: child abuse as an example*

high fraction, entailing far too many false accusations of families, the committee revised the legislation, dropping the screening program from the mandate of the new agency.

In 1974 President Nixon signed the revised bill into law, creating NCCAN. It was the last bill he signed before resigning.

The Fitchburg Public Schools Calendar

The public schools of Fitchburg, a city of 40,000 people in central Massachusetts, faced rapidly rising energy costs during the winter of 1979–80. An energy conservation committee, consisting of school administrators, teachers, representatives of local utilities, and concerned citizens, was formed to study the problem. Its report, issued in March 1980, focused on the savings that could be made by altering the school calendar (Feeney 1980).

The proposed changes included starting the school year in late August rather than in September, extending vacations at Thanksgiving and Christmas, closing schools on Mondays during February and March, and adding a vacation in April. In addition, the school day would be 15 minutes longer in order to meet state time requirements. If adopted, this program would save an estimated 65,000 gallons of fuel oil annually.

The Fitchburg School Committee wished to gauge community sentiment before proceeding with the program, so school administrators made plans to survey the city. A questionnaire outlined the proposed calendar and asked for the respondent's reaction to each of the major changes. It also asked for some demographic information in order to determine differences in feelings between households with one parent home during the day, households where both parents worked during school hours, single parents, and households with no schoolchildren. The survey was printed in a local newspaper that enjoys wide circulation in the area, and copies of the questionnaire were also sent home with schoolchildren.

Only 116 households responded to the newspaper survey; of the more than 6,000 questionnaires distributed to schoolchildren, 2,205 were returned. This response rate is higher than it might appear, since the many families with more than one child in the school system received multiple copies of the questionnaire. Since analysis showed no difference between returns from the newspaper and returns from parents, the responses were combined.

Overall, the changes received substantial support. Only 17 percent of those responding found fault with the proposed modification, a level of support of almost five to one. However, when the responses were broken down demographically, some significant patterns emerged. More than 20 percent of single-parent households and households where both parents work claimed they would have a major problem with the Monday closings and the April vacation, while opposition to all portions of the plan was negligible from households with one parent at home. Comments accompanying the survey forms indicated that many of the objections stemmed from anticipated problems of finding child care during the new closing times.

The survey results were submitted to the school committee. At the same time a poll of the teachers' union revealed support for the revisions on the order of five to one. The two surveys were sufficient to convince the committee to go ahead with calendar reform. In reaction to the concerns expressed by working parents, the April vacation was shortened, and Monday closings in March were dropped in favor of a one-week vacation during that month.

The proposed calendar was submitted to the Massachusetts Department of Education with the survey results attached as supporting documentation. The changes were approved, and the new calendar went into effect in August 1980 on a one-year trial basis. During this trial period, observational studies were conducted to examine the level of energy savings and look for effects on student achievement and teacher and pupil absenteeism.

Enacting Laws to Help Small Business

The gubernatorial election year of 1978 in Minnesota stimulated much discussion of the state's supposedly poor business climate. Some groups charged that the state was discouraging entrepreneurship, that state regulations and taxation policy were driving businesses away and preventing the success of new ventures.

To bring objective information into the increasingly emotional debate, the Minnesota Planning Agency commissioned the College of Business Administration at the University of Minnesota to "examine the most significant problems faced by Minnesota small businesses and, where feasible, to recommend specific steps Minnesota's state government can take to assist small business." The study would also assess the importance of small business to the economy of the state and determine public perceptions of the importance of state programs to assist small business (University of Minnesota 1979).

The University of Minnesota team marshalled information from four sources: the relevant literature, including both academic and government studies; interviews with persons believed to have special expertise in the problems of small business; detailed case studies of twelve selected small businesses; and questionnaires administered to over 300 financial institutions dealing with small businesses.

For the interviews with experts, the investigators used a questionnaire to conduct personal interviews with fourteen persons, including officials of the U.S. Small Business Administration, bankers, accountants, and prominent investors. Each interview took between an hour and a half and two hours to complete, and several individuals had follow-up interviews. The interviewers themselves were experts in business management, and the interviews were structured to elicit in-depth responses. Although they used a standardized questionnaire and asked all questions on this form, interviewers were free to ask follow-up questions in order to gain further insight. As a supplement to this process, they informally interviewed over twenty small entrepreneurs, accountants, bankers, legislators, and government officials with small business experience.

Because financial organizations such as banks, insurance companies, and commercial credit firms are often focal points for local business activities, providing managerial advice in addition to capital, the investigators sought the views of individuals working for these firms. They devised and mailed a written questionnaire to 1,610 financial institutions throughout the state that were believed to have dealt with small businesses in the past. The chief executive officer of each institution receiving a questionnaire then sent it to the person in the firm most knowledgeable about small business. A cover letter signed by the governor of Minnesota explained the importance and purposes of the survey.

The mailing elicited 303 usable responses, a response rate of 19 percent. Limitations on time and money prevented follow-up of nonrespondents. The response rate was highest among banks and lowest among savings and loan associations. As banks generate over 95 percent of all capital provided to small business, this overrepresentation of banks was not serious.

In a three-volume report on the problems facing small business, the investigators found that the data obtained from the expert interviews, the case studies, and the survey of financial institutions were in substantial agreement. Six key findings emerged:

√ Small business is vital to the economic future of Minnesota.

√ Removal of current restrictions on business activity will help business more than new assistance programs.

√ Lack of capital is a major problem for most small businesses.

√ Government paperwork and regulations create a major problem for many small enterprises.

√ High taxes, Workers' Compensation, and Unemployment Insurance are major problems for small businesses.

√ State programs to assist small businesses are poorly publicized and are therefore little known and underutilized.

Interest in the report was great. Leading newspapers in the state editorialized on its recommendations, several of which were enacted into law during the 1979 legislative session. These included:

√ Provisions for increased state procurement from small businesses.

√ Establishment of a state business assistance center.

√ Changes in income and inheritance tax laws intended to aid small businesses.

√ Tax credits for pollution control and provision of pollution control loans.

√ Provisions to hold down the cost of the Workers' Compensation and Unemployment Insurance systems and to simplify the administrative procedures involved.

In addition, the Minnesota Planning Agency and Department of Economic Security set up an information system to systematically measure small business formation and development.

FEATURES OF THE SAMPLE SURVEY

Sampling helps a policy analyst understand the characteristics of a population. To see how a sample survey can deliver useful information, we turn now to different ways of selecting a sample.

Kinds of Samples

A policy analyst can select, or have access to, part of a population in various ways—as a by-product of some program (fortuitous), through the judgment of an expert, or by scientific design (probability sampling).

"YES - THIS IS A TYPICAL
EXAMPLE OF THE HOUSES
IN THIS NEIGHBORHOOD."

Fortuitous Samples

Data are often available on a small part of a population, where the policymaker had little or no say about the makeup of the sample. For example, many large-scale federal programs involve volunteers. CETA job training, community mental health centers, and Head Start are three examples. An analyst who wishes to study the effects of these programs without designing a new, controlled intervention must use data from volunteers. Such fortuitous samples may be useful in generalizing about a program's value for a larger population of volunteers, but their validity for generalizing to broader populations, or to populations with nonvolunteers, is questionable.

Expert Choice

Judgment sampling gives a second method of selection. A policy analyst chooses a subgroup of people or places from a large population, using a variety of criteria. Often the aim is to produce a "representative sample"—one that resembles the population in all the ways that matter. Unfortunately, the term "representative sample" lacks a precise meaning and has been abused by people who want to bestow an air of respectability on a sample that has no scientific basis. William Kruskal and Frederick Mosteller (1980) have examined the meanings that various writers intended by this term; they summarized the range of usage in *nine* distinct meanings, each illustrated by a sketch. Of these meanings, we illustrate, both with a cartoon and a quotation, five that have special relevance to our work, their meanings numbered 1, 2, 3, 5, and 7.*

*Illustrations of meanings reproduced with the permission of the editor of the *International Statistical Review*.

Meaning 1. General, usually unjustified, acclaim
for data: The emperor's new clothes.

". . . private and municipal museums are, if my sampling has been representative, a little better than all but the most prestigious state museums." Douglas J.
Stewart, "Two Cheers for the Tombaroli," *The New Republic* 28 (April 28,
1973): 21.

Sometimes it may be appropriate to require that the sample be
chosen according to certain rules, such as from locations where a new
program is most likely to succeed or from patients most eager to co-
operate with the new regimen. For example, in a planned variation
study of Follow Through (a follow-up to Head Start for young children), each of ten organizations (the sponsors) was asked to try out its
curriculum at four sites. The sponsors chose their own sites, and so

one might guess they selected the sites they felt were best matched with the program. The results from such a sample may give a policymaker valuable insight into what happens when a sponsor tries out a program at a specially selected place. They tell much less about what would happen if this sponsor's program were implemented at a broad variety of sites.

Probability Sampling

Probability sampling imposes some mathematical and procedural rules upon the sampling process. The key idea is that every individual or group of individuals in the population has a known and nonzero probability of being selected. *Random sampling*, a special kind of probability sampling, requires that each possible sample of a given size from a population have an equal chance of selection. We cannot count on this unless specific steps have been taken to ensure it. Other complex schemes to strengthen inferences from a sample are based on prior knowledge or judgments about the population.

Steps in Organizing a Sample Survey

Regardless of the type of sample, a policy analyst should take certain steps to organize it. Cochran (1977) provides a good summary:

1. *State the objectives clearly.* For example, the objective may be description ("What fraction of white males over age 50 are anemic?") or inference ("How well are patients doing with a new medication versus those with an old one?") or both.

2. *Specify the exact population to which inferences will be made.* This should be the aggregate from which the sample is chosen. Notice that, for policy inference, a sample that is not appropriate for a certain population may be appropriate for a slightly different one. For example, although a sample of hospital patients tested for hypertension may not provide a good estimate of the prevalence of hypertension in the entire American adult population, the sample might support a useful estimate of prevalence for a broad hospital population.

3. *Indicate how precise a result is needed.* This is particularly important for analyses preceding policy decisions, many of which require precise estimates. Political decisions often require precision as well. For example, allocating a political campaign's scarce resources across many states now requires close estimates of how well a candidate is doing in each state. As few as five percentage points can tip the scale toward mounting or abandoning a campaign.

Meaning 2. Absence of selective forces: Justice
balancing the scales.

"Ehrenberg was, of course, aware that his sample was not representative of
Krupp employees as a whole because of their long time employment with Krupp,
their higher average income and their occupational distribution. . . . He was,
however, willing to sacrifice this criterion in favor of obtaining precise data."
Susanna Petra Schad, *Empirical Social Research in Germany 1848–1914* (The
Hague: Mouton, 1965, p. 84). The quotation, of course, illustrates the presence
of selective forces.

Other decisions require only rough estimates. For example, the
Gallup Poll regularly measures voters' attitudes toward the two major
political parties on a variety of issues, such as how well the government is handling inflation. Most analysts simply want to look at the
pattern of responses to see whether a party's ratings are generally high

or generally low. A five-percentage-point difference probably would matter little.

Why is this a useful distinction? Because sample surveys always have some uncertainty in their results. Part of this comes from sampling fluctuations (since surveys collect data on only a part of the population), and part comes from imprecision of measurement (since people often fail to respond accurately). Sampling fluctuations can be reduced by taking bigger samples, and imprecise measurement can be made more precise through careful and in-depth probing. But both solutions increase costs. Thus, the policymaker must choose between cost and precision and inform the survey designer of this choice.

4. *Choose a sampling unit.* Many situations offer the possibility of defining the population and its individual units in more than one way. If we want to know the distribution of income in the United States, we have to choose between persons and households. Should we take a sample of wage earners, or should we sample adults regardless of whether they are wage earners, or should we use the total earnings of the family unit? All have been done.

5. *Construct a frame.* A frame is a complete list of sampling units for the entire population. It could come from existing management records, or it might have to be assembled especially for the new survey—a far more expensive proposition. An accurate frame is crucial to selecting probability samples. Policy analysts should not accept an existing frame without checking on its accuracy and currency. How likely is it to be incomplete? How likely is it that the items left out of the frame are precisely the items we most want to learn about?

6. *Decide how information will be collected.* Data on children's reading performance may come from school records, from a standardized test administered to groups of students, or from individual testing.

WHAT THE SAMPLE SURVEY IS NOT

A sample survey is not good at assessing causality. Surveys can assess the frequency of a certain attribute such as high blood pressure, or the average level of a continuous variable, such as income, or the degree of association between two characteristics, such as ethnicity and the presence of sickle cell anemia. But they can almost never firmly establish a clear causal link between a treatment and an outcome.

For example, the Equal Educational Opportunity Survey, commissioned by Congress as part of the 1964 Civil Rights Act, and conducted by James Coleman and colleagues in the mid-1960s, involved a sample of several hundred thousand students in schools throughout the United States. Coleman's team collected information about the students' backgrounds, families, and friends; about the schools they attended, their level of spending, and their resources; and about students' performance in school. Many relationships were uncovered, including some that policymakers emphasized, such as the relationship between classroom composition and the academic performance of poor or minority students. But like most sample surveys, this one involved no formal intervention on the part of the policymaker. No new program or treatment was introduced. Instead, the Coleman survey assessed existing educational curricula. Thus, while it described and compared the levels of resources that different children were exposed to, the Coleman survey told nothing in a causal sense about the possible effects of reallocating those resources. For example, while the survey tells about how students in schools with large libraries perform relative to their peers in schools with small libraries, it is inappropriate to make an inference about how purchasing more school library books will change student performance (Coleman et al. 1966).

STRENGTHENING SAMPLE SURVEYS

Many ways of selecting and analyzing a sample can strengthen the results of a survey. These methods minimize the bias of a survey procedure or improve the precision of a measurement. For example, if each of several surveys of income undertaken by the Bureau of Labor Statistics underestimates the true average income of wage earners, other things equal, we would prefer the survey that underestimates the true average by the smallest amount. Further, if the Bureau of Labor Statistics estimated the average family income in Boston in 1981 as almost certainly falling between $5,000 and $30,000, we might decide that such a wide interval is indeed correct but useless for making policy.

So strengthening sample surveys means either reducing the bias of a survey procedure or increasing the precision of an estimate of the true value in the population.

For the policy analyst charged with organizing a study, the most practical methods of strengthening a sample survey fall into three categories:

1. Reduce the uncertainty of estimates by considering alternative designs, utilizing such techniques as stratified or cluster sampling.

Meaning 3. Miniature of the population: Model
train set.

"As a portrait should be like the person portrayed, so should a representative
House be like the people whom it represents. . . . [An] authority has told us that
our House of Commons should be the mirror of the people. I say, not its mirror,
but its miniature." Anthony Trollope, *Phineas Finn* Vol. 2 (New York: Dodd,
Mead, 1893, p. 130).

2. Reduce errors and the possible biases that might result from non-responses.

3. Use repeated measurements to improve the quality of information.

Refinements in Survey Design

A random sample, the simplest kind of probability sample, is common
in research directed to policy decisions. It has the virtue that, once a
policymaker has access to the frame for the target population, a random sample is easily selected by using a table of random numbers. A
random sample is usually fairly easy to define, analyze, and explain.

But several other survey designs have been available for decades; and major sampling organizations, in both the private and public sectors, are well prepared to carry them out routinely.

Stratification

Populations can often be divided into nonoverlapping subpopulations called *strata*. An example would be classifying all the patients in a hospital into two subgroups: those with hypertension and those without. Stratified random sampling divides the population into such strata, selects a simple random sample from each one, and then combines the information into an overall estimate for the whole population.

Stratified sampling offers at least three advantages. First, it guarantees some representation from each stratum. This virtue may be particularly important in policy settings to marshall political support for an activity. For example, in a recent survey of children's nutrition programs, the Food and Nutrition Service of the U.S. Department of Agriculture emphasized the importance of collecting information from every region of the country. This was less a statistical than a political necessity. Second, information may be easier to collect if we use different methods for data gathering in different strata. Third, stratified samples often give more precise results than simple random samples, thus helping the policy analyst to pin down more tightly some features of a large population.

When does stratified sampling have its greatest advantage? It happens when the strata are homogeneous internally with respect to the characteristic under investigation and heterogeneous from one to another. This suggests that, when policymakers have options about how to stratify for any problem, they should choose those strata that are most homogeneous internally. An extreme example shows the advantages. Suppose a product is sold in a variety of retail outlets: a few large department store chains, several medium-size general stores, and many small specialty stores. To estimate the total sales of this product, a policymaker might do well to divide the population of stores into three strata by store size. Stratum 1 would include the few large retail chains, stratum 2 the more numerous medium-size stores, and stratum 3 the many small stores.

As a sampling strategy, a good plan would be to collect data from most or all of the large chain stores, from a smaller fraction of the medium-size stores, and from an even smaller fraction of the many small stores. Since the majority of sales actually comes from the few large stores, collecting relatively complete information from this stratum would yield the bulk of the information. Data from the smaller samples in the other two strata would round out the sales picture.

Meaning 5. Coverage of the population: Noah's
Ark.

"To ensure a reasonably representative sample of knowledgeable scholars, each
field was divided into six or more common subspecialities (for example, in
law—constitutional law, criminal law, taxation, and so on). Originally the deans
were asked to provide the name of a knowledgeable person in each subspecial-
ty. . . . Where a follow-up letter did not bring a response, names of representative individuals were selected from the current catalog of the university." "The
Cartter Report on the Leading Schools of Education, Law, and Business," *Change*
(February 1977): 44.

Clustering

A second refinement of probability sampling is cluster sampling. The
analyst divides a population into subgroups, called *clusters*, and randomly selects some of the clusters from the entire group. Clusters can
occur naturally—for example, schools could be clusters—or the policy
analyst can construct them. Cluster sampling has a single overriding
advantage relative to both random and stratified sampling: for the
same amount of information it is usually cheaper. If, for example,

clusters are geographic units and travel costs for a survey are substantial, choosing only a few clusters and collecting extensive data in each is much cheaper than selecting people randomly from a large and geographically dispersed population.

When is cluster sampling most effective? Aside from the low cost, the statistical estimates that it generates are most precise when each cluster is internally heterogeneous. Thus, cluster sampling works best precisely where stratified sampling is at its worst.

Furthermore, a policy analyst collaborating with a survey design specialist may be able to determine how clusters are constructed. For example, if the goal is to collect information throughout a large geographic area, it may be up to the policy analyst to create the group of clusters within that area. With sufficient flexibility, it may be possible to design clusters that are relatively heterogeneous internally, and thus to benefit from the lower costs of cluster sampling. This is gerrymandering at its best.

Multistage Samples

It is possible—indeed, it is rather common—to employ several sampling methods in a single survey. This is usually called a multistage sample.

An important issue in multistage sampling is how to allocate resources among the stages. A general rule for surveys is to concentrate resources most heavily on stages where the outcome variable shows the most variation. For example, the policymaker who wants to learn something about the productivity of small businesses in different states can select either many businesses within a few states or a few businesses from each of many states. The choice rests on whether variation in productivity is greater within or across states. Here, a policymaker and survey designer who understand the characteristics of small business productivity will have a large advantage over a novice with little or no such knowledge.

Dealing with Nonresponse

Assuming that a survey is well organized and well designed, the ultimate use of its findings for policy must await collection of data. We turn now to issues concerning data collection. Even well-designed sample surveys rarely succeed in achieving a 100-percent response rate. What might cause nonresponses?

1. People are not at home when the interviewer visits or telephones.
2. People are at home but choose not to respond.

3. People are unable to respond; for example, a language barrier may separate the interviewer and the respondent, or the respondent may be ill.
4. People are "not found." They may have moved, for example, since their address was included in the survey frame.

If nonrespondents do not share the attributes or opinions of respondents, the sample reflects only a subpopulation, not the whole intended population. Worse, the extent of the difference is unknown. This is called *nonresponse bias*. When few sampled members respond, this bias may be huge. Nonrespondents may also differ from respondents as to their background characteristics, sometimes called *predictors* by statisticians. For example, they may be poorer, or less educated, or older. For these reasons, it is important to make an effort to correct for possible nonresponse bias.

It should not be assumed that nonresponse is a problem only with samples of people. Samples of physical items can pose similar troubles. W. Edwards Deming reports that a telephone company in Philadelphia was sampling equipment contained in its manholes to justify a rate increase. The city had recently paved over some manholes. The company's petition to dig out the sampled manholes was declined. The judge ruled that equipment in nonresponding manholes should be assigned a lower value than those responding. This ultimately hampered the plea for a rate change (Deming 1950, pp. 13–14).

Let us turn to some ways of strengthening survey results by dealing with nonrespondents.

Call Backs

Call backs pursue people or institutions who did not respond on the first try. A person may not have been home. An organization may have refused to respond. There may have been repeated refusals to return a mail survey questionnaire. So calling back may involve a second or third or fourth try. Usually some additional data can be picked up from these follow-up efforts. Indeed, although it may appear that repeated follow-ups are not promising, the statistician Leslie Kish has pointed out that, while the first call yields the most responses, the second and third calls often have higher rates of response per call (Kish 1965).

When making a series of call backs, it is particularly valuable for an analyst to track the results of each. This information may give insight into the pattern of nonresponse. We may have a trend in response, wave by wave. For example, if on the first call 50 percent of those responding favor a certain policy, while on the second call 30 percent of the respondents and on the third call 20 percent favor that policy, we might well assume that among those not yet reached, few favor the policy. The trend seems clear.

Sampling Nonrespondents

When the first call or mailing of a questionnaire results in a high rate of nonresponse, it may be valuable to select a random sample of non-respondents and work very hard to track down their responses. This is especially useful in a large mail survey, where often the response rate is low. If personal interviews yield a high response rate from a small sample of nonrespondents, the results from this random sample can be generalized to all the nonrespondents and ultimately used to improve the survey estimate. This procedure may reduce or eliminate nonre-sponse bias. If it is used, however, the confidence intervals around sample estimates will be wider than they would have been if the first wave had achieved the ideal 100-percent response.

Replacing Nonrespondents

Some large survey organizations use nonrespondents from earlier sur-veys as replacements for people who are nonrespondents in a current survey. This procedure is especially useful for organizations that con-duct repeated surveys and maintain files of nonrespondents from past surveys. The idea behind this procedure is that nonrespondents to dif-ferent surveys have at least nonresponse in common, and a good fall-back strategy for estimating what a nonrespondent would have said in the current survey is to coax a nonrespondent from an earlier survey to respond this time.

Existing Sampling Organizations

A policymaker who needs survey information should remember that, in addition to the many federal agencies, such as the Bureau of the Census, that routinely collect sample information (see Chapter 9 on official statistics), various nongovernment organizations specialize in designing samples to answer policymakers' questions.

Prominent among sampling organizations affiliated with universi-ties are the Institute for Social Research at the University of Michigan and the National Opinion Research Center at the University of Chi-cago. Prominent firms in the private sector include Westat Inc.; Yanke-lovich, Skelly, and White, Inc.; Louis Harris Associates; and the Gall-up Organization. Applied social research firms include Abt Associates Inc., Educational Testing Service, Rand Corporation, Research Tri-angle Institute, Stanford Research Institute, Systems Development

Meaning 7. Some specific sampling method: The
Sampling Department in action.

"Quite often . . . one knows the ratios N_j/N, while the N_j and the $\sigma_j(V)$ are not
known. In such cases it has been an accepted practice to choose the n_j proportional to N_j/N . . . [and such a] stratified sample . . . is called a representative
sample. . . ." Z. W. Birnbaum, *Introduction to Probability and Mathematical
Statistics* (New York: Harper, 1962, pp. 183–184).

Corporation, The Urban Institute, and Westat Inc. Dozens of other
organizations also do first-class survey work. A policymaker should
seriously consider the risks of trying to mount a one-shot effort when
so many organizations are experienced in conducting policy research.

We stress this last point. Over many years, social scientists have developed many ways to gather data. The field of sample surveys has led to a network of institutions—government agencies, academic groups, and private enterpreneurs—which routinely gather data in a way that builds upon experience and provides results with known reliability. These organizations have built upon years of experience in dealing with pitfalls and potential troubles. For a policy analyst who needs to make a major decision based on survey data, it can be frustrating to have access only to survey data collected on an ad hoc basis by an inexperienced group of samplers. The reliability of these data may be unknown, and little experience will be available to judge how good they are. It is perilous for a policymaker to ignore the many first-class survey organizations when planning a sample survey. If he or she is able to specify the questions that need answering and the population that must supply the information, then close collaboration with an experienced sampling organization should either provide reliable results along with solid documentation of their reliability or show how and why the results fail to be informative. Not being misled is a primary goal in data gathering.

MERITS OF SAMPLE SURVEYS

Sample surveys are usually at their best when the goal is to describe certain features of a population. Although a census or full count of the population might seem to be a policymaker's first choice, a partial enumeration offers several advantages.

First, a sample survey is usually much cheaper to conduct than a full census. Second, it can usually be done much more quickly. Third, more comprehensive data can be obtained for each unit in a sample. Extensive or in-depth information can be gathered for relatively few people rather than a small amount of information for many people. For example, the decennial census mandated in the U.S. Constitution first used sampling in 1940. A 5-percent sample of people were questioned about the national origin of their parents, military status, family size, and occupation.

A fourth advantage of sampling relative to a full census is that it reduces destructive testing. For example, in quality control of manufactured products, a sample from a large shipment of bullets can give information about the quality of the shipment without destroying more than a small portion.

Fifth, as experience with sample surveys continues to accumulate, archives are now being developed to store survey findings for future reanalysis. These archives will help historians understand changes in American attitudes and values. They will also help future policy-makers who want to do case studies and retrospective analyses to determine why and how policies have succeeded or failed. The extra bit of funding such archives will require seems well worth spending, because the stored survey data will provide a record for future genera-tions of how our society has changed.

WEAKNESSES OF SAMPLE SURVEYS

We have already argued that sample surveys are weak at assessing causality. They have other potential weaknesses as well, although not all of them are unique to samples; some may occur in a full census.

First, the actual population from which a sample is drawn may differ from the intended population. (This parallels the failure of an experiment to deliver the intended treatment to subjects.) If a survey of women's attitudes toward female corporate executives relies on per-sonal interviews conducted during the day with women who are at home, the views of working women will be left out, and the resulting data will be a biased representation of what all women think.

Second, people may intentionally give inaccurate information, particularly if they believe that it is in their interest to misstate a characteristic, such as income, and that an untrue answer will not be penalized. For example, if corporate executives being questioned about their income over the past few years were told the informa-tion was being collected for Dun and Bradstreet, their responses might differ from those provided in a survey for the Internal Revenue Service.

Third, people may give inaccurate information unintentionally. Perhaps they cannot recall the correct information, or the questions are confusing. Researchers conducting a survey in Rome were left wondering about the shape of a building in which the Italian family downstairs reported an area of 60 square meters and the English couple upstairs reported 100 square meters. This potential weakness has been widely studied, and good survey organizations are well aware of it. From extensive experience in conducting complex surveys, these organizations have learned how to develop and pretest survey instruments that minimize confusion and are able to detect inconsis-tent responses.

QUALITY CHECKLIST

We now discuss a series of questions that a policymaker should keep in mind when assessing the value of a sample survey.

1. *Is there a clear statement of the question?* In developing a sample survey, it is useful to start with a clear idea of the knowledge you wish to acquire. While we all know of accidental discoveries—and these may be more common than scientists appreciate—it is easiest to get information you have set out to look for. Most surveys seek to collect specific information. The question to be answered should be clearly expressed, ideally in measurable terms. Words such as "desirable," "should," "ought," "valuable," "bad," and "good" are often not easily measurable. Such vague notions as "normal diet," "disability," "emotional health," "stress," and "safe driving" require reformulation into measurable terms. Does "safe driving" mean no involvement in automobile accidents during the preceding twelve months, no involvement in accidents other than those in which the other driver is found at fault, or no arrests for moving violations? What about members of the study population who do not own cars or do not have driving licenses?

2. *To what population will the results be generalized?* Sometimes the information obtained in a sample survey or census is not used just to describe one precise population at a single point in time. Both investigators and readers wish to generalize the findings beyond the study population. The results of the census may seem to apply only to the population measured, but a census population can be thought of as a sample in time. For example, in 1979 we still used the results of the U.S. census for 1970, extrapolating them to the U.S. population in 1979. This is usually done without much further thought, although it is possible to make corrections based on projections of population shifts from past censuses.

The investigator or reader must determine to what extent information from the study population can be generalized to the wider population. We may have more faith in the generalizability of information derived from a population of patients cared for in Veterans Administration hospitals if the subject under study is cancer of the prostate or arthritis than we would if it were African sleeping sickness or the complications of pregnancy.

Persons who volunteer to participate in a study may differ in some respects from those who do not volunteer, and findings from a population of volunteers may not necessarily apply to the population at large. Patients in a hospital or medical facility are likely to have health problems causing them concern and are probably atypical of the general population.

It is difficult to relate the sample to a wider population. Some survey reports describe specific aspects of the study sample so that the reader can easily consider this question. For example, a report may give the percentage of each sex or the distribution across ages.

Usually, information about the general population is unclear. We know that there are about as many women as men in the overall population, but is this true of automobile drivers? On a per-mile basis are there more men than women? If so, how many more? How many more men than women drive professionally? Such questions are not easily answered and are frequently not addressed in sample surveys, but the reader must keep them in mind when determining (1) to what population the results can be generalized, and (2) whether the study population is an appropriate one for the expected generalization.

3. *If you had the results of a census, could you answer the question?* A census may be thought of as a sample survey when the sample approaches 100 percent. A survey with careful probability sampling should give much the same results as a census, with the possible exception that rare events may not be uncovered.

4. *Does the question ask about causation rather than simple existence or association?* A survey collects information systematically as it is naturally found. The investigator does not ordinarily manipulate the subjects of study by exposing or withholding from them a treatment under investigation. For this reason, surveys are good at demonstrating the existence of subjects studied, and they can give a great deal of information concerning association of various occurrences.

5. *Are rare events expected or sought?* A study of rare events is especially difficult because the precision of our knowledge about them depends on the number of such events observed rather than the number of subjects surveyed. As mentioned above, if a rare event is sought, a sample survey will require a very large number of individuals in the sample. Some events are simply too rare for a sample survey to be practical. Sometimes other methods can give useful information about rare events. In studying handicapped people, lists may be available. People with a rare condition may know others with the same trouble.

6. *Is the sampling technique specified clearly?* The value of a sample survey is in large part determined by the method used to draw the

QUALITY CHECKLIST

1. Clear statement of question?
2. Population for generalization?
3. Would census answer it?
4. Causation or association?
5. Rare events?
6. Sampling technique specified?
7. What sampling method?
8. Population size known?
9. Instrument appropriate?
10. Quality controls?

sample. A sample can be described only in terms of the method by which it was derived, and unless we are told this, it is almost impossible to guess at the reliability of the results.

7. *How would you describe the sampling method: probability, random, stratified, haphazard?* Unfortunately, the reader cannot rely on the statement "random sample," but must go back to the investigator's description of what actually happened to determine what method was used. "Random," used by an investigator, may have little meaning in practice, in part because of the everyday use of the word to indicate "without deliberate bias," and in part because many people who draw samples are careless with technique. They may use a method, refer to it as the random method, and even think it is random, when actually it is something else like "systematic" or "haphazard."

8. *If aggregate rather than average values are needed, is the size of the sampled population known?* If one wishes to know the total purchasing power of families in Greater Boston, the average family income is no help without some idea of the population or number of families in Greater Boston.

9. *Is the survey instrument described clearly? Does it seem an appropriate means of addressing the study question?* What was actually asked of the sample? Do the data recorded seem appropriate to the overall question? For example, in the Coleman Study of Equality of Educational Opportunity, the records did not directly connect teachers to their students, only to the schools, thus making it difficult to associate teachers with their students' performances.

10. *Are there quality controls on fieldwork?* A beautifully designed survey will not provide good information if data are collected poorly. For example, if several researchers who are out in the field gathering data on bank deposits define certain types of deposits (time deposits, demand deposits, certificates of deposit) in different ways, their aggregate findings will be messy. Checks should be instituted to make sure that data are collected in a systematic way at different places and by different people. Often the data collectors receive training as a single group.

POLICY IMPLICATIONS

Sample surveys represent one area of statistics that has become institutionally embedded in American life. In contrast to large-scale field experiments, for example, sampling is done routinely in many contexts. Businesses use sampling routinely for purposes of quality control. Many federal agencies collect sample information regularly to maintain official statistics and use these data for major policy decisions. Reports on unemployment, consumer prices, housing starts, and other such fundamental economic data that are routinely read by policymakers all come from sample information. Thus, sample surveys are fairly well understood by both policymakers and the general public; their results tend to be accepted.

At the same time, amateurish sample surveys are easily criticized, and the criticisms redound to spoil the reputation of both those who carry them out and those who commission them.

The policymaker has a special responsibility to make sure that the sampling frame—the basic population to be sampled—actually represents the population that is to be studied. This responsibility, and the compromises that are required to make the task of carrying it out practical, cannot be delegated to those carrying out the sample survey. No matter how impeccable the study design is in other respects, if the wrong population is studied, the study is seriously weakened.

The policymaker may also have some responsibility for completeness of response. A high rate of nonresponse can destroy an otherwise well-designed study. The policymaker can take steps in advance to make sure that funds for follow-up will be available, and perhaps that pressure can be brought to bear to ensure respondent cooperation. For example, a letter from the head of an agency will elicit many more responses than one from a polling organization. In some sorts of studies, especially regulatory ones, the law may even require response. The policymaker must decide at what level the pressure for response can or should be set. In 1980 the Internal Revenue Service planned to audit a sample of returns. A high school student with a simple return was drawn into the sample. In response to journalistic criticism, the agency explained that it wanted to avoid deviations, presumably nonresponse. As the media continued to attack, the IRS finally made a new rule excluding the high school student and others from the audit. It is clear that the public did not understand the nonresponse issue, but perhaps the reporting burden and negative public opinion costs outweighed the value of the information.

Because a sample survey is ordinarily a rather public venture, policymakers must almost always share the results with a broader audience, and they should be prepared to be comfortable with that publicity. As we discuss in Chapter Nine on official statistics, several agencies now go out of their way to make their findings widely available. Thus, their work contributes to further studies which in turn tend to raise the general quality of information in a field.

CONCLUSION

Sample surveys are the standard method of gathering information about characteristics or attitudes of a population without measuring each individual. When the sample follows probability principles, statistical methods of analyzing the results will yield estimates with known precision. Often only a small fraction of the population must be included in the sample to produce accurate estimates, and this economy permits the survey to probe in much greater depth, more carefully, and more quickly than a census. A variety of methods, such as stratification and cluster sampling, have been developed to gain efficiency from the structure of the population.

Even with a sound basic design, a survey can encounter a variety of biases and other difficulties—poor access to part of the population, nonresponse, inaccurate recall, and intentional misinformation. Fortunately, many survey organizations have developed expertise in avoiding these problems or minimizing their effects.

With careful planning and interpretation, a sample survey can give a policymaker timely and accurate information about a population as it stands. Thus, if a census would provide the information needed, ask whether a sample survey could reduce the burden on the responders and the costs of collection and analysis.

REFERENCES

Cochran, W. G. 1977. *Sampling Techniques*, 3rd ed. New York: John Wiley.

Coleman, J. S. et al. 1966. *Equality of Educational Opportunity.* Washington, D.C.: Office of Education, U.S. Department of Health, Education, and Welfare.

Deming, W. E. 1950. *Some Theory of Sampling.* New York: John Wiley.

Feeney, D. 1980. Interview with Superintendent James Angevine, Fitchburg, Massachusetts, April.

Gil, D. 1973. *Violence Against Children: Physical Abuse in the United States.* Cambridge, Mass.: Harvard University Press.

Kempe, H. 1962. The Battered Child Syndrome. *Journal of the American Medical Association* 181: 17–24.

Kish, L. 1965. *Survey Sampling.* New York: John Wiley.

Kruskal, W., and Mosteller, F. 1980. Representative Sampling, IV: The History of the Concept in Statistics, 1895–1939. *International Statistical Review* 48, no. 2: 169–195.

Light, R. J. 1973. Abused and Neglected Children in America: A Study of Alternative Policies. *Harvard Educational Review* 43 (November): 556–598.

University of Minnesota. 1979. *Small Business in Minnesota.* Report submitted to the Minnesota State Planning Agency by the College of Business Administration.

FURTHER READING

Bradburn, N. M., and Sudman, S. 1979. *Improving Interview Method and Questionnaire Design.* San Francisco: Jossey-Bass.

Cochran, W. G. 1977. *Sampling Techniques*, 3rd ed. New York: John Wiley.

Davis, J. A. 1971. *Elementary Survey Analysis.* Englewood Cliffs, N. J.: Prentice-Hall.

Hyman, H. H. 1972. *Secondary Analysis of Sample Surveys.* New York: John Wiley.

Kish, L. 1965. *Survey Sampling.* New York: John Wiley.

Rosenberg, M. 1968. *The Logic of Survey Analysis.* New York: Basic Books.

Sudman, S. 1976. *Applied Sampling.* New York: Academic Press.

Williams, W. 1978. *A Sampler on Sampling.* New York: John Wiley.

Yamane, T. 1967. *Elementary Sampling Theory.* Englewood Cliffs, N.J.: Prentice-Hall.

CHAPTER 6

Longitudinal and Panel Studies

In the preceding chapter on surveys we focused on one-shot efforts. Even in multistage samples, the respondent (person, school, company, or whatever) is asked only once for data.

For some policy questions, data collected repeatedly over time from the same people may be particularly useful. The key here is to use the same respondents. For example, suppose public support for a proposed new law is vacillating and legislators want to understand people's views more fully. A public debate is scheduled, and legislators commission sample surveys both before and after it to get a reading of public opinion. Two ways might serve: commission two separate surveys, each of which selects a random sample of citizens; or commission two surveys of the same group of people, one conducted before and one after the debate.

The second way illustrates a panel study. It has one clear purpose: soliciting information from the same individuals more than once to see who changed their minds and in what direction. If two separate surveys of different people showed that support for the new law increased from 45 percent of respondents to 55 percent, that would be valuable knowledge. But we would know only this net change in support and would have far less information on how it came about. Perhaps 10 percent of the respondents switched from opposition to support; or perhaps 20 percent switched toward support, while 10 percent switched the opposite way, leaving a net 10-percent switch.

A panel study enables the policymaker to explain a net change. We can not only figure out how many people switched each way, but also identify those who switched—maybe the switch occurred entirely among the elderly or disproportionately among the poor.

Longitudinal studies can be viewed as long-term and particularly detailed panel studies. Although these two kinds of studies are often described interchangeably in the research literature, it is helpful to think of longitudinal studies as being longer term and involving more repeated measurements of people or institutions. Indeed, when the sample consists of people, the aging or maturation process may be of fundamental interest.

The simplest form of panel study—taking two measurements over time for the same group of people—is particularly well suited to estimating the details of changing opinions or circumstances near an event. The more elaborate longitudinal investigation can help policymakers understand the behavior of the units being measured over time. For example, if we want to understand the caseload handled by a family service agency, it is important to know how often families need assistance, what kind of assistance they need, and how these demands are distributed among families. Organizations that provide human services have noticed that often relatively few families account for nearly all the demand for such services. Longitudinal information can make this observation both concrete and quantitative.

EXAMPLES

Habitual Offenders in Philadelphia

To learn what factors lead to criminal behavior and what types of intervention prevent such behavior, the Law Enforcement Assistance Administration of the U.S. Department of Justice commissioned a study in the late 1960s of almost 10,000 men (Wolfgang, Figlio, and Sellin 1972). A research team from the University of Pennsylvania retrospectively followed these men through both institutional records and interviews in an effort to learn what factors distinguish the habitual criminal from the nonoffender.

The researchers began with juvenile careers. Recognizing that the usual retrospective study of a select group of offenders could not provide much information on the factors distinguishing them from nonoffenders, they decided on a longitudinal study of an entire population. The group selected was defined as all males born in the year 1945 who resided in the city of Philadelphia continuously between the ages of 10 and 18. To identify the members of this cohort and get information about them was a difficult and laborious task. School records provided the bulk of the information and identified a group of 14,313 male students born in 1945. Some of these students did not meet the residence criterion and could be eliminated. However, complete records could not be found for 3,700 students, largely because of transfers between public and parochial schools. To complete these records, the files had to be checked by hand at each of the city's 401 public, parochial, and private schools. The files of the police department were checked, and records of offenses were matched with the school records. Finally, the records of the Selective Service System confirmed residence in the city at age 18. Of the 14,313 boys investigated, 9,945 met the criteria for inclusion in the study, and 3,475 of these had had contact with the juvenile justice system at some point. Only 31 boys were excluded from the study because of incomplete information.

From school records, the investigators obtained information on the race, IQ, scholastic achievement, school behavior, and truancy of members of the cohort. From police files, they obtained a list of offenses, descriptions of the offenses, and disposition of cases for each of the boys.

In this phase of the study the researchers found that the primary variables distinguishing offenders from nonoffenders were socioeconomic status and race, with nonwhites and the poor much more likely to commit crimes than the rest of the population. More important, certain habitual offenders, 627 of the 9,945 boys, accounted for over half of all juvenile offenses. Of those with police records, 46 percent had been arrested for only one offense, and an additional 35 percent had only two arrests on record. The policy implication is that intervention aimed at the population at large or following first or even second contact with the police might well be wasteful and that greater attention should be paid to the habitual offender.

As a follow-up to this study, Wolfgang and Collins (1978) took a sample of 10 percent of this original cohort and interviewed as many as could be located (more than half). Records from the Philadelphia Police Department and the Federal Bureau of Investigation revealed the criminal behavior of this sample up to age 30. This portion of the study confirmed the existence of a small group of chronic offenders. Those earlier identified as habitual juvenile offenders were responsible for between 60 percent (from interviews) and 80 to 85 percent (official records) of the offenses committed by the entire cohort. The measure of offenses obtained from interviews can be expected to be lower than the actual number.

These reports were completed at the same time as a number of other studies documenting the existence of a class of habitual offenders. While it is impossible to assess the effect that any one of these studies had on official decision making, in recent years both the federal government and local law enforcement agencies have created many new programs to deal with habitual offenders. This example illustrates the point made earlier that a few individuals or families may create much of the load on a social system.

Unemployment Statistics

A second example providing policy insights comes from a longitudinal study, conducted by Parnes (1980) for more than ten years, that has been analyzed by many economists. Parnes and his colleagues found that gross unemployment statistics gave an incomplete picture of the employment situation in America. Over many months during which the unemployment rate held steady at about 7 percent, the economists found that the hard-core unemployed did not account for most of that 7 percent; instead, more than 20 percent of the U.S. labor force was unemployed at some time during a year, and these people were unemployed about one-third of the year, on the average. This gave the U.S. Department of Labor a very different picture of the structure of unemployment in America than most people had guessed. Instead of a small group of hard-core unemployed persons who never can find a job, it now appears that roughly 20 percent of Americans in the work force are marginally employed, moving in and out of insecure jobs, and moving in and out of the welfare system. Only a longitudinal study could have revealed this more detailed picture.

MERITS OF LONGITUDINAL STUDIES

As an examination of changes, the longitudinal study shows the individual changes in a cohort, not just the net changes. For example, longitudinal studies can be used in marketing to appraise brand loyalty or in politics to determine party loyalty. In studying unemployment, one can find out how many people are unemployed for long periods, how many for short. One can study the vicissitudes of income for families or the changes in profits of companies.

Over a long period, a longitudinal effort allows us to study the development of such processes as disease or delinquency, and especially processes that develop slowly, for example, the effects of aging on the demand for welfare services. It also helps us identify predictor variables. Continuous data over time provide information about which predictors are especially valuable, so that, for example, a policy analyst can validate predictions about which families are most likely to need social services in the coming year.

One of the most famous longitudinal studies, and one that illustrates the strengths of this type of research, is the Framingham study (Dawber 1980). Organized in 1949 and still in operation today, this study of the epidemiology of atherosclerotic, or coronary heart, disease was organized in 1949 by Dr. Gilcin F. Meadors, then a young officer in the U.S. Public Health Service. Residents of Framingham, Massachusetts, between 30 and 59 years of age were recruited to participate, and the study group began with 5,127 people, all free of coronary heart disease. Participants were followed up every two years, even those who changed residence. The overall loss to follow-up was an extraordinarily low 2 percent.

Data collection during each biennial patient visit included a medical history, a physical examination, blood studies, and other laboratory work. Symptoms of illnesses were reviewed, and interim hospitalization or medical visits noted. An ongoing record was thus kept for each participant.

Findings from this longitudinal effort have greatly influenced the medical community. The Framingham study uncovered a series of major risk factors related to coronary heart disease, including hypertension, blood lipids (elevated levels of blood cholesterol), cigarette smoking, lack of physical activity, obesity, and diabetes mellitus.

T. R. Dawber concludes his detailed historical examination of the Framingham study with a strong statement of the virtues of such a longitudinal effort for improving public health:

In summary, it is evident that, largely as a result of epidemiologic studies in cardiovascular disease, the attitudes of the medical profession continue to change. The pessimistic view that atherosclerotic disease is an inevitable result of the aging process has been replaced by a far more optimistic concept that atherosclerosis can be prevented—or its onset significantly delayed. This can be achieved only by concern for the health of the well population long before any evidence of overt disease is apparent. (Dawber 1980, p. 229).

WEAKNESSES OF LONGITUDINAL STUDIES

Since longitudinal studies provide detailed information about changes over time in a population, why not always use them for ongoing policy analyses? There are several reasons. First, it is much more expensive to follow up a large group of people repeatedly than to use a series of one-shot samples without worrying about who moved or dropped out.

Second, the behavior of respondents may change simply because they know they are part of an ongoing study. Regardless of whether the change is positive or negative, these people may, over time, become less and less like others in the population from which they were drawn.

A third difficulty is selecting a genuine random sample from a population to participate in a panel study. Assuming that participation is voluntary, the people who agree to participate in a repeated series of interviews may not be similar to those in the larger population.

Fourth, it is often difficult to find sustained funding for a longitudinal study. By and large, organizations that sponsor studies want quick results to use for further work. Projects that pay off twenty or thirty years down the line are usually difficult to fund; and even if they are initially funded, when the original enthusiasts for the work die off or move to other agencies or activities, financial support may be withdrawn. In 1980 long-term environmental effects of chemicals seemed to be a major problem for the nation, yet few longitudinal studies were launched.

Fifth, long-term follow-up of a specific therapy or reform, especially one having a strong technological aspect, may not seem worthwhile because technology changes so rapidly. Researchers may expect something much better to come along very shortly and replace whatever they are doing. These judgments have some merit, but we tend to be optimistic about the speed of technological improvement. Shortly after World War II, many experts were confident that foreign languages would easily be translated into English using electronic computers. We are still waiting, and we no longer expect this accomplishment in the near future. We need some additional studies of the rate of change associated with technological developments to help appraise questions of this sort.

Sixth, we return to the specific maintenance problems created by attrition and the high cost of follow-up. Nearly 20 percent of Americans move to new homes each year; merely keeping track of people requires considerable effort and can be expensive. Some people do not care to be found, perhaps for reasons directly related to the study—for example, some individuals are not eager to have their income reported. To keep track of people, then, requires considerable active effort. Although various kinds of detective work are often successful, the longer the study goes on, the more expensive this work becomes.

UNDERSTANDING RARE EVENTS

Panel surveys can help us identify and understand relatively infrequent occurrences, such as the unemployment example mentioned earlier. A series of new random samples taken over time may accurately estimate the frequency of a rare event—lead paint poisoning, iron-deficiency anemia, or truancy from school. A panel study also can provide background information on those people who at some point in the series of measurements begin to display the rare characteristic. For example, we might notice that an abnormally high fraction of families reporting marital problems had, at the previous measurement, reported that the husband had been laid off from work.

REFRESHING AND ADJUSTING PANELS

Seymour Sudman (1976), who has broad experience in working with panel studies, reminds us that, while at first look it may seem necessary to keep the panel intact and to minimize changes and dropouts, this may not be a good idea. He points out that panel samples come from a carefully defined population, which can change over time in important ways. For example, in the past decade the term "head of household" has increasingly been used to describe women.

Thus, we must view a population as dynamic, and such a perspective has implications for panel samples. Indeed, if when first measured a sample is a good representation of the population, we would expect it to change along with the population. For example, we would expect roughly a similar fraction of families in our panel sample to move each year as move in the population. We would expect the divorce rates to be roughly similar. And so on. This conception of the panel sample as a dynamic representation of the population means that, rather than being frustrated by changes in the sample, a policy analyst should view these changes as providing important information about similar changes that are probably taking place in the population. From this perspective, allocating substantial resources to following people who move or become divorced may be an excellent investment.

For the same reason, panels should be refreshed. If the population from which a panel was selected in 1981 consists of all full-time working women, we should not be surprised if some new women enter this population by 1983. Thus, in long-term studies it seems useful to update and expand a panel over time to include an appropriate representation of new entrants into the population.

PITFALLS

The nature of longitudinal studies suggests that certain biases or errors can creep in, and an alert investigator can anticipate some of them. First, people answering the same question repeatedly can be influenced by the very process of answering. Perhaps respondents will hesitate to change their answers over time because they believe consistency a virtue and do not want to appear undecided or changeable. Also, thinking about a question may create or solidify an opinion that was only vague before. Simply being asked a question may cause people to think harder than they normally might about this topic, and will thus change their opinion or behavior. They may then report a change to the investigators, who receive a correct report. But if investigators generalize from the study respondents to a broader population of individuals who have not each been asked that same question, they may seriously overstate the prevailing opinion.

A second pitfall is collecting information from different members of an organization at different times. For example, an annual survey of families might have different family members responding in different years. In a business firm it would not be surprising if the senior vice-president in charge of personnel changed every year or two. Between the first and second years, a learning effect may occur if the same person is interviewed, but if in the third year a new person is interviewed, the learning effect disappears.

A third pitfall involves tracking people who move. To alleviate this difficulty, the survey researcher might ask each respondent at the beginning of the longitudinal study to name several relatives or friends who would always know how the respondent could be contacted. Freedman, Thornton, and Camburn (1980) did this in the 1960s for a survey on women's family plans. They were successful nine years later in locating 94 percent of the original women. Over one-third of these women were found by using information provided by a relative or friend.

POLICY IMPLICATIONS AND CONCLUSION

Longitudinal studies that have been well executed over a period of many years are rare. An important one is the Framingham study. Carrying out such an effort requires serious long-term funding support and staff commitment. It is much easier logistically to commission an occasional one-shot sample survey to assess income or attitudes, with-

"I thought it was me, but maybe the school's no damn good."

out worrying about following up old respondents or tracking down those who have moved.

Longitudinal studies detect changes over long periods of time and help policy researchers tie predictor variables to outcomes. These are important strengths. However, a poorly executed longitudinal study is likely to be a waste of money. So planners should think hard about the high level of commitment that such studies involve, and go ahead only if they foresee long-term support.

REFERENCES

Dawber, T. R. 1980. *The Framingham Study: The Epidemiology of Athero-sclerotic Disease.* Cambridge, Mass.: Harvard University Press.

Freedman, D. S.; Thornton, A.; and Camburn, D. 1980. Maintaining Response Rates in Longitudinal Studies. *Sociological Methods and Research* 9: 87–98.

Parnes, H. 1980. *The National Longitudinal Survey.* Report prepared for the U.S. Department of Labor, Manpower Administration. Washington, D.C.: U.S. Government Printing Office.

Sudman, S. 1976. *Applied Sampling.* New York: Academic Press.

Wolfgang, M. E., and Collins, J. J. 1978. *Offender Careers and Restraint: Prob-abilities and Policy Implications.* Report prepared for the U.S. Department of Justice, Law Enforcement Assistance Administration.

Wolfgang, M. E.; Figlio, R. M.; and Sellin, T. 1972. *Delinquency in a Birth Co-hort.* Chicago: University of Chicago Press.

CHAPTER 7

*Case Studies**

Case studies differ in an important way from most of the other methods of data gathering because they have little statistical theory behind them. Parts of such studies could use almost any sort of data, and they have no special methodology of their own. Professional schools use case studies heavily in their teaching, and their students usually find this method of instruction attractive. Cases offer the tang of reality, touching on topics of current interest and even urgency. However, the problem of appropriate generalization must be recognized, and students should guard against a mistaken emphasis on an unusual or appealing feature. Worst and best cases and human-interest situations lend the strength of reality and weakness of rarity and atypicality to case studies.

We can speak only in the vaguest way about when the method is especially appropriate—perhaps when we want to repeat almost exactly what "the case" has successfully, or even unsuccessfully, done in a slightly different setting.

Sometimes the hope is that the case study makes it possible to understand a process under observation, because the case offers a microcosm. The following quotation, translated from a Chinese publication (*Statistical Reporter*), puts the idea in a most engaging light:

The survey of typical cases is an important method to find out the circumstances and study the problems. Through the statistical tables, enormous phenomena may be understood but the causes of these phe-

*Harvey V. Fineberg has kindly given us the benefit of both medical and policy criticism.

nomena and the problems behind them, and the means of solution cannot be found out simply from these data, and a detailed survey is indispensable. Therefore, besides making correct statistical tables, statisticians are asked to go deep into the realities of life and among the masses and conduct systematic and careful surveys of certain typical factories, shops and people's communes and acquaint themselves with the actual situation. For instance, where the statistical data of a certain area show an imbalanced fulfillment of the plan between the enterprises, we would select three typical cases, the good, bad and medium, for further investigation, analysis and comparison, to make clear the reason why the good one is good and the bad one bad. In China there is a proverb: "The sparrow may be small but it has all the vital organs." After having "dissected" a few sparrows, one may have an idea about sparrows in general. With such rich and concrete materials, when combined with the figures from reporting tables, we can study problems, give the problems better explanations, and make suggestions on how these problems can be solved. (State Statistical Bureau of the People's Republic of China 1980, p. 135)

EXAMPLES

The Swine Flu Affair

In 1977 the United States seemed to be threatened by an epidemic of swine flu, or possibly a pandemic. About the time of World War I, the same virus had caused an influenza pandemic, and 1 million people had died in the United States. The evidence for a possible pandemic was modest, but it included an estimate that epidemics occur about once every eleven years, and the expected danger point was approaching.

Public health officials then had to consider whether to create and prepare substantial amounts of the vaccine, which requires a long lead time, and they also had to decide whether to propose mounting a program of vaccination among very large numbers of people. The vaccine was prepared, and the public health officials persuaded the elected officials to declare in favor of a national vaccination campaign.

Several difficulties arose, including in rare cases the Guillain-Barré syndrome, which produced a form of paralysis leading to death for a few and to partial or complete recovery for others. Whether this syndrome had occurred in earlier vaccination programs is unclear, but the swine flu program involved so many millions of people and was so carefully monitored for side effects that such rare events were easy to detect.

A second difficulty was that the pharmaceutical manufacturers declined to accept responsibility for adverse consequences of the vaccine not due to their negligence, and the insurance carriers balked as well. Thus, the federal government was forced to accept responsibility for the outcomes. The insurance obstacle was apparently a surprise to those planning the vaccination campaign, yet over the years people have become more and more inclined to undertake litigation when unfortunate consequences follow public and private health measures.

Three people in Pittsburgh died of cardiovascular complications almost immediately following their vaccination. Some analysts have declared that, in a program as large as this one, such an occurrence might have been expected to occur by chance alone and, by implication, that the public could have been better prepared for it. Others said that this event was most unusual and some unexpected and rare factor must have been the cause.

At any rate, after millions of people had been vaccinated, the campaign was called off. No epidemic or pandemic occurred, nor is it clear that either would have occurred without the program. (Some cases of A-Victoria influenza were diagnosed in a nursing home in Miami. The

SWINE FLU: QUANTIFYING THE "POSSIBILITY"

We need better rules for translating everyday language into quantities and vice versa, especially in the area of probability. Philip M. Boffey (News and Comment, 14 May, p. 636) reports that President Ford, in referring to the campaign against swine flu, spoke of an epidemic as a "very real possibility." Boffey consulted at least four experts and reports their responses concerning the probability of a swine flu epidemic in the 1976–77 season as being, respectively, 2 percent, 10 percent, 35 percent, and "less than even," which I translate as "less than 50 percent." The 2 percent responder regarded his number as plucked out of the air; we were not told how the others regarded theirs.

Boffey then says. "Those probability estimates, though far lower than the official rhetoric of the campaign would lead one to expect, do not necessarily mean that the vaccination campaign is a foolish endeavor." I wish to address the question of whether the estimates are far lower than the official rhetoric should have led us to expect. Since Boffey emphasizes Ford's concern about the " 'very real possibility' of a dangerous epidemic in the United States next fall and winter," I regard the phrase "very real possibility" as the official rhetoric needing quantification. Boffey has done the fieldwork of consulting experts for their guesses. Judith Selvidge (1) found, from responses of Harvard Business School students to a questionnaire, that for the median student the word "possibility" in probability estimation had a value of 20 percent (with quartiles of 10 and 50 percent). Thus about half the students thought "possibility" meant 20 percent or less. Cliff (2), in his

A-Victoria vaccine was available only in a combination with the swine flu vaccine. Then Secretary of Health, Education, and Welfare Califano called a special public meeting of experts to deal with this late threat, which we shall not discuss here.)

Richard E. Neustadt, a professor at the J. F. Kennedy School of Government at Harvard University, and Secretary Califano thought that it would be useful to have the swine flu story written up as a case study, because much could be learned about handling such problems by studying the events. Neustadt and Harvey V. Fineberg, a physician with public policy training, wrote a report entitled *The Swine Flu Affair: Decision-Making on a Slippery Disease* (1978).

We can scarcely do justice to a several-hundred-page book in a few pages here, but we do wish to indicate the kinds of recommenda-

article "Adverbs as multipliers," found that the multiplying effect of "very" is about 1.25. I have no way of knowing the multiplicative effect of "real," but "decidedly" has a factor of 1.16, "unusually" of 1.28, and "extremely" of 1.45. I personally would consider "decidedly" as similar to "real" in multiplicative effect. This would give as a median estimate $1.16 \times 1.25 \times 20 = 29$ percent (with quartiles of 14 and 73 percent). (A more careful effort would require a transformation that would keep all percentages between 0 and 100.) Is not 29 percent one reasonable summary of the four estimates 2, 10, and 35 percent and "less than even"? If so, the official rhetoric seems to be right in line with the reported probability estimates, at least for the populations studied. I would like to see us much better able to make translations of the sort Boffey tries to make, and to encourage others to inform us of work done in this area of quantifying everyday language.

Frederick Mosteller

Department of Statistics,
Harvard University,
Cambridge, Massachusetts 02138

1. J. Selvidge, "Assigning probabilities to rare events," thesis. Harvard University (1972).
2. N. Cliff, *Psychol. Rev.* 66, 27 (1959).

tions that evolved from the detailed case study, as well as some of its strengths and weaknesses. For a book whose conclusions depend on opinion and interpretation, one would not expect uniform agreement from readers. Thus we are presenting the findings not in the spirit of endorsement, though we find them instructive, but as an illustration of the kinds of things that can be learned from a case study. It does seem to us that, whenever one takes massive precautions against a small chance of a large disaster and the threatened event does not actually occur, one's efforts are likely not to be appreciated by an ungrateful citizenry. Had the influenza pandemic occurred, the public health officials responsible for initiating the vaccination program would have been heroes. Nevertheless, Neustadt and Fineberg's proposals might be wise even if the pandemic had arrived.

Neustadt and Fineberg made several points (which we have simplified and shortened). First, we need to conduct research on influenza, which is a "slippery" disease for the following reasons:

1. It changes all the time, yet the vaccine needs to be precisely geared against the current strain of virus.
2. The severity is unpredictable.
3. Vaccine effects are short-lived and difficult to measure.
4. Symptoms are easily confused with those of other diseases, and outbreaks of flu-like illnesses may be caused by other organisms.
5. The many causes of flu-like diseases make the impact of the disease and the vaccine hard to estimate.

Second, for the actual swine flu decision, they felt that the specialists were overconfident, even though the data were inadequate; for example, the evidence for an eleven-year cycle was weak.

Third, the personal beliefs and agendas of specialists may influence their decisions more than is appropriate. Neustadt and Fineberg want a system or mechanism that does not depend so heavily on the particular individuals operating it.

Fourth, the specialists may tend to make more decisions than have to be made at a particular time. The policymakers could have set deadlines for making particular decisions.

Fifth, the uncertainties that surround these decisions should be addressed openly and systematically. The idea is to maintain an open planning process and establish dates for reconsideration at each stage of the process.

Sixth, the enterprise did not question adequately the scientific logic and the prospects for implementation. For example, could children be treated in only one dose, or did they have to receive two doses? Also, in a national vaccination program the problems of recall for second administrations can be substantial, particularly in a not very regimented country.

Seventh, it is important to understand the media and to maintain the credibility of the institutions. Neustadt and Fineberg suggest that if the public had been properly warned, public reaction to the three deaths in Pittsburgh would have been less severe. (Our view is that this particular item is hard to treat, even though the general point about the media is a good one. If officials had warned that in a large-scale vaccination program there were bound to be accidental deaths in peculiar clusters from chance alone, how would the press have reacted? Probably variously, but some headlines would surely have announced, "Officials expect deaths in bunches following vaccination!" and this would not have been a crowd-soother.)

What makes the swine flu case study potentially useful? We feel that the inferences are short in distance and compelling because:

1. The Center for Disease Control (CDC) and related organizations continue to have the same responsibilities with respect to influenza as they did in 1977.
2. Making the population immune continues to be one of the CDC's major jobs.
3. Influenza continues to be an important disease with the slippery properties identified by Neustadt and Fineberg.
4. The mechanisms of distribution, manufacture, insurance, legislation, and communication are likely to continue to be much the same as before. But we note that one major difficulty in the swine flu affair was a changing system of justice, with a large award for damages going to a patient against a drug manufacturer for a paralytic condition that may or may not have been caused by the drug. A weakness of the case study, including this one, is that it is often hard to recognize that times have changed unless and until you are the primary target of the change. The insurance companies recognized the change, but the government officials apparently did not realize what it would mean to their vaccination program.
5. The findings may also be applicable to many other mass public health programs.
6. The swine flu case study offers many perspectives on a complicated series of events that no one saw in its entirety.

To use a classic cliché, the danger of the case study is that it tells you how to fight the last war but not the next one. It does suggest some things that will be useful to do next time, but you may not be able to tell whether they will be effective, and surprises are inevitable.

Project Sappho: Industrial Innovation

Collections of case studies can be useful for comparative purposes, but used in this way they partake of the features of sample surveys or observational studies. The following (Mosteller 1981) illustrates this idea.*

The Science Policy Research Unit at the University of Sussex (1972) studied the reasons for success and failure in industrial innovation. Using a combination of a matched pair approach and a case

*From *Science* 211, February 27, 1981, pp. 884, 885. Copyright 1981 by the American Association for the Advancement of Science. Reprinted with permission.

study approach, the investigators selected twenty-nine pairs of technological innovations that had been introduced to the chemical or scientific instruments industries. In each pair one innovation had been successful, the other unsuccessful. The case study method was used to describe the details of both the successful and unsuccessful innovations. Since much work had already been carried out in this field, the investigators had several hypotheses to test.

The main finding was that no one variable seems to distinguish successful from unsuccessful innovations. Five statements summarize the other findings. Successful innovators:

√ better understand user needs;

√ pay more attention to marketing;

√ develop more efficiently, but not necessarily faster;

√ make better use of outside technology and advice;

√ have responsible individuals with greater seniority and authority (mostly the business innovator rather than the technical innovator).

Many features often mentioned in business lore did not seem relevant: size of firm, management techniques, use of qualified scientists and engineers, timing (being first or second to market the innovation), initial familiarity with markets and technology, structure of research, in-house versus out-of-house ideas, market pressures. Something called management style could not be assessed in this study.

This sort of observational study is not unlike research that might be conducted by an epidemiologist investigating why some groups of people suffer from a disease by matching pairs of places with differing rates and comparing the properties of the paired sites.

Airplane Crash Investigation

When a disaster such as a commercial airplane crash occurs, the government usually conducts or commissions a substantial case study to obtain a description of what is believed to have happened. The purposes of the investigation are (1) to allocate blame, (2) to find the cause, and perhaps (3) to regulate so as to prevent repetition. Among other methods, the actual process of the case study may employ:

√ interviews with witnesses, participants, and other personnel;

√ scientific or engineering tests;

√ reports from maintenance organizations and/or manufacturers;

√ reviews of tape recordings made at the time of the incident;

√ hearings;

√ historical information.

The results of the investigation may lead to further inquiries, such as sample surveys or scientific and engineering experiments.

Although repetitive events such as airplane crashes may provide an opportunity to standardize case studies, each investigation has an exploratory character, much like a detective mystery, so that the direction of the study is largely determined by the information as it is obtained. Birds on the runway, equipment or instrument failure, remarkable coincidences, and human error are among the reasons for accidents.

Pre-Election Polls of 1948

Although the pre-election polls of the *Literary Digest* in the 1936 Roosevelt-Landon election have been widely publicized, the failure of the 1948 polls in the Truman-Dewey election offers more scope for a case study. By that time, the polls had had a long sequence of successes in presidential, state, and local elections, and some pollsters felt that pre-election polling was easy, now that a scientific basis for the work had been established. The sample survey had become a major tool in social science and market research. The failure of the 1948 forecasts by several major polling agencies raised serious questions about the methods used, as well as about the honesty of the pollsters. Some journalists felt that they should return to their old ways and abandon sample surveys. Concerned about the influence of polls on elections, Congress considered whether it should impose legal constraints in spite of the First Amendment.

In response to these concerns among pollsters, social scientists, journalists, lawmakers, and the general public, the Social Science Research Council set up a blue-ribbon investigating committee, together with a staff of experts, to try to find out what happened.

The investigators used a variety of research methods—further sample surveys, interviews with the polling organizations and their workers, studies of the records, and so on—and produced a book-length explanation (Mosteller et al. 1949). Although many people thought they knew precisely why the polls failed, a major finding of the case study was that no single reason explained the mishap. Instead, several reasons combined to create the error, and not always the same reasons for each polling organization.

One lesson of this study was "When someone offers a simple plausible explanation for a complicated event, don't grab for it. More likely, complicated things occurred." For example, when a column of figures in a table does not add up correctly,* one may wonder whether misreading a 3 for an 8, say, could be the explanation for an error of 5, but it is not wise to assume that this is the reason. Troubles frequently arise through a sequence of events or coincidences that one is not likely to have anticipated or even thought probable.

For example, in the 1948 polling the sampling plan itself did not seem to be at fault at the level of the sampling points used by the three polling organizations, Crossley, Gallup, and Roper (Mosteller et al., p. 114). The quota method of sampling probably contributed to the error, as did the last-minute changes of mind, and for one polling agency, a plan to produce compensating biases (which had previously been rewarded by good outcomes) contributed to the error. For agencies that used probability sampling methods, the nonresponse would have contributed to an error of estimate. For most forecasters, lack of attention to potential error from many sources led to unqualified forecasts.

The debacle and the case study had several consequences:

1. Congress did not pass a law.
2. The polling organizations engaged in a substantial research program.
3. Forecasts were reported with more caution.
4. Probability sampling methods came into wider use.

FEATURES OF THE CASE STUDY

The concept of a case study has classical origins in the medical and legal areas, where the study of an individual afflicted with a disease or of a single legal conflict plays the title role. For purposes of policy analysis, we use the concept in a more general sense: a case study is an analytic description of an event, a process, an institution, or a pro-

---

*When rounded correctly, percentages should *not* always add up to 100.0 (Mosteller, Youtz, and Zahn 1967).

gram. How the description is carried out depends on the particular case, just as the variables in an experiment are determined by the subject of study. However, certain general features of the case study can be enumerated.

Specificity

If preservation of the alligator as an endangered species is the program under study, it is wise to keep it separate from the corresponding program for preserving redwoods or whooping cranes. In the case study the great push is for specificity. Generalization may flow from collections of case studies or from loosening an inference, but extending the case study to many cases ordinarily asks too much of this method of data collection.

Description of the Parties and Their Motives

Sometimes the accident or development of common causes, often for different reasons, is part of the message; other times it is the process of winning and losing that is instructive. For example, the long, slow process that industry has often used to resist changes that would protect or clean up the environment has become an instructive pattern. Similarly, the innocence with which the neophyte do-gooder approaches complicated problems offers a warning to us all. The methods used to change motivation may be useful in parallel circumstances. Understanding both successes and failures can be valuable in future work.

Description of Key Issues

In addition to a set of parties, a set of issues may underlie the event or program. The resolution and details of these issues and their treatment and effects on the different parties may help someone analyze a future policy problem.

Solutions

The case study may suggest possible moves toward solutions, together with their pros and cons.

Levels of Applicability

Readers will benefit when authors try to indicate the applicability of their methods to similar or new problems. These applications may occur at varying levels. For example, Mosteller and Wallace (1964) carried out a large-scale data analysis to determine the authorship of the disputed *Federalist Papers*. This observational study was also a case study in method, though not necessarily for policy. The analysts wanted to see how a special statistical method called Bayesian analysis worked in a large-scale problem, and their conclusions had several levels:

1. The authorship of the *Federalist Papers*.
2. Statistical authorship studies.
3. Practical Bayesian inference.

Thus, the author of a case study should suggest circumstances in which the conclusions might or might not generalize to new situations.

WHAT THE CASE STUDY IS NOT

A case study is not an experiment or a sample survey, but these might be conducted in association with a case study. For example, a description of how the Salk polio vaccine led to a nationwide immunization experiment on children could be a valuable case study. But for the purpose of policy analysis, one would look at the social forces underlying the experiment, the tensions that led to two simultaneous versions of the study (one a randomized experiment, the other a comparison of second graders with first and third graders), and the consequences of the Cutter incident (a batch of vaccine that may have contained live virus). We would try to find out what lessons this experiment had for preventive medicine, especially such preventive treatments as vaccines applied to children. For example, why were we able politically to get usable data from this experiment, whereas the work of the previous summer on another vaccine, gamma globulin, did not produce useful data? The Salk vaccine experiment focused on the outcome—what was the difference in rates of polio among comparable groups? A case study would be more likely to focus on the processes leading to the experiment or to implementation following the experiment—for example, how do we explain the changeover from the injected Salk vaccine to the oral Sabin vaccine with its attendant dangers?

Thus the Neustadt-Fineberg study of the swine flu program uses that case as a device for considering what actions could be improved in future mass prevention programs. This sort of study ought to be especially valuable because it can be oriented toward almost identical medical circumstances for almost identical organizations in the future—except, of course, for the unanticipated variable, which often seems so obvious in retrospect.

STRENGTHENING CASE STUDIES

As for any historical effort, good records and documentation make case studies particularly valuable. When history can be carefully collected as a study or demonstration proceeds, facts can often be better established. For example, some military units have historians attached.

Comparative case studies and collections, as illustrated by Project Sappho, can offer a good deal more than a single case study. Several additional devices and materials strengthen the case study:

√ interviews with participants and observers,

√ historical documents and working drafts of plans for a project,

√ contemporary newspaper reports,

√ management records,

√ biographies of participants,

√ organization charts for institutions,

√ time-line of events,

√ parallel cases.

MERITS AND WEAKNESSES OF CASE STUDIES

Because the merits and weaknesses of case studies flow from almost identical features, we present them in one section rather than two.

Relevance and Similarity to Future Problems

We can choose to do case studies that deal with problems almost identical with those we will have in the future. For example, if the U.S. Postal Service were planning to improve its operations, it might study the handling of one or a few complaints and write a history, not as an amusing article for the *New Yorker* but as an instructive piece that would focus on where things go wrong and how they might be fixed.

In discussing the usefulness of the swine flu case study for the CDC, we noted the short step between the case study and the decisions needed, but we did not mention the common situation of a case study undertaken for the express purpose of aiding immediate or imminent decisions. For example, the Office of Technology Asssessment (OTA) often makes case studies as a result of requests from congressional committees. Their study *Assessing the Efficacy and Safety of Medical Technologies* (Office of Technology Assessment 1978) reviews the current knowledge about seventeen medical treatments and procedures, including pap smear for cervical cancer, amniocentesis, mammography, skull x-ray, electronic fetal monitoring, surgery for coronary artery disease, tonsillectomy, and cast application for forearm fracture. Several items on the list illustrate that medical technologies have often been widely used before their safety and efficacy have been evaluated.

Since these requests usually come from several committees with related missions, the OTA conducts case studies of interest to the several committees. These collections of case studies then form a basis for suggesting policy options. Of course, a collection of case studies, such as Project Sappho produced, begins to resemble a sample survey or an observational study.

The OTA study of safety and efficacy also illustrates the problem of choosing case studies. The OTA panel found it difficult to choose a set of studies that would be regarded as representative of the population of all medical technologies. The investigators chose studies from surgery and medicine, from treatments for young and old, from diagnosis, prevention, and treatment for the sake of variety, or what Kruskal and Mosteller (1980) call coverage (see Chapter 5). The OTA investigators chose items that are expensive or widely used to achieve a measure of importance.

Each of the studies is sufficiently important to stand in its own right. Since they deal with current technologies, presumably they can offer a collective basis for thinking about legislation.

Pilot demonstration projects offer another opportunity to conduct case studies if a program is to be implemented in many places. The demonstration project may inform us by encountering many of the difficulties that will arise in the full program so that we can take advantage of the experience. You may have noticed that nearly everything runs poorly the first time around.

Vividness and Reality

The journalist commonly introduces difficult articles on science, policy, banking, or statistics with an engaging story of what has happened to a particular person or family. Many of us find this lead-in much easier to grasp than the general idea that the article is trying to convey. The emotional impact of such stories does much to communicate the idea and to persuade the reader that the matter is important and that something can and should be done.

One must remember that the journalist has probably chosen the most extreme story available as the "case." Its features are likely to be more memorable for the reader than the general ideas presented in the article. Thus, in a program that has served thousands of people uneventfully, the biggest foul-up of all time is likely to be what is reported. The difficulty is not the injustice, but rather that the event that is so well remembered may cause the organization to spend substantial resources on preventing difficulties that rarely arise and that little can be done about, where equal funds and attention might prevent or redress more frequent, though less dramatic, difficulties.

Case studies may be rich in background letters, quotations from the people involved, newspaper articles, official documents, details of studies and reports, and so forth.

Complexity

Many case studies illustrate the complexity of causation, such as an airplane crash or the failure of the 1948 pre-election polls. Programs and policies are often strongly influenced by personalities and their clashes, and these may be treated in detail. The pressures of politics and time (deadlines, change of legislators, cessation of funding) complicate the story and frequently produce strange actions. Irrational things do occur, but the authors of case studies tend, unfortunately, to tidy them up.

The complexity invites an explanation of why a process works, or how a program has evolved and what actually leads to its successes and failures. Case studies have the advantage and unerring logic of hindsight. But even when correct, the inferences may not apply to a similarly complex situation at another time and place. For example, knowing how to install a successful clinic in a city in 1930 may not be of much use in 1980, when neighborhoods and ethnic groups insist on local control of such facilities.

On the other hand, Barbara Rosenkrantz's (1972) heartrending description of the failure of Henry Bowditch's 1873 housing program for the lower and middle classes does not sound unlike the outcome of public housing programs in 1980. Bowditch hoped that the tenants would adopt a more salutary mode of life than had previously characterized the housing block, with its high rates of drunkenness, crime, and disease. Rosenkrantz quotes Bowditch as saying that, after originally favorable signs, "we saw some boys grow up to be thieves, and girls fall into unchaste lives, in spite of any effort we as a committee could exert."

Teaching Tool

The case study is widely believed to be a good teaching tool, illustrating general problems through the mechanism of a concrete example. The decision about the F-111 military airplane (discussed below) illustrates the general problem of military defense and the development of expensive weapons while underlining the traditional differences and rivalries between branches of the U.S. armed services.

Wilson (1979) has noted the high costs of data collection in the long case study and its disadvantage as a teaching tool. "Case studies are too long; and because they are often not directly relevant to the person's present concerns, they are low in priority" (1979, p. 451). Wilson cites Fritz Mulhauser as saying that front-line practitioners and high-level policymakers do not have time to read detailed case study reports. The very richness and complexity of the case study seem to reduce the readership and thus the effectiveness of this method. Perhaps the great case study is summarized by word of mouth.

Laurence Lynn says that for teaching purposes case studies should be long to bring out the complexity of a situation and to give the student an opportunity to study many different issues in the same case.* It also forces the student to discriminate between relevant and irrelevant material.

Longitudinal

Sometimes case studies cover a long period of time. The setting for the event is intended to aid in its appreciation.

*Personal communication.

Utility and Value

Although we would like to think of research as value-free, a case study is likely to reflect the value system of the author. This may or may not influence presentation of the facts. A politician who writes the history of legislation he or she has sponsored is not likely to assume the role of villain of the story, but opponents of the legislation may not fare so well.

The authors of the swine flu case study wanted to improve the process of making important public decisions, and we would expect them to emphasize publicity, timing, and the relationship between health professionals and elected officials, with perhaps less attention to the scientific side of the investigation.

In their case study of the failure of the 1948 pre-election polls the authors, as social scientists, were interested in preserving the sample survey as a research and policy tool. James Conant, then president of Harvard University and a former chemist, said of the failure: "It is like an explosion in a laboratory. It doesn't stop research on a problem or even discontinue the method of research, but it certainly sets things back for a while."* Whether these special interests destroy all objectivity or merely emphasize some aspects of the findings readers must judge for themselves in each instance.

Wilson (1979) points out that the usefulness of a case study depends on the value system of the reader. Material that reinforces the reader's beliefs is generally better remembered and more likely to be acted upon than material that opposes the reader's established value system. People who are concerned about unemployment of youths do not want to hear about the possibility of lowering the minimum wage, because that seems to oppose the labor movement, which they also favor.

As another example, the humanist would like to believe that the suicide rate in England and Wales was reduced by about one-third between 1964 and 1970 thanks to the Samaritans, a society established to help troubled people. An alternative explanation, attractive to technologists but rather cold, is that a less toxic gas was used as the domestic gas supply during that period. The number of suicides from poisoning by domestic gas declined from about one-third of the total to zero (see *Lancet* 1978).

*Personal communication.

Counterexample

In mathematics and in the "exact" sciences, the counterexample provides a constructive proof that a theorem or theory is not universally true and should therefore be abandoned or at least reformulated to exclude the offending example. Developing counterexamples is a standard part of creative research to determine the limitations of a proposed theorem.

In less exact situations, an example of a program that did not work as desired may point to serious shortcomings in the system and its procedures or to the possibility of bizarre cases that the system was not designed to handle. If these cases are rare, they can often be ignored. However, if the example points to a failure that could affect an important segment of the program participants, a change in the system or its procedures may be required. The routine reporting and investigation of unwanted outcomes is a common method for identifying deficiencies in a system; presumably these investigations will lead to changes in policy or procedures to reduce the chances of recurrence. Some examples are the reporting of all maternal deaths (in childbirth); the reporting of all cases of "reportable" diseases, such as smallpox; and the Civil Aeronautics Board's investigation of all commercial airline accidents.

When examining a counterexample, an administrator should consider the following issues:

1. Does the case fall within the purview of the program? Sometimes language problems introduce discrepancies between the intent and the wording of a regulation, so that, for example, some people are eligible for a program not intended for them.
2. If the problem affects only a few people, particularly if the effect is small, the costs of a change may outweigh its benefits.
3. As with any policy or procedural change, changes suggested by counterexamples must be examined for other possible effects on the system. A change in eligiblity requirements may change the number and distribution of participants and hence the utilization patterns of the service centers, leading to budgetary problems.

Ease

Most people feel that they can prepare a case study, and nearly all of us believe we can understand one. Since neither view is well-founded, the case study receives a good deal of approbation it does not deserve.

To assist us in appreciating what the case study method is especially suited for, Marjorie Olson reviewed several case studies used in the public policy program at the J.F. Kennedy School of Government at Harvard University. From this review she developed a list of contributions a study might make and then applied her list to five of these case studies, which represent a variety of policy areas. Before discussing the list and its application, we briefly describe each of the five.

The Detroit Fiscal Crisis (Parts A, B, and sequel) was written in 1977 by William Mates and William B. Marcus under the supervision of Laurence E. Lynn, Jr. This study discusses the fiscal crisis faced by the City of Detroit at the beginning of 1976. Part A probes the city's historical background, demography, government, relations between races, economic dependence on the manufacture of automobiles, and the spread of urban decay accelerated by the movement of middle-income people to the suburbs. Appendices vividly describe the general deterioration of the city (one neighborhood in particular) and its positive attributes. Part B analyzes the economic crisis in greater detail under five headings: city appropriation patterns, revenue sources, imbalance between appropriations and revenues, possibilities for cutting city expenditures, and possible sources of revenue. The sequel delineates the patchwork set of provisions that saved Detroit from financial disaster in fiscal year 1976–77.

The Massachusetts Department of Correction (Parts I, II, and III) was prepared in 1977 by Alan Konefsky, Richard Peers, and Donald Simon under the supervision of Philip B. Heymann. This is a rather extensive case study of the term of John Boone as head of the Massachusetts Department of Correction, his subsequent firing by Governor Sargent, and the failure of the state administration to institute prison reform. Part I describes the Department of Correction and the eight Massachusetts correctional institutions in 1972. The authors give a comprehensive picture of correctional officers, prison social structure and social control, disturbances and unrest, and the details and difficulties of prison reform. Part II discusses the Boone administration, including Boone's selection by Governor Sargent; his early term; political, prison, and media opposition to him; the Omnibus Correctional Reform Act; and strife at Walpole prison. Part III discusses the erosion of Boone's support among the administration, his firing, and his replacement by Frank Hall. The case study closes with various quotations from participants looking back upon the episode.

The Massachusetts Medical School (Parts 1, 2, 3, and 4) was prepared under the supervision of Graham Allison in 1975. Part 1 presents the dilemma faced by the Sargent administration in 1969 as to whether, and if so how, to proceed with plans to construct a Massachusetts Medical School in view of disagreement over need and site, and rapidly escalating costs. The dilemma is posed in the form of a charge from the lieutenant governor to a policy analyst (and to the student being taught by this case) to prepare recommendations in light of two reports, one by a researcher, Leon S. White, and one from the Office of Comprehensive Health Planning. These reports are included in the case study. Part 2, the sequel, tells us that Sargent approved the proposal to build the medical school in Worcester, and reproduces his letter of explanation to the Chairman of the University Board of Trustees. Parts 3 and 4 (notes to teacher and students, respectively) focus on the problems of implementation and incorporating implementation considerations into the practice of analysis, and offer guidance for the intellectual work required by the analyst.

TFX: The Commonality Decision was prepared by John Robinson and revised by Gregory Mills in 1974 under the supervision of Joseph L. Bower. Written as a chronological history, this case study documents the failure, over a ten-year period, of a plan by then Secretary of Defense Robert McNamara to build the F-111 airplane for common use by the Air Force and Navy. McNamara felt that, in addition to providing substantial performance advantages over previous fighters, the new airplane should be more dependable and less expensive to build. He thought these goals could best be accomplished by designing and building a plane to be used by both the Navy and the Air Force. The case study describes McNamara's background, the concerns of the Department of Defense at the time, the disparate goals of the Air Force and Navy, and the competition for the contract between General Dynamics/Grumman and Boeing. After the award of the contract to General Dynamics/Grumman, despite the preference of the military for the Boeing plan, development of the plane was begun amid great controversy, both political and ideological, between the Air Force and Navy and their congressional allies. This controversy, combined with differences over such design difficulties as drag and approach speed, stalled the program, which was further hampered by the departure of McNamara as Secretary of Defense and congressional membership changes. The project was eventually killed by lack of funding.

Beth Israel Hospital Ambulatory Care (Parts A and B) was written in 1976 by Judy Smith and Lynn Homeier under the supervision of Harvey Fineberg. This case study recounts the successful reorganization of Boston's Beth Israel Hospital to improve the delivery of ambulatory care. Part A discusses the greater demand for ambulatory (outpatient and emergency) services nationally, and the increased costs of delivering such services. It treats the effect of these trends on Beth Israel Hospital in the early 1960s and several other issues that played a part in decisions concerning the hospital's ambulatory care. Part B describes how Beth Israel, in 1970, set out to alter its outpatient department in order to provide accessible, continuous, and reasonably priced medical care. The financial aspects of the change, organizational details, and overcoming opposition are discussed. The case study includes an appendix prepared by Dr. Thomas Delbanco, Medical Director of Ambulatory Care at Beth Israel, advocating the creation of first-class ambulatory care programs.

We return now to Olson's list of the potential contributions of a case study. The word or phrase in parentheses following each item is the short heading used for it in Table 7-1, which summarizes Olson's application of the listed items to the five case studies.

Marjorie Olson's list was primarily oriented to the contributions that case studies can make. John P. Gilbert prepared a list of guidelines for authors of case studies. Inevitably, the Olson and Gilbert lists overlap. Although it could have been presented in the section on strengthening the case study, Gilbert's list includes questions of interest to anyone who wants to know about the study. Gilbert applied his list to the same five case studies Olson used. The results appear in Table 7-2. Again, each item in the list is followed by a word or phrase used as a heading in the table.

QUALITY CHECKLIST

Our list of questions concerning the quality of a case study, potential or completed, follows:

1. *What is the special competence of the authors?*

2. *What are the special biases of the authors?*

3. *Who sponsored the study and why?*

4. *What charge was given to the authors, if the study was sponsored?*

5. *Does the study deal with the whole problem or only parts?*

6. *How long did it take to complete?*

7. *Have other studies of the problem been conducted? If so, what are their findings?*

8. *If the matter is controversial, will key parties respond to the study?*

SOME ASPECTS OF A CASE STUDY by MARJORIE OLSON

1. It can explain why an innovation worked or failed to work. (innovation and result)

2. It can explain the reasons for a problem, the background of a situation, what happened, and why. (what and why)

3. It has the advantage of hindsight, yet can be relevant in the present. (hindsight, relevance)

4. It can illustrate the complexities of a situation—the fact that not one but many factors contributed to it. (complexities)

5. It can show the influence of personalities on the issue. (personalities)

6. It can show the influence of politics on the issue. (politics)

7. It can show the influence of the passage of time on the issue—deadlines, change of legislators, cessation of funding, and so on. (time)

8. It can include vivid material—quotations, interviews, newspaper articles, and so on. (vividness)

9. It can suggest to the reader what to do or not do in a similar situation. (applicability)

10. It can evaluate, summarize, and conclude, thus increasing its potential applicability. (evaluation)

GUIDELINES FOR REPORTING LARGE CASE STUDIES by JOHN P. GILBERT

1. What was the core issue? (core issue)

2. What was the time span? (time span)

3. Who were the decision makers? (decision makers)

4. What were the arguments for the issue? (arguments for)

5. What were the arguments against it? (arguments against)

6. What sources of information were used? (information sources)

7. Were there differences in how the issues were interpreted? (interpretation differences)

8. Were there studies or experiments that were or might have been done? (studies, experiments)

11. It can discuss and evaluate alternatives not chosen. (alternatives)

12. It can cover many years and describe how the preceding decades led to a situation. (time span)

13. It can spell out differences of opinion on the issue and suggest how these differences have influenced the result. (differences of opinion)

14. It can obtain information from a wide variety of sources. (sources)

15. It can present information in a wide variety of ways (for example, interview excerpts and mathematical or political analysis) and from the points of view of different groups—politicians, managers, program recipients, taxpayers. (presentation)

16. It may or may not be influenced by bias on the part of the author. (bias)

17. It may fail to include all the material needed by the reader to evaluate the innovation or problem. (completeness)

18. It can examine a specific instance but illuminate a general problem. (generality)

---

9. What were the decisive factors leading to resolution? (decisive factors)

10. What factors were speculative or probabilistic in nature? (speculative)

11. What techniques of data gathering and processing were used? (data gathering)

12. Were there issues of timeliness, either real or perceived? (timeliness)

13. Were costs, risks, and benefits considered? (costs, risks, benefits)

14. What was the monetary scale of the issue (or other measures of importance)? (monetary scale)

15. Are there any quotable statements? (quotes)

TABLE 7-1 Olson contribution summary

	Detroit	Massachusetts Correction	Massachusetts Medical School	TFX	B.I.H.	Summary Totals
1. Innovation and result	no	yes, mostly failed	innovation proposed and decided upon	innovation failed	innovation succeeded	innovation: 3 yes, 1 proposed, 1 no; result: 2 failed, 1 succeeded
2. What and why	yes	yes	yes	yes	yes	5 yes
3. Hindsight, relevance	yes	yes	no hindsight, relevant	yes	yes	hindsight: 4 yes, 1 no, relevance: 5 yes
4. Complexities	many	very many	very many	many	some	2 very many, 2 many, 1 some
5. Personalities	somewhat important	very important	important	very important	important	2 very important, 2 important, 1 somewhat important
6. Politics	important	very important	very important	very important	important	3 very important, 2 important
7. Time	not especially important	important	important	important	not especially important	3 important, 2 not especially important

8. Vividness	vivid	vivid	vivid	somewhat vivid	vivid	4 vivid, 1 somewhat vivid
9. Applicability	to some extent	to some extent, negative and positive	to some extent	to some extent, negative	yes, positive	1 yes positive, 4 to some extent
10. Evaluation	some	no	no	no	some	2 some, 3 no
11. Alternatives	no	no	yes	no	no	1 yes, 4 no
12. Time span	3 years and background	4 years and background	11 years and background	7 years and background	3 years and background	3–11 years and background
13. Differences of opinion	many	very many	very many	very many	some	3 very many, 1 many, 1 some
14. Sources	many	many	many	many	many	5 many
15. Presentation	varied	varied	less varied	varied	varied	4 varied, 1 less varied
16. Bias	not evident	not evident	not evident	not evident	not evident	5 not evident
17. Completeness	seems complete	seems complete	not complete (by intention)	seems complete	seems complete	4 seem complete, 1 not complete
18. Generality	yes	yes	yes	yes	yes	5 yes

TABLE 7-2 Gilbert guideline summary

	Detroit	Massachusetts Correction	Massachusetts Medical School	TFX	B.I.H.	Summary Totals
1. Core issue	fiscal crisis	reform mostly fails	to build?	fails	succeeds	1 problem, 2 attempts that fail, 1 that succeeds, 1 presentation of facts for decision making
2. Time span	3 years and background	4 years and background	11 years and background	7 years and background	3 years and background	3–11 years and background
3. Decision makers	government administration	governor's administration	governor	Secretary of Defense, armed services, aircraft companies	hospital trustees, administration	4 public administration, 1 private
4. Arguments for	not applicable	many	many	many	many	4 many, 1 not applicable
5. Arguments against	not applicable	many	many	many	many	4 many, 1 not applicable
6. Information sources	many	many	many	many	many	5 many

7. Interpretation differences	yes	yes	yes	yes	yes	5 yes
8. Studies, experiments	studies were done	probably not	many studies were done	many studies and experiments were done	studies were done	4 studies done, 1 probably not
9. Decisive factors	no resolution	yes	yes; may have been inevitable	yes	yes	4 yes, 1 no resolution
10. Speculative	yes	yes	yes	yes	yes	5 yes
11. Data gathering	much fiscal	little	much	much	much fiscal	2 much fiscal, 2 much, 1 little
12. Timeliness	some	much	much	much	little	3 much, 1 some, 1 little
13. Costs, risks, benefits	some	none	a lot	a lot	a lot	3 a lot, 1 some, 1 none
14. Monetary scale	large	not much	very large	huge	large, but came close to breaking even in end	1 huge, 1 very large, 2 large, 1 not much
15. Quotes	some	many	some	none	some	1 many, 3 some, 1 none

9. *How solid are the data and documentation?*

10. *Is the study oriented to policy; can it be used in considering policy options, regulation, or legislation?*

11. *Is it sufficiently respectable and convincing that it can be used as support for policy decisions?*

12. *How much did (would) it cost?*

13. *Can the results be generalized to other situations?*

POLICY IMPLICATIONS

Because of its detail, the case study treats its subject more nearly as a complete entity than any other method, and consequently is likely to give good information about the political aspects of the event, institution, or process studied. The detail and realism of the case study usually make the story more appealing and compelling than do other methods. Indeed, it is often too compelling; if used to explain why something succeeded or failed, the case study may suggest a causal explanation that does not stand up under repeated trials. (See the Project Sappho example.)

If the case study is used to describe and evaluate a demonstration unit for a planned program, the policymaker should recognize that, although first-time efforts have their rocky moments, the demonstration is likely to have been carried out by better qualified and more enthusiastic staff and with more resources than will be available for the full program. Thus, the effects of enthusiasm and money will be diminished later.

If the case study is designed to help with later decisions about a program, the commissioner of the study should recognize that this method is one of the easiest for an author to bias, and the choice of author may well determine the ultimate policy implications of the study.

CONCLUSION

The case study is a maverick among methods of data collection. Persuasiveness and human interest can make it effective if length does not deter readers. The method has severe biases in even the best of hands

QUALITY CHECKLIST

1. Competence of authors?
2. Biases of authors?
3. Sponsor?
4. Charge to authors?
5. Whole problem or part?
6. Time required?
7. Other studies?
8. Replies from key parties?
9. Documentation?
10. Oriented to policy?
11. Convincing?
12. Cost?
13. Generalizable?

because of problems of values, slant, omission, and emphasis. The case study is an important teaching device, and it can be especially useful if what one wants to do next is almost exactly what the study treats. It can produce a false sense of security because, in spite of the detail offered by the case study, new situations produce new problems. Nevertheless, the case study should reveal many difficulties and opportunities that the armchair analyst would not appreciate. It provides proof of possibility by documenting the existence of a successful venture and provides analogues of counterexamples, and thus disproofs, in other contexts.

Collections of case studies begin to resemble sample surveys or observational studies.

REFERENCES

Kruskal, W., and Mosteller, F. 1980. Representative Sampling, IV: The History of the Concept in Statistics, 1895–1939. *International Statistical Review* 43 (November): 556–598.

Lancet. 1978. Suicide and the Samaritans (editorial). October 7: 772–773.

Mosteller, F. 1976. Swine Flu: Quantifying the "Possibility." *Science* 192 (June 25): 1286, 1288.

_____. 1981. Innovation and Evaluation. *Science* 211 (February 27): 881–886.

Mosteller, F., and Wallace, D.L. 1964. *Inference and Disputed Authorship: The Federalist.* Reading, Mass.: Addison-Wesley.

Mosteller, F.; Youtz, C.; and Zahn, D. 1967. The Distribution of Sums of Rounded Percentages. *Demography* 4: 850–858.

Mosteller, F. et al. 1949. *The Pre-Election Polls of 1948.* Social Science Research Council Bulletin 60.

Neustadt, R.E., and Fineberg, H.V. 1978. *The Swine Flu Affair: Decision-Making on a Slippery Disease.* Washington, D.C.: U.S. Government Printing Office.

Office of Technology Assessment. 1978. *Assessing the Efficacy and Safety of Medical Technologies.* Washington D.C.: U.S. Government Printing Office, 052-003-00593-0.

Rosenkrantz, B. 1972. *Public Health and the State.* Cambridge, Mass.: Harvard University Press.

Science Policy Research Unit, University of Sussex. 1972. *Success and Failure in Industrial Innovation.* London: Centre for the Study of Industrial Innovation.

State Statistical Bureau of the People's Republic of China. 1980. Statistical Work in New China. *Statistical Reporter* (1980).

Wilson, S. 1979. Explorations of the Usefulness of Case Study Evaluation. *Evaluation Quarterly* 3: 446–459.

FURTHER READING

Wilson, S. 1979. Explorations of the Usefulness of Case Study Evaluation. *Evaluation Quarterly* 3: 446–459.

CHAPTER 8

Management Records

In the normal course of work, government, business, and other institutions generate and record vast amounts of data. Each record contains potentially useful information for policymakers. Modern society has always generated such management records, and the widespread use of computers makes these data increasingly available for further analysis. When we can find relevant data, they can sometimes save us from having to do a costly and time-consuming study.

Management records provide a source of policy information, even though they may have been collected for an entirely different reason from that under consideration. For example, public health officers might use school attendance records to measure the local intensity and course of a flu epidemic.

On many occasions, management records can answer questions beyond those that originally stimulated their collection. We begin by describing three examples.

EXAMPLES

The first example involves the use of police records to study the effect of a change in staffing policy. Police records customarily serve to monitor crime levels but are not designed to monitor staffing policy. The second example considers the use of hospital records to study regional variations in the frequency of surgical operations. The primary purpose of such records is individual patient management, but statewide collection of data makes them more broadly available for health policy studies. The third example describes how Social Security records can monitor the effectiveness of job training programs. These records serve principally to monitor payroll taxes and to determine eligibility for benefits. Ultimately, they proved useful for policy research.

Police Manpower

Municipal governments, as well as city dwellers in general, want to reduce crime. Will increasing the level of police protection help? Since extra police cost money, a policymaker needs to know how effective a proposed increase might be before implementing it. Press (1972) reports the results of a quasi-experiment on this question based on the records of the New York City Police Department.

In October 1966 New York City increased the average number of patrolmen working in the 20th Precinct from 212 to 298, while making no marked changes in the number of patrolmen in neighboring precincts. To assess the impact of this policy decision, Press compared

the crime rates before and after the manpower increase for the different types of crime in the 20th Precinct with changes observed over the same time period in neighboring precincts. The New York City police report crimes of various sorts on a form that records the type of crime and whether a passerby could have observed it from the street (outside crime) or not (inside crime). The police made minor changes in the form shortly before the manpower change in the 20th Precinct. In his analysis Press adjusted for the effects of this change in reporting as well as for seasonal fluctuations in the frequency of different types of crime.

Press found a decrease in crimes visible from the street, such as robbery, grand larceny, and auto theft, but no significant change in the rates of other types of crime, such as burglary. He points out that one would be more inclined to generalize these results to other situations if more precincts had been studied and if the manpower level could have been varied several times in each of the precincts.

In reviewing this study and its use of an existing data base, we see that:

√ The investigation was feasible because reporting is a part of the regular duties of the police. The study probably would not have been possible if it had required special reporting.

√ The investigators could study only those categories of crime that the police normally report. The findings of the study would not have been possible if they had required a special reporting mechanism.

√ Because the investigators had access to data from previous years, they did not need to delay the manpower change until they had collected sufficient prechange data from the trial and control precincts.

√ The example is particularly interesting because the study included a policy change—increasing the number of patrolling officers. Some studies based on management records will not have this feature.

Variations in Surgery Rates

In discussions of policies intended to contain medical costs and maintain the quality of health care, legislators are uncertain about which procedures and services government should pay for. What could reasonably be included in a proposed national health insurance plan?

Some claim, for example, that large numbers of surgical operations are unnecessary. Because we rarely have a way to demonstrate that an operation is unnecessary for a particular person, indirect investigations using routine hospital records can provide helpful evidence.

Gittelsohn and Wennberg (1977) gathered data on how frequently different operations were performed in various regions of Vermont, where the population is fairly homogeneous in ethnic and socioeconomic background. Gittelsohn and Wennberg divide the state into thirteen hospital catchment regions and compute rates of operations for each region, properly adjusted for the ages of the residents.

Table 8-1 shows some of their findings. They note substantial variation in the rate of certain surgical operations from region to region. Tonsillectomy and adenoidectomy (T & A) varied from a low of 16 per 10,000 population to a high of 135 per 10,000, an eightfold variation. The table also shows rates for other groups in the U.S. and abroad.

Other operations showed less variation, but rates for several commonly performed operations varied more than threefold. Such variation in itself proves nothing, but it does raise some questions. Why, in a fairly homogeneous territory, do such variations occur? Sampling fluctuations cannot explain them. Using the same hospital records, Gittelsohn and Wennberg found that some physicians performed many more tonsillectomies and adenoidectomies than did others. Because these operations are often carried out by physicians not formally trained as surgeons, the variation seems to be more a matter of physician and patient preference than of a physician with specialty training doing most of the operations.

None of this proves that some operations were unnecessary—indeed, we must emphasize that we have no measure of outcome here. Perhaps even more surgery would be beneficial; or perhaps alternative methods of treatment have comparable merit, and we are observing simple variation in treatment preferences. But the records clearly show that the phenomenon of surgical variation leaves something to be explained. Deeper analysis of the records shows some sources of variation and lays the groundwork for further inquiry.

To conduct such a comparative study of records, uniformity of record systems across institutions—here, hospitals—is essential. Ordinarily, uniformity can be achieved only through lengthy negotiations among willing participants or with powerful political or fiscal pressure. For example, after two-score years of negotiation, the United States in 1979 achieved a well-defined and agreed-on uniform hospital discharge data sheet consisting of about ten items, such as name, age, and sex of patient.

TABLE 8–1 *Surgical procedure rates per 10,000 population, 13 Vermont hospital service areas, 1969–71, selected populations (all ages)*[*]

Area	T&A	Appen-dectomy	Prosta-tectomy (males)	Inguinal Hernia (males)	Mas-tectomy (females)	Hyster-ectomy (females)	Cholecys-tectomy (females)
1	66	15	32	50	29	39	27
2	23	15	15	38	16	30	19
3	63	20	29	38	22	30	29
4	54	14	25	38	20	33	30
5	54	25	23	52	24	32	30
6	41	21	21	45	35	48	38
7	135	30	27	54	22	41	53
8	41	31	22	45	27	51	25
9	69	18	28	47	24	60	29
10	46	18	23	47	22	41	32
11	60	25	24	49	22	40	24
12	31	14	32	41	18	43	28
13	16	23	20	51	20	30	18
Vermont	46	19	25	45	22	41	29
Saskatchewan	87	32	27	34	21	63	56
U.S.A.	63	20	20	51	26	52	na
England & Wales	32	22	9	29	15	21	na
U.S. Employees BC/BS	75	22	23	48	28	49	na
Group	20	10	11	30	19	24	na

[*]Age-adjusted rates computed without decrementing population for prior removals.

From A. M. Gittelsohn and J. E. Wennberg, On the Incidence of Tonsillectomy and Other Common Surgical Procedures. Chapter 7 in *Costs, Risks, and Benefits of Surgery*, J. P. Bunker, B. A. Barnes, and F. Mosteller, eds., New York: Oxford University Press, 1977, p. 100. Copyright © 1977 by Oxford University Press, Inc. Reprinted with permission.

The difficulties of agreeing on standard records stem partly from history and partly from disparity of purposes. For example, a hospital that defines length of stay in a particular way is reluctant to use another definition, because the change will disturb the comparability of its statistics from one period to another and will require retraining of record keepers. Similarly, difficulties in definition may flow from the differing interests of concerned parties. Should number of days in hospital count both day of admission and day of discharge? How one counts can make a substantial difference in judging the efficiency of use of hospital beds.

Through the years a constant effort persists to define and classify procedures more precisely. New medical knowledge changes the appropriateness of some categories. Inevitably, changes interfere with comparability of records across time periods.

Job Training Programs

The U.S. Department of Labor (DOL) constantly faces the problem of measuring the effectiveness of its job training programs. For fiscal year 1981, over $10 billion was budgeted for job training, including over $4 billion for youth programs. The DOL has commissioned several surveys and field studies to examine its job programs; at the same time, it has used management records to provide information. Believing that the information from these records had helped considerably in evaluating training programs, the DOL sought outside confirmation from the National Academy of Sciences. The Academy reviewed DOL procedures and issued a report confirming that the DOL's use of management records was a highly effective tool for policy (National Academy of Sciences 1974).

The DOL procedure for assembling Social Security earnings data involves matching earnings records on file at the Social Security Administration with Social Security numbers taken from job program trainee records. To compare the trainees with a comparison group, the trainees' records are compared with data from a random sample of nontrainees taken from the Continuous Work History Sample, a 1-percent sample of the basic Social Security master file.

Social Security data include a longitudinal earnings history. The National Academy of Sciences report points out that such factors as education, family background, motivation, and achievement determine a person's expected lifetime earnings. Therefore, records of prior earnings reflect these variables. Using an earnings history prior to program involvement controls for labor market influences of sociodemographic variables.

The Department of Labor wanted to see, first, whether the Social Security records were a useful source of information about program effectiveness and, second, how these data compared with information gathered by other means. Their conclusions, listed below, are instructive and are given here because similar questions might be asked of management records at other levels of government.

Using these management records offers the following advantages:

1. The cost per unit of observation is extremely small.
2. The data are reasonably accurate.

3. The data are longitudinal, with each wage earner as the unit of data collection.
4. There is little nonresponse bias due to missing observations or variables. (There may be unreported earnings.)
5. The data embody a comparison group as good as any that has been used in other studies.
6. The sample sizes are very large.

The disadvantages of using these data are:

1. Earnings are reported, rather than hours of work and wage rates.
2. Reported earnings are truncated for those earning above the Social Security maximum.
3. Social Security coverage varies as a function of age, possibly affecting the completeness of the control group.
4. Only a limited number of sociodemographic variables is available.
5. There is some time lag in the full reporting of the data.
6. Maintaining confidentiality of the data is difficult.

The National Academy of Sciences report points out that, after fifteen years of massive expenditures on manpower training programs, relatively little is known about their educational and labor market effects. Legal restrictions requiring programs to accept all volunteers often make it impossible to conduct a randomized field trial. When it is possible to select a subgroup of volunteers for a program, the selection process chooses those volunteers judged most likely to succeed, and leaves the others for the control group. These are design problems, and no data collection methodology alone can overcome them.

Social Security records are limited in the types of information they provide, and they have the specific shortcoming of being truncated at the Social Security earnings maximum. If a person earns more in a year than the maximum Social Security base, we do not know how much more he or she earns. But the data are accurate, inexpensive, and truly longitudinal. The longitudinal structure is crucial to the analysis of investments in training.

In light of the history of manpower training studies, the National Academy of Sciences report judges that Social Security management data are at least as good a source of comparison groups as tailor-made sample surveys. In some respects the Social Security data are even better, because it may be possible to match pairs of observations on selected employee characteristics, in particular an employee's prior earning pattern.

The National Academy of Sciences report recommends that these management records continue to be used for the evaluation of manpower programs, especially those that primarily serve young males.

FEATURES OF A MANAGEMENT RECORDS STUDY

Administrators routinely record information about individuals, physical goods, transactions, and processes. For instance, a loan application form helps a bank officer to decide whether to lend money to an applicant. Hospital charts help physicians manage patient care and aid hospital administrators in determining personnel needs. An hourly tally of the number of automobile parts produced in each area of a factory allows the plant manager to locate potential bottlenecks in the assembly process. The design of these record systems facilitates the day-to-day management of a complicated process.

Such information may also provide answers to questions that were not foreseen by the person collecting the data. A study of last year's loan applications may help a bank determine its effective service area. Hospital records may tell whether a new medical treatment has been successful. Hourly factory records may indicate which part of the plant needs expansion.

We define a management records study as one that relies on and draws conclusions from data already gathered for an administrative purpose. Generally, this original purpose differs from the new purpose of the retrospective study of the records. Ordinarily, then, the information available is not exactly what an investigator starting from scratch would have collected.

This definition suggests that a management records study is usually a special type of observational study. Recall that an observational study lacks intervention or control in the assignment of subjects to treatments. Similarly, since a management records study relies on previously gathered information, the investigator cannot control assignment as in an experiment. The features, strengths, and weaknesses of observational studies have been discussed in Chapter 4. The present chapter concentrates on issues unique to management records.

MANAGEMENT INFORMATION SYSTEMS

Management information systems are computerized systems for data management that allow managers to monitor and control an ongoing process. These systems consist of management records and computer procedures to summarize them. For example, many fire departments routinely use a computer-linked system to deploy their resources in response to multiple fires. A computer keeps track of special hazards of the site and of the location of fire-fighting equipment stored at the site, and relays this information to the company en route to the fire. Because all this information is electronically recorded, the computer can provide monthly summaries of fire incidents and the department's responses. The usefulness of a management information system depends a lot on its design. When the users of the system communicate their data needs to the system's designer, the resulting information is more useful for policy as well as management decisions.

This chapter concerns the use of management records, one component of a management information system, for policy studies outside the original reasons for collecting the data. For instance, fire department records may allow the fire chief to evaluate the reduction in response time due to a new allocation of equipment to fire stations, or these records may provide data for a simulation study to decide which company should respond to a given alarm.

STRENGTHENING MANAGEMENT RECORDS STUDIES

Sampling

Management files tend to be voluminous. Frequently we do not need to analyze all the data available. Scientific sampling, as discussed in Chapter 5, can help one deal with such large amounts of data.

As an example, consider the case of the Massachusetts Superior Court, which has been saving all its court records since its inception in 1859 (Hindus, Hammett, and Hobson 1979). In 1977, 40,000 cubic feet of records were stored in various locations throughout the state. Through the years, some records have been lost due to fire, flood, or lack of interest. Reviewing a stratified sample of about 3500 files, a committee of historians determined that, although 10 percent of all the files had historical value, 19 percent of those files thicker than 1.25 inches were historically valuable. The committee reasoned that by saving the thick files (17 percent of the total number of files) they could preserve 31 percent of the historically interesting files. The historians recommended saving both a random sample of all files to preserve the profile of the legal process and a separate set of thick files to preserve historical details.

An important side effect of the study was to make a random sample of 3500 files available for historical research.

Whenever we use sampling, we must carefully consider the sampling frame, and this is no less true for sampling management records. In the case of the court files, a docket book enabled the committee to construct a list of all files. In the absence of a list, researchers sometimes sample by selecting all records active on a certain day or set of days. This selection procedure tends to select longer cases than average, essentially because longer cases are each active for more days and have a greater chance to be included in the sample. This effect is known as "length-biased sampling." If the sample of legal records had been selected in this way (for example, all files active on January 1 of each year ending in zero), the sample would have included a larger proportion of the thick and historically interesting files, because such cases usually take longer to hear in court.

Researchers frequently use systematic sampling to study management records. One technique is to take every record whose unit number ends in, say, 7, to get a 10 percent sample, or, say, 42 or 67, to get a 2 percent sample. This technique works well and is easy to carry out as long as the mechanism for assigning numbers to records does not depend on any attribute of the record itself. For example, the court clerk may find it convenient to number all of the new cases each week on Friday afternoon, starting with the final digits 00 for the most serious cases and numbering the rest in decreasing order of seriousness. A researcher who later unknowingly samples all cases ending in 03 will find a extremely high proportion of serious cases in the sample.

Records are sometimes sampled physically. For instance, a ruler is used to find the files located at exactly 3, 6, and 9 inches in a drawer of supposedly randomly ordered files. This scheme tends to emphasize thicker files, and, as we have seen in the court example, these are often different from the rest. Furthermore, the cases may not be randomly arranged, and the problems associated with systematic sampling may also occur.

Generally, the effects of length-biased and systematic sampling of records are not glaring enough to be recognized simply by looking at the final results alone. But they may be strong enough to distort these results. Careful consideration must be given in advance to the type of sampling to be applied. Talking with the clerks who maintain and use the records usually helps to avoid many difficulties.

File Structure

A major difficulty in using management records is that the information is arranged in the file in a fashion that may be convenient for administrators but inconvenient for policy studies. In particular, information about one case may appear in numerous locations in one file or in many different files, and it may be identified slightly differently in each location. The following devices help to sort out the information and make it usable.

File Organization

Before a study can start, we may have to reorganize or sort the records in the file to bring together the data relevant to a case. Thus, one might sort a file of births so that all children born to the same parents are together.

Record Linkage

When records dealing with the same case are in two (or more) files, the analyst must match, or link, these records, using an identifier common to both (or all) files. Suppose, for example, that one planned to use monthly data from each precinct to study the relationship between police manpower and outside crime. One would probably find the monthly manpower reports for each precinct in one file, and the monthly crime reports by precinct in another. One would need to match the two files by precinct and month before proceeding with the analysis. When the cases to be matched are based in part on a person's name, there may be differences in how it is recorded—for example, J. Paul Jones, John Paul Jones, or John P. Jones.

Redundancy Checking

An investigation can greatly increase the certainty that correct linkages are made by using redundant information when it exists. Thus, if J. P. Jones and John Jones are both 37 years old and naval officers, they are more likely to be the same person than if they differ in age and occupation.

Splitting Data for Trial and Test

Large sets of management data can often be split into two or more groups to assess the reliability of the study findings. One group is used to develop a hypothesis and the other(s) to test this hypothesis on fresh data.

Adjustments

In studying the relation between presumed causal factors and their presumed effects, the association can often be clarified by adjusting for other contributing factors. For example, in studying the effect of police manpower on reducing crime, Press adjusted for time of year. As another example, if the school records in our possession have twice as many third graders as second graders, we can recalculate averages to reflect a more even distribution. Prior knowledge helps identify contributing factors.

Ancillary Studies

When a management record study is conducted because a special study is not feasible, interpretation of the findings may depend upon untested assumptions. For example, was the distinction between inside and outside crimes recorded accurately? Such specific issues can be resolved by investigating a small part of the total enterprise. Thus, one could review a sample of crime reports in detail to see if inside and outside crimes had been categorized accurately.

MERITS OF MANAGEMENT RECORDS STUDIES

The merits of studies based on management records flow from the nature of the original records: we have them in hand, frequently in computerized form.

Timeliness is a special merit of management records studies. We distinguished these studies as a special class of observational studies that use historical rather than prospectively gathered records as raw material. By using available management records, we can avoid spending a long time observing a process before carrying out the analysis. If we must decide on a policy question quickly, a study based on historical records may be the only type that can be carried out soon enough to help.

Management records studies are relatively inexpensive. Few or no resources are necessary for data gathering, fieldwork, or a central staff for data collection. Some may be needed to gather information about the reliability and peculiarities of the collection system. Frequently, the data are already coded, cleaned, and available in a form directly accessible by a computer. Since data gathering and coding frequently require a substantial financial effort, already collected and possibly computerized records can drastically reduce the cost of a study.

Management records may provide a window on the past that may not otherwise be available. Parish records of births and deaths are the sole source of information on fertility and mortality in pre-industrial Europe. The Massachusetts Superior Court records shed light on the state's legal and social history since 1859. Last year's hospital records may be the only source of information on the outcomes of an obsolete treatment.

Depending on the original purpose for collecting the records, the data they contain may be more accurate than other sources of data.

Some reasons are:

1. Administrative records usually record the event or transaction at about the time it takes place. Except for background information, respondents are not asked to recall events that happened months or years ago.
2. The respondents may have more incentive to complete a management record accurately. If they believe their answers will affect an administrative decision rather than go into a file for an undefined research purpose, they are more likely to treat the questions seriously and provide accurate answers.
3. Generally, more is at stake in a management situation than, for example, in the corresponding sample survey situation. Respondents may gain or lose benefits as a result of their replies, and they know that their accuracy might be checked. This situation leads people to think more carefully about their answers, and could lead to more honest and accurate answers.
4. Management records are often required by law or administrative procedure. Completion of the record may be a precondition for receipt of a benefit or service. These features lead to less serious nonresponse problems for management records studies than for other types of studies.
5. Since respondents do not know they are taking part in a study, they have no incentive to shade their answers one way or another to influence the outcome of the study. They may, however, try to influence the primary management purpose of the record.

WEAKNESSES OF MANAGEMENT RECORDS STUDIES

Like the strengths, the weaknesses of management records studies also arise because the data have already been collected. Each strength enumerated in the preceding section suggests a corresponding weakness.

It may be difficult or impossible to make inferences to the situation at hand, because the investigator did not control either the population studied or the information collected. An investigator should consider the differences between the actual and desired populations, and perhaps adjust for the effects of potential differences in composition of the populations. The investigator often must substitute proxy variables for the ideal variables when the latter have not been measured. Spanish surnames used in lieu of Hispanic origin or earnings records rather than hours worked are examples.

A researcher may misunderstand or have to guess about the definitions of the population and the variables. Especially when computers are involved, adequate documentation may be hard to obtain since one must know how the data were coded as well as their definition.

The practical aspects of using management records may also pose difficulties. The data may be (and frequently are) stored in inconvenient places, and the structure of the files may be difficult for an outsider to understand. The organization may store records for the same case in different places. It may be hard to find the desired facts when the records are thick file folders of handwritten forms and papers.

Individual records are frequently missing from the file, sometimes because a previous researcher found them interesting and removed them. One would not be surprised to find the chest x-ray of the only Legionnaires Disease patient this year to be missing from the file. Sometimes organizations keep only selected cases. A company may keep only the files of accounts active in the last two years, or a hospital only the records of Medicare patients. Investigation frequently reveals that such selected cases differ substantially from the remainder.

Investigators using management records must be taught to respect the privacy of the individuals who supplied the information and the confidentiality of the material in the records. Chapter 16 discusses the legal, ethical, and practical aspects of these concerns.

Sometimes the original reason for collecting the data weakens a study based on existing records:

1. The respondent who completes a management record during the course of an event may be hurried rather than thoughtful and accurate.
2. Since the respondent has more at stake than in other types of studies, there may also be more incentive to give incorrect answers if they would be beneficial to the respondent. Tax forms are a familiar example: the IRS says that many fewer people overestimate than underestimate their income.
3. Sometimes strong incentives exist for not completing administrative records. The U.S. Census Bureau finds it difficult to count the population of some areas because of the large number of illegal immigrants who are afraid that the Immigration and Naturalization Service will use census records to track them down. The nonresponse problems encountered in analyzing such records can be very serious if respondents differ from nonrespondents.

Often these weaknesses can be surmounted, but they must all be considered when evaluating the validity of a study based on management records.

QUALITY CHECKLIST

1. *Why were the original records collected, and how are they likely to be biased?* According to the original administrative purpose of the records, respondents may have had an incentive to bias their answers systematically. Department of Motor Vehicles records probably reveal better eyesight among 18-year-old males than do the records of the Selective Service Board. By considering the purpose of the records, we can often guess the direction of the bias, perhaps even estimate its magnitude, and partially adjust the results of the study accordingly.

2. *From whom were the original records collected, and were possible respondents omitted?* The participants in a program that generates records sometimes differ substantially from the population that interests the policymaker. Medicare data files provide information on health costs, but only for an elderly population. The effect may be more subtle. Cities often use telephone and utility company records to help estimate migration into the city since the last census. But doing so may not accurately reflect the number of new arrivals who are poor. If something is known about the missing people, adjustments are sometimes possible.

3. *Were all of the original records saved, or could deletions bias the results?* If some records have been removed, the reason for their absence could alter the composition of the remaining records. For instance, the removal of records for court cases that have been appealed to a higher court leaves the remainder different from the whole in many respects.

4. *If the records were sampled from a larger group, did the sampling method introduce any biases?* Random sampling requires that all records—and also all samples—have the same chance of being selected. If records are physically larger, or if the cases they represent were active longer, or for some other reason, some cases are more likely than others to be selected for the sample. If so, the sample may differ from the total group of records in a substantial way.

5. *Did the organization of the records allow easy and accurate transcription?* Complex records are obviously harder for an outsider to

read, understand, and organize. Because of updating, they may contain multiple entries of interest, and the reader must determine which entry is most current or otherwise the one of major interest. Poorly organized, voluminous records often conceal important information.

6. *Was linking of records necessary? If so, was it done well? What percent could not be matched?* Record linking is most accurate when a unique identifying number is present on all records. Otherwise, it may be difficult to link individuals in one data source with the same individuals in another source. The presence of accurate, unique numbers is unusual in the United States. Even the Social Security number is not unique or universal. Some individuals have two or more numbers. Some numbers have more than one owner.

Record linking by name and demographic characteristics is possible, but is hampered by nonuniqueness of names and by the tendency for people to use different versions of their names at different times.

Even small percentages of mismatches in linkage studies can cause major difficulties. The U.S. Bureau of the Census links census records with lists of driver's licenses, tax rolls, and so on to help estimate the fraction of residents missed by the census. They can match all but a few percent of the people on the lists, but the proportion of mismatches is about the same as the proportion of people actually missing. Thus, the resulting undercount estimate is relatively uncertain.

7. *Were important variables present, or did the investigator need to use substitutes?* The lack of exactly appropriate variables is a major weakness of management records studies. Payroll taxes for Social Security are not perfect substitutes for income—because there is a maximum yearly payment, people with incomes of $50,000 and $500,000 make the same payment. In environmental studies, pollution measures recorded by a regulatory agency investigating a potential violation of standards usually do not reflect average levels for that plant or region.

If the appropriate variables are not available, one must use substitutes. Sometimes analytic adjustments are possible. At the least, an investigator should try to estimate the direction of potential bias introduced by using the available data.

8. *Would the proposed study violate anyone's privacy or the confidentiality of these records?* Privacy and confidentiality are important ethical and legal issues that arise whenever we consider the use of data

QUALITY CHECKLIST

1. Purpose of the original records?
2. Omitted respondents?
3. Deleted records?
4. Sampling method?
5. Organization and complexity?
6. Record linkage?
7. Substitute variables?
8. Privacy and confidentiality?
9. Observational studies checklist.

gathered for another purpose, especially if the original purpose was administrative. Promises of confidentiality are often given when information is collected for administrative records, and it must be honored in subsequent studies using the information. In addition to important ethical factors, the quality of the data is often better if respondents believe that confidentiality will not be compromised. Honoring the confidentiality of records is important in the long term to preserve the validity of surveys, management records studies, and other sources of data for policy decisions. For a fuller discussion, see Chapter 16.

9. *All questions from the observational studies checklist.* Because they usually lack controlled intervention, management records studies are special types of observational studies. The checklist in Chapter 4 helps to assess the validity of inferences drawn from these studies.

POLICY IMPLICATIONS

The main advantage of studies based on management records is that the raw material already exists. The data are the records generated in the day-to-day business of an agency. If the records are relevant to the study, they may be easily, inexpensively, and quickly assessed and analyzed. Many of the problems of collecting, editing, and storing the information have already been solved. If the data are useful, no new burden falls on the supplier of the information.

The ease of access to the data depends, in part, on who collects and controls the information. It is generally easier for policymakers to get information from a data collecting branch of their own agencies than to get it from other agencies, for both bureaucratic and legal reasons. It often takes bureaucratic clout to get the time and attention of the busy computer staff that knows how to access the data. The policymaker must often convince the person directly in charge of computer operations that the data serve a common purpose and are valuable. Concern for the confidentiality of stored management records may also inhibit certain uses of management records data (see Chapter 16).

Since management records are generated in the course of regular administrative activity, they often refer directly to the population of interest rather than to a special study group. This can make the results easier to generalize and seem more appropriate to the situation at hand.

CONCLUSION

Our institutions record vast amounts of management information daily. Such records contain data with many potential uses. A management records study is a special form of observational study, without intervention on the part of the experimenter or observer. The available data never exactly match what one would have in a study planned for a specific purpose, because someone else designed the records.

Nevertheless, the available information may be more accurate and complete than in other studies. Moreover, management records sometimes provide the only data about a historical situation.

Timeliness and relatively low cost constitute the major benefits of management records studies. Both come from using previously collected data rather than slowly and expensively gathering new data. If a decision must be made quickly, management records may be the only available source of relevant information.

REFERENCES

Gittelsohn, A. M., and Wennberg, J. E. 1977. On the Incidence of Tonsillectomy and Other Common Surgical Procedures. In *Costs, Risks, and Benefits of Surgery,* J. P. Bunker; B. A. Barnes; and F. Mosteller, eds. New York: Oxford University Press.

Hindus, M. S.; Hammett, T. M.; and Hobson, B. M. 1979. *The Files of the Massachusetts Superior Court, 1859–1959: An Analysis and a Plan for Action.* Boston, Mass.: Judicial Records Committee of the Supreme Judicial Court.

National Academy of Sciences. 1974. *Final Report of the Panel on Manpower Training Evaluation: The Use of Social Security Earnings Data for Assessing the Impact of Manpower Training Programs.* Washington, D.C.: National Academy of Sciences (January).

Press, S. J. 1972. Police Manpower Versus Crime. In *Statistics: A Guide to the Unknown*, J. Tanur et al., eds. San Francisco: Holden-Day.

FURTHER READING

Boruch, R. F., and Cecil, J. S. 1979. *Assuring the Confidentiality of Social Research Data.* Philadelphia: University of Pennsylvania Press.

CHAPTER 9

Official Statistics

Official statistics and indices are related to the general family of censuses and sample surveys. The key feature of these statistics is that they are already gathered, usually either for a purpose different from that of the investigator or as general-purpose statistics of use to many people. Governments frequently publish official statistics as a by-product of their own administrative or regulatory information-gathering activities (see the previous chapter on management records). We call such data "official" because they are usually commissioned and published by government order, although semipublic or private agencies do issue some as well.

Making policy or other decisions based upon these data requires their analysis, and this book deals with data gathering, not with analysis. Nevertheless, the policymaker must be aware of available sources, in order to take advantage of them when appropriate. Perhaps the situation does not allow time for other specific data gathering. Perhaps available official statistics will directly answer the question. Perhaps the problem, while interesting, is not sufficiently important to undertake an expensive, more sharply focused search for data.

GUIDES TO DATA

Where can official statistics be found? For the United States, good starting places are:

1. *Guide to Federal Statistics, A Selected List* (Washington, D.C.: U.S. Government Printing Office, 1980). Published by the Bureau of the Census, this ten-page publication is a "guide to guides"; it lists and describes the publications, catalogs, indexes, bibliographies, and references from the major U.S. statistical agencies. It also provides an overview of the data available from the federal government.

2. *American Statistics Index: A Comprehensive Guide and Index to the Statistical Publications of the U.S. Government* (Washington, D.C.: Congressional Information Service, Inc.). In 1973 the Congressional Information Service began to identify, catalog, describe, index and announce the data and publications available from the federal government. This annual guide and index has monthly supplements, is current, and is available in most major libraries. It indexes publications by subject, author, title, category, and agency report number.

3. *Statistical Abstract of the United States* (Washington, D.C.: U.S. Government Printing Office). Published annually since 1879, this summary of statistics on economic, social, and political conditions is such a popular book that in recent years it has been distributed both by the government and by private publishers. It presents statistics in over 1300 tables and charts from government, private, and international sources. Each volume includes a guide to sources, listing 800 statistical publications on over 50 major subjects. The *Statistical Abstract* cites the sources of data in each table and in a general review at the end.

4. *Guide to U.S. Government Statistics*, 4th ed. (John L. Andriot, McLean, Virginia: Documents Index, 1973). This annotated guide, arranged by department and agency, lists the various official publications containing statistical data and provides agency, subject, and title indexes. It covers more than 3200 titles in the major statistical numbered series and gives notes for over 1700 serial publications.

5. *Social Statistics in Use* (Philip M. Hauser, New York: Russell Sage Foundation, 1975). This book gives, for many areas of study, a chapter on the kinds of statistics available and what organization has them, as well as illustrations of the sorts of studies that are available. It also provides information on how official statistics are used. Its particular

advantage is an in-depth treatment of population, vital statistics, education, economic and social indicators, and many other areas of social statistics.

6. *Statistics Sources,* 6th ed. (Paul Wasserman, Detroit: Gale Research Company, 1980). This large, annotated bibliography is designed as a user's guide to statistics sources. It presents more than 26,000 citations on 12,000 subjects. Arranged in dictionary style, with numerous cross-references, *Statistics Sources* cites government publications, annuals, yearbooks, and directories, as well as trade and professional societies and other organizations. Both the United States and other countries are covered.

7. *Statistical Reference Index: A Selective Guide to American Statistical Publications from Sources Other than the U.S. Government* (Washington, D.C.: Congressional Information Service, Inc.). Publication of this guide to nonfederal statistics began in 1980. It is issued monthly. Indexes are cumulated annually, with an annual edition for the preceding year issued each spring. The Congressional Information Service has published a similar guide and index to statistical publications of the U.S. government, beginning in 1973, in a similar annual index, with monthly supplements. The *Statistical Reference Index* focuses on U.S. publications from sources other than the national government. It covers state governments; trade, professional, and other nonprofit associations; businesses; commercial publishers; and independent research organizations. Excluded are local government sources. Publications are indexed by subject, name, category, issuing source, and title.

First-class research libraries are excellent sources of information, and experienced reference librarians are often ingenious at figuring out where good numbers can be found. The *World Almanac,* other almanacs, and encyclopedias may also prove useful.

In addition to consulting general guides and library sources, investigators can approach government statistical agencies directly.

While virtually every country in the world publishes official statistics, and many of the larger countries publish data comparing countries, a principal source for international information is the United Nations, which issues annual publications catalogs in several languages (address: Room A 3315, New York, New York 10017 U.S.A., or Palais des Nations, 1211 Geneva 10 Switzerland). *United Nations Publications in Print 1979–1980* is the current English-language listing of publications, with information on price, availability, and language

"WHY DIDN'T WE CHECK
THOSE RUSSIAN CLIMATE DATA?"

of all United Nations materials. This covers both printed and mimeographed documents, as well as microfilm and microfiche, in the areas of economics, trade, finance and commerce, social questions, law, communications, atomic energy, disarmament, narcotic drugs, demography, public finance, and other international statistics. A statistics yearbook is published annually, as are yearbooks of international trade statistics, national account statistics, construction statistics, industrial statistics, and world energy supplies.

Another source for international statistics is the Organization for Economic Cooperation and Development (headquarters: 2 rue André-Pascal, 75775 Paris, France; U.S. Information Office: 1750 Pennsylvania Avenue, N.W., Washington, D.C. 20006). This organization publishes data in a variety of fields, such as general economic surveys, international development, employment, energy, agriculture, environmental problems, and education. It issues a variety of serial publications, as well as special reports.

The organization of U.S. statistics is difficult to describe, because the system is decentralized, with a large number and variety of agencies generating numerical series according to their particular areas of interest. Some statistical series are used widely by the public to meet greatly varying needs. For the last forty years there has been a central coordinating agency, now the Office of Federal Statistical Policy and Standards of the Office of Management and Budget. This office is responsible for providing general policy guidance on the development of an integrated statistical system. While perhaps a hundred separate federal agencies conduct information inquiries that might be thought of as statistical, the Office of Federal Statistical Policy and Standards* has developed a list of thirty-eight that play a key statistical role; we describe twelve of them below.

FEDERAL STATISTICAL AGENCIES

Three statistical agencies collect data of general interest, both across departments and across functional areas: the Bureau of the Census (Department of Commerce); the Statistical Reporting Service (Department of Agriculture); and the Bureau of Labor Statistics (Department of Labor).

1. *The Bureau of the Census, U.S. Department of Commerce, Data Service Division* (telephone: 301-763-7662) is the central agency in the U.S. federal statistical system. Its most important activity is conducting the decennial census of the entire U.S. population, as specified in the Constitution. The budget and staff of the bureau are the largest among U.S. statistical agencies. The Bureau of the Census also provides special studies, tabulations, and a variety of other statistical services, both within and outside the Department of Commerce. Some projects require developing and conducting individual surveys, while others use existing surveys as a vehicle for preparing additional data or special tabulations. The primary purpose of the bureau is to collect general statistics, meeting a wide range of needs for data. The bureau collects and publishes basic statistics about the population and economy of the nation in order to assist the development and evaluation of economic and social programs. Periodic censuses include the Census of Population and Housing, taken at ten-year intervals, and the Census of Agriculture, the Census of Governments, and economic censuses, all taken at five-year intervals.

*In February 1982 the name was Statistical Policy Branch.

2. *The Statistical Reporting Service of the U.S. Department of Agriculture* (telephone: 202-447-4415), is the principal statistical group for the Department of Agriculture. It collects a wide variety of current agricultural data, generally on a continuing basis. Cooperative agreements are maintained with forty-eight states and similar agencies that collect and publish data for smaller geographic units. The principal mission of the Statistical Reporting Service is to supply current general-purpose agricultural statistics at the national and state levels, and to conduct analyses on food, agriculture, rural resources, and communities. It supplies official estimates of acreage, yield and production of crops, stocks, value of farm commodities, and inventory of livestock, as well as analyses of later stages in agricultural processing and marketing.

3. *The Bureau of Labor Statistics in the U.S. Department of Labor* (telephone: 202-523-1239) collects and analyzes data on labor and price statistics. These are defined broadly, resulting in general-purpose statistics. The findings of special analytic studies are published regularly in *Monthly Labor Review.* The Bureau of Labor Statistics covers employment, unemployment, occupational health and safety, employee compensation, wages, productivity, and labor relations, in addition to wholesale, retail, export, and import prices.

All three of the above agencies collect data as a major part of their overall programs and are not limited to statistical needs in a particular functional area. The budgets of these three agencies combined equal nearly 50 percent of the total U.S. government statistical budget for current programs.

Other federal statistical agencies sponsor one or more major data collection efforts in an area of general interest.

1. *The Energy Information Administration in the Department of Energy* (telephone: 202-252-8800). Prior to the founding of the Department of Energy in 1977, approximately fifty government agencies collected and analyzed energy data. The Energy Information Administration now has responsibility for carrying out a central, comprehensive, unified energy information program to collect, analyze and publish data. As both a collection and analytical agency, it collects and publishes statistics on petroleum supply, production, and stocks, as well as statistics on refineries, primary terminals, pipeline companies, and importers. It covers all phases of domestic and foreign energy-mineral resource development, as well as electrical energy production and dis-

tribution. It conducts broad-ranging analyses of energy: sources of availability and processing, transmission and distribution, cost and price, imports and exports, and short-term supply/demand balances.

2. *The National Center for Health Statistics* (NCHS) (telephone: 301-436-8500) is the federal agency with principal responsibility for the collection, analysis, and dissemination of vital and health statistics. NCHS produces data on the extent of illness and disability in the population, the supply and use of health services, and other measures of health and health status. As the source of the nation's official vital statistics on birth, death, marriage, and divorce, NCHS releases these data in publications, special tabulations, public use data tapes, and through collaborative research projects. Several regular publication series, such as the *Vital and Health Statistics* series, *Vital Statistics of the United States, Monthly Vital Statistics Report,* and *Advance Data* present survey findings, methodological studies, or detailed compilations of data. The health data yearbook, *Health, United States,* reports to Congress on the state of the nation's health. The findings of biennial surveys of the supply and use of health resources are presented in *Health Resources Statistics* and the *Nation's Use of Health Resources.* To obtain publications catalogs, a guide to data tapes, or the center's source book of health statistics, *Facts at Your Fingertips,* contact the Scientific and Technical Information Branch, National Center for Health Statistics, Room 1-57, 3700 East-West Highway, Hyattsville, Maryland 20782.

3. *The National Center for Education Statistics, Department of Education* (telephone: 301-436-7900) maintains cooperative arrangements with state education agencies and, through them, with local education authorities. In the past, the National Center for Education Statistics acted as a general purpose statistical collection agency, but in the last decade its mission has been expanded to include a variety of analytic functions. It is charged with compiling a periodic report on the condition of education in the United States, and with assisting state and local agencies in improving and automating their own statistical and data collection activities. It also supports the National Assessment of Educational Progress, a periodic survey for various agencies of the educational performance of samples of the general population.

4. *The Bureau of Mines in the U.S. Department of the Interior* (telephone: 202-634-4770) collects, compiles, and prepares statistics on all phases of domestic and foreign mineral resource development, except fuels, including reserves, production, consumption, inventory, price, and exports and imports. It conducts special analytical services dealing

with mining and metallurgy products, with helium and its distribution, and with various safety aspects of mining.

5. *The Bureau of Justice Statistics of the U.S. Department of Justice* (telephone: 202-724-7765) supports the collection, tabulation, evaluation, and preparation of statistics on U.S. law enforcement. Statistics are compiled on criminal victimization, law enforcement, judicial administration, corrections, and overall criminal justice functions.

6. *The Division of Statistics of the Internal Revenue Service in the U.S. Treasury Department* (telephone: 202-376-0216) collects a vast amount of data produced as a by-product of the tax collection process. As a matter of policy, tax forms are not used as vehicles for collecting data, other than those needed to support the tax collection function. However, as the tabulator of tax forms, the Division of Statistics provides important statistical support for other Treasury Department offices concerned with the analysis and forecast of tax receipts and the development of tax policy. In addition, the division supplies income and related data to other analytical offices, such as the Bureau of the Census and the Federal Trade Commission.

7. *The Department of Housing and Urban Development's Office of the Assistant Secretary for Policy Development and Research* (telephone: 202-755-5600) gathers statistics and information on housing and mortgage markets as part of its general research and development effort. This office oversees an annual housing survey, surveys of mortgage lending, statistics on interest rates on home loans, and surveys of new home completions and apartment occupancy.

8. *The Bureau of Economic Analysis in the U.S. Department of Commerce* (telephone: 202-523-0777) prepares the economic accounts of the United States and interprets economic developments. These provide a quantitative view of the production, distribution, and use of the nation's output in a framework of an interrelated system of debts and credits. The national accounts are supplemented by various measures for forecasting international developments. Because the accounts provide a disciplined and realistic quantitative description of the economy, they have become a primary tool for economic analysis and decision making. The measures and analyses prepared by the Bureau of Economic Analysis are published in *Monthly Survey of Current Business* and in periodic supplements to the *Survey.*

9. *The Office of Research Demonstration and Statistics within the Health Care Financing Administration of the U.S. Department of Health and Human Services* (telephone: 301-594-6702) serves as

the primary federal statistical office for the compilation of economic data on health care. It publishes statistics on health care costs and expenditures for specific goods and services. This office currently issues seven serial publications on health care financing.

The statistical system of the U.S. government is decentralized and sometimes seems hard for an occasional user to penetrate. Like most large institutions, the government undergoes periodic reorganization. Agency names change, roles are reassigned, tasks dropped or added. Personnel, addresses, and telephone numbers change.

The *Federal Statistical Directory* (Washington, D.C.: U.S. Government Printing Office, 1979) is a telephone book that includes "Tables of Organization" for federal statistical agencies, and it is issued every few years. Frequently, you can find the proper person or office for specific data by checking this directory. Other times a telephone inquiry to one office will bring quick referral to the right source.

The investigator working with official statistics faces many problems similar to those faced in the use of management records.

Inevitably, the constraint placed by official statistics on scholars is that they must make do with what is available. However, what is available does go well beyond the material published in books and reports. Such organizations as the Bureau of the Census, the National Center for Health Statistics, and the National Center for Education Statistics have gone to considerable effort to make their data accessible to users. Thus, they have tapes that researchers can use to make special analyses, and some organizations are willing to help qualified research workers get improved access to the data collected by an agency. For a user charge, many statistical agencies will do special analyses in response to individual requests. The Bureau of the Census and the Bureau of Labor Statistics, for example, will make various cross-tabulations of information from their existing data tapes, tabulations they do not publish routinely. Beyond this, some organizations can help the researcher by adding questions appropriate for analyses of mutual interest to the studies they regularly carry out.

Thus, it is possible to get at much data that is not published in printed form, but it does require an analytical effort on the part of the user.

Frequently, official statistics form a useful time series—as when the same questions are asked in repeated censuses or surveys over time, so that recent data can be readily compared to those previously obtained. For example, a few of the questions in the 1980 U.S. census were asked in the census of 1790. Of course, the scope and number of questions have increased greatly in the last 190 years, and although some care has been taken to maintain the comparability of data from one census to another, the user must be constantly on guard for changes in questions and definitions.

ADDITIONAL SOURCES

Private agencies also publish time-series data. We follow stock market prices with the Dow-Jones Index. We observe changes in the availability of bank-lending funds by following the prime interest rates of our larger banks. The American Medical Association has regularly published data on physicians in the United States for many years.

Occasionally, time-series data arise from panel studies; that is, not only are the same questions asked repeatedly over time, but they are asked of the same persons. Some of the Department of Agriculture crop-reporting data arise from measures of the production of the same fields each year. The Consumer Products Safety Commission surveys a panel of hospital emergency rooms repeatedly and publishes data on accidental injuries over time.

In addition to federal agencies and national organizations, many state, county, and local groups collect and publish data. The resources tend to vary so widely from one state or locality to another that specific local inquiry is usually required. Generally, if approached, those who have collected data are only too eager for it to be used. A telephone inquiry to various likely state or local government offices may well uncover unpublished or unexpected sources of official statistics. Frequently, one's first call will turn up only suggestions of other persons or agencies to contact, but people will usually be eager to help, and eventually one will be referred to the right office or person. Sometimes a state or national compiler will know of a local source for more detailed data for a city or county.

INTERPRETATION

Having located a source of promising data, one must then decide what to make of the information. Without going too deeply into issues of analysis, let us consider some basic steps. Since official statistics are generally collected for a purpose other than that of the researcher, it is important to know how these data were collected, and what possible biases may be present because of their intended use. A good source for a number will usually provide a note explaining what the number is supposed to represent and how it was obtained. A slight change in definition can make a substantial difference, and numbers from different sources may be differently defined. In addition to the definition and source of the number, one must consider its reliability. For example, data from the Internal Revenue Service based on pooled individual income tax returns probably do not overestimate income or underestimate deductions.

In *Statistics: A New Approach* (1956) W. Allen Wallis and Harry V. Roberts compared estimates in almanacs of the number of people in the world speaking various languages. The most spectacular percentage difference was for Arabic-speaking people: one almanac estimated 29 million and another, 58 million. The discrepancy is explained in part by the fact that one almanac estimated the number of native speakers, the other, the total number of speakers.

Just because official statistics are supplied by somebody else does not mean they are easy to use. First, finding the appropriate data is not always easy. Second, you have to understand how and why they were gathered, and identify their likely strengths, biases, and weaknesses.

An official statistic is, of course, derived from something—perhaps from the government's own management records, perhaps from a sample survey or census, perhaps from a forecast. The source of the number affects its suitability for policymaking. A number derived from a sample survey and published as an official statistic has all of the strengths and weaknesses of sample surveys, so the individual using this statistic should be familiar with the material covered in the chapter on sample surveys.

Although they are published as indices or as tabulations, official statistics are derived from raw data, such as answers to individual survey questions. Some statistical agencies make available to qualified users the raw data themselves (for example, in the form of data tapes), perhaps deleting only information that might identify specific individuals. As one goes along the continuum from raw data, through tabulations, to derived indices—that is, as the raw data are processed to make them more generally useful—the problems of definition increase. The raw data are usually specific, but the information can be tabulated in various ways, and these tabulations are further manipulated to produce indices, such as the consumer price index. Unless users understand how the tabulations or indices were made, they can misunderstand their meaning.

In preparing sample estimates of major economic and social indicators, accuracy matters. The Council of Economic Advisers to the President estimated in 1978 that because of cost-of-living adjustment clauses in the contracts of large unions, as well as Social Security and other such transfer payments, each .1 percent increase in the consumer price index had the effect of increasing payments to individuals by over $1 billion; 60 percent of unionized workers are now covered by such clauses. Thus, the precision of economic series, such as the consumer price index, becomes important in direct monetary terms, because it affects the income and welfare of many people.

THE INFORMATION INDUSTRY

While most use of official statistics is made directly from the source to the user, in the last ten or fifteen years an industry has grown up devoted in large measure to helping its customers make better use of official statistics. The largest firms in this field focus their activities on large-scale economic studies. Because of the difficulty and expense of such studies, individual clients usually find it impractical to commission much brand new data gathering and are forced to rely on information collected and published as official statistics. Such organizations as Data Resources Inc., Wharton Econometrics, and Chase Econometrics serve as middlemen, helping their customers solve economic problems.

These companies work for clients in both the private and the public sector; they may be commissioned to do a study for an individual corporate client, a trade association, or a government agency. While they do some special data gathering, their work involves extensive analyses of official statistics. They may, drawing on published data, make special studies of future demand, price, and availability of individual commodities. For example, they may help a housing trade association determine the likely future prices of finished wood products, using official statistics of present timber production, present and forecasted housing starts, the overall state of the economy, and changing family size. Thus, their elaborate computer modeling of future economic conditions relies heavily on official statistics drawn from a variety of government agencies. These companies are analogous to survey-research organizations in that they serve as expert intermediaries between the data source and user. Their experience and familiarity with the availability and quirks of official statistics make their work particularly valuable for complicated analytical jobs.

REFERENCE

Wallis, W. A., and Roberts, H. V. 1956. *Statistics: A New Approach.* Glencoe, Ill.: The Free Press.

FURTHER READING

Martin, M. E. 1981. Statistical Practices in Bureaucracies. *Journal of the American Statistical Association* 76: 1–8.

CHAPTER 10

*The Explosion in Computer-Assisted Library Searches**

In the last decade a quiet revolution has taken place in library searches. Scholars and research workers, even those connected with major universities and research institutes, are likely to be surprised at the extent of this transformation in seeking published information.

This area is moving rapidly. The authors' purpose is to alert you to these continuing developments so that you can investigate your local library resources to make sure you are taking full advantage of them.

We who work at Harvard University were surprised at what we learned. We went to the Harvard University Library to find out what was available. In addition to the central library, we consulted the libraries at Harvard's graduate schools of education, business, medicine, health, government, and law.

Today, one uses a computer instead of poring through catalogs or bound indexes of periodical literature. Rather than searching printed indexes by year for separate subject headings, the user asks a computer to search entire data bases at once for many different terms and years. The computer provides rapid retrieval of citations, printing the bibliographies it finds and usually an abstract of the work, something indexes rarely include. The computer accomplishes the inquiry through machine-stored bibliographies and periodical indexes in only a few minutes.

*Anne Church Bigelow was responsible for much of the preparation of this chapter.

HOW A SEARCH WORKS

Different data bases cover various fields of endeavor. Once the user selects the appropriate data base, a research librarian can help pick out key subject terms, journal titles, and/or authors' names. These are then connected by AND, OR, or NOT. When two subject terms are linked by AND, a citation must mention both of them to be retrieved. If the terms are joined by OR, a citation has to include only one of them. In this way one can hunt for synonymous terms or related concepts. Using the word NOT ensures that specific terms will not be retrieved. (These expressions involving AND, OR, and NOT are Boolean logic statements.)

Many data bases permit the user to interact with the computer. The computer will print out on the terminal a brief selection of the results of a search—perhaps the first 5 or 15 citations found (title, author, source, date), together with a count of the total number that satisfied the search instructions. You review these and perhaps modify the instructions. Maybe 1600 references will be produced. Rather than drown in this flood of paper, you modify the search to seek only those in the English language, or only those published in the last 18 months. Perhaps you find, on reviewing the sample printout, that the references being retrieved are not what you want at all. You can then revise your search instructions to seek other citations. Some data bases will supply an abstract for some, or all, citations. You may review a sample of these to see whether you are on the right track. Thus, a search may be a repetitive, exploratory process as instant feedback from the computer to your terminal lets you refine your search instructions to get what you seek.

Example: Stability of Africa

A government or corporate policymaker, concerned about the stability of Africa, might run a search on "Ideologies of National Liberation with reference to Angola, Mozambique, Algeria, Guinea-Bissau, and the Third World." *Social Scisearch* would be an appropriate data base to use. It covers every area of the social and behavioral sciences, indexing every significant item from the 1,000 most important social science journals throughout the world, as well as selected social science articles from 2,200 other journals in the natural, physical, and biomedical sciences. Produced by The Institute for Scientific Information in Philadelphia, it includes 765,000 records, from 1972 to the present, with monthly updates. *Social Scisearch* also provides a retrieval technique that allows you to search the references that an author cited.

Near the end of 1980, a search for "Liberation" in the title drew 580 citations. "Third World" OR "Angola" OR "Mozambique" OR "Algeria" OR "Guinea" OR "Ideology" resulted in 4,259 references. When the computer combined the two commands, searching for articles whose titles satisfy both, it retrieved 22 citations. At that stage, we listed half of them to see what we were collecting:

1. "Idealism and Revolution—New Ideologies of Liberation in Britain and the United States," *Political Studies.* English. (Book review)
2. "Namibia—The Ideology of National Liberation," *IDS Bulletin—Institute of Development Studies.* English.
3. "Liberation and National Reconstruction of Mozambique," *Argument.* German.
4. "Idealism and Revolution—New Ideologies of Liberation in Britain and the United States," *American Political Science Review.* English. (Book review)
5. "Idealism and Revolution—New Ideologies of Liberation in Britain and the United States," *Sociology—The Journal of the British Sociological Association.* English. (Book review)
6. "People in Power—Account from Angola Second War-of-National-Liberation," *African Affairs.* English.
7. "National Liberation and Development of Socialism in Africa (Angola, Guinea-Bissau, Mozambique)," *Canadian Journal of Political Science.* French.
8. "Aspects of Ideology of Gay Liberation Movement in New Zealand," *Australian and New Zealand Journal of Sociology.* English.
9. "Health and National Liberation in People's Republic of Mozambique," *International Journal of Health Services.* English.
10. "Some Notes on National Liberation Wars in Angola, Mozambique, and Guinea-Bissau," *Military Affairs.* English.
11. "Revolution of Damned—Struggle for Liberation in Guinea-Bissau," *Argument.* German.

In this list eight articles are in English, two are in German, and one is in French. Article 8, on gay liberation in New Zealand, highlights a loophole in the strategy, which we want to correct. Already, we know that this project will involve foreign language skills and some pruning of irrelevant liberation movements or a revision of tactics. Proceeding in this iterative fashion, we could request that the list of eleven remaining citations be mailed to us and then continue our investigation with the introduction of AND "Violent" NOT "Gay" NOT "Britain" NOT "United States," for instance.

When using data bases through a library, you first consult a reference librarian, who helps you formulate a search statement and interact with the computer. The cost differs according to the various data bases used, the computer time consumed, and the number of citations retrieved. For those who do not have regular access to a research library that provides this service, it is often available at a surcharge to members of the public.

TYPES OF DATA BASES

Data bases come from various sources. Many are maintained by government agencies. For example, *Child Abuse and Neglect* comes from the National Center for Child Abuse and Neglect in the Children's Bureau of the U.S. Department of Health and Human Services. Since 1965, it has covered research project descriptions and bibliographies, plus references and service program listings. At present, it includes some 9,000 citations.

Other data bases are offered by societies, associations, or institutions. For example, *Enviroline*, at the Environmental Information Center in New York, covers the world's environmental literature. It indexes and abstracts more than 5,000 international primary and secondary sources, including such fields as management, technology, planning, law, political science, economics, geology, biology, and chemistry as they relate to environmental issues, with 80,000 citations.

These and similar data bases are supplied by information-retrieval-system companies. Librarians refer to such companies as "data base vendors." For instance, DIALOG Information Retrieval Service, a division of Lockheed Missiles and Space Company, offers over 110 data bases, with more than 40 million records. Research libraries, government agencies, businesses, hospitals and other institutions contract with information retrieval systems. The computer terminal in a library or in a client's office is connected by telephone to the computer operated by a data base vendor, such as DIALOG. The selected abstracts and citations can be printed at the receiving terminal, or they can be mailed.

Law libraries and law firms use a data base called LEXIS, supplied by Mead Data Central. Instead of scanning by citation, LEXIS has entire libraries it searches word by word. For example, the Federal Securities Library is made up of federal cases, statutes, legislative history, and rulings on U.S. securities legislation. LEXIS follows a different strategy and produces a concordance. A concordance, like those to the Bible or to the Works of Shakespeare, is an alphabetical list setting forth the location of each appearance of the listed words in the particular text. A LEXIS concordance lists the words in a file of cases or other legal materials.

For example, one might look for all U.S. Federal Court opinions in which "ice" and "sidewalk" appear within 15 words of each other. The computer can then display up to 999 words on either side of the search words. It will also engage in a dialogue with the user to provide instructions when needed and to allow modification and follow-up then and there. It also recognizes and corrects typographical errors and misspellings or tells the user how to deal with other mistakes. LEXIS thus takes the data base service one step further in that a major research task can be completed right at the computer terminal.

From the many different data bases, we reproduce below some examples of those available in 1981. This field has expanded rapidly in the last few years, and it continues to do so at an ever faster rate. Since what we describe here will soon be outdated, you will want to investigate current possibilities for yourself.

DATA BASES AT ONE UNIVERSITY

The following list of data bases includes all titles we found at Harvard University in January 1981. For those items that policymakers might be especially interested in, we have given a description; for the rest, only titles are provided.

ABI/INFORM (Abstracted Business Information)
1971–present, updated monthly
Stresses general decision sciences information that is applicable to business management and administration; 400 business and business-related publications are scanned for articles to be abstracted and included in the data base.

ACCOUNTANTS INDEX

AGRICOLA
1970–present
From the National Agricultural Library, covers worldwide journal and monographic literature in agriculture and related subject fields. The Food and Nutrition section of the file contains abstracts.

AIM/ARM (Vocational and Technical Education)

ALCOHOL USE/ABUSE
1968–present
Alcoholism. Hazeiden Foundation.

AMERICA: HISTORY AND LIFE

AMERICAN STATISTICS INDEX
1973–present, updated monthly
A comprehensive index to the statistical publications of the U.S. government, with citations to the publications of over 400 federal agencies, including the Bureau of the Census, the Department of Labor, and the National Center for Education Statistics.

BIOSIS PREVIEWS
1970–present
Provides access to over 2.3 million citations that have appeared in BIOLOGICAL ABSTRACTS and BIOLOGICAL ABSTRACTS/RRM (formerly BIORESEARCH INDEX).

BOOKS INFO
Books currently in print.
Contains approximately 800,000 citations indicating author, title, publisher code, price, subject descriptors, LC card number, and ISBN number.

CA CONDENSATES (Chemistry)

CA SEARCH (Chemistry)

CHILD ABUSE AND NEGLECT
1965–present, updated semiannually
Produced by the National Center on Child Abuse and Neglect. Divided into three subfiles: ongoing research projects, service program descriptions, and bibliographic references. The first two subfiles, consisting of descriptions of methodology, services, funding, and clientele, are purged and updated annually. The third subfile includes bibliographic references to conference proceedings, journal articles, books, and research reports; it is updated semiannually.

COMPREHENSIVE DISSERTATION INDEX
1861–present, updated monthly
Includes nearly all dissertations accepted for academic doctorates in the U.S., with selective coverage of Canadian and other foreign dissertations. The printout does not include abstracts, but for all disserta-

tions available through University Microfilms, it will indicate the volume and page in Dissertation Abstracts International, where the abstracts can be found.

COMPUTER AND CONTROL ABSTRACTS

CONGRESSIONAL INFORMATION SERVICE
1970–present, updated monthly
An index to the publications of the U.S. Congress, CIS covers hearings, reports, committee prints, documents, and special publications of congressional committees and subcommittees.

DISCLOSURE
Indexes and extracts reports filed with the Securities and Exchange Commission by approximately 11,000 publicly owned companies. Access is by company name, location, officers, SIC codes, subsidiaries, assets, revenues, etc.

DOW JONES NEWS/RETRIEVAL

DRUG INFO

ECONOMIC ABSTRACTS INTERNATIONAL
1974–present
Covers the world's literature (books, reports, and articles) on markets, industries, country-specific economic science. Half the material is in English.

EIST: KEY TO ENVIRONMENTAL IMPACT STATEMENTS
1977–present
Contains citations to environmental impact statements from federal, state, county, and municipal agencies.

ELECTRICAL AND ELECTRONICS ABSTRACTS

ENERGYLINE
1971–present
Includes books, articles, conference proceedings, reports, and surveys on energy-related research. Special emphasis is on policy and planning, resources and reserves.

ENVIROLINE
1971–present
Similar to ENERGYLINE. Includes air and water pollution, land use, environmental design, transportation.

ERIC (Educational Resources Information Center)

EXCEPTIONAL CHILD EDUCATION RESOURCES (ECER)

FEDERAL INDEX
1976–present, updated monthly
Coverage of new federal regulations, bill introductions, speeches, hearings, executive orders, and contract awards. Indexes the *Washington Post*, *Congressional Record*, presidential documents, and *Commerce Business Daily*.

FOUNDATION DIRECTORY

FOUNDATION GRANTS INDEX

FOUNDATIONS, NATIONAL

GPO MONTHLY CATALOG
1976–present, updated monthly
Corresponding to the printed Monthly Catalog of U.S. Government Publications, this data base indexes public documents generated by the U.S. federal government and printed by the Government Printing Office.

HISTORICAL ABSTRACTS
1973–present
Indexes articles, dissertations, and books in the field of modern world history; excludes U.S. and Canada.

INFORM (Abstracted Business Information)

THE INFORMATION BANK (*New York Times* and other major newspapers)

INSPEC (Physics, Electronics, Computers)

LANGUAGE AND LANGUAGE BEHAVIOR ABSTRACTS (LLBA)

LEXIS (Law)

M.L.A. BIBLIOGRAPHY (Literature and Language)

MAGAZINE INDEX

MANAGEMENT CONTENTS

MARC SERIALS (Library of Congress Serial Records)

MEDLARS
1966–present
Index Medicus is produced from this data base, which provides access to the world's biomedical literature.

MEDOC
1976–present
Provides comprehensive coverage of U.S. government documents in health-related subject areas.

MONTHLY CATALOG (U.S. Government Printing Office Catalog)

NATIONAL FOUNDATIONS

NATIONAL INSTITUTE OF MENTAL HEALTH (NIMH)
1969–present
A unique collection of mental health literature selected from approximately 950 journals, symposia, government reports, and other sources. Covers biomedical and social science topics.

NATIONAL NEWSPAPER INDEX

NICEM (National Information Center for Educational Media)

NICSEM/NIMIS (National Information Center for Special Education Materials/National Instructional Materials Information System)

NTIS (National Technical Information Service)
1964–present, updated biweekly
Includes government-sponsored research, development, and engineering. NTIS is the central source for research reports, analyses, and technical information from local, state, and federal agencies, as well as their contractors or grantees. Includes material from H.H.S., HUD, Department of Commerce, and some 240 other units. Corresponds to the printed Government Reports Index.

PAIS (Public Affairs Information Service)
1972–present, updated quarterly
Contains records from the PAIS Bulletin (1976–present) and the PAIS Foreign Language Index (1972–present), covering issues of public policy regarding international relations, economics, public administration, law, education, social welfare, and social anthropology.

PHARMACEUTICAL NEWS INDEX

PHILOSOPHERS INDEX

PHYSICS ABSTRACTS

POPULATION BIBLIOGRAPHY
1966–present, updated monthly
Covers all aspects of population studies, including abortion, demography, migration, family planning, fertility studies, policy, population

education, and population research and methodology. Includes articles from journals, technical reports, government documents, and dissertations. Emphasis is on socioeconomic aspects of U.S. and developing countries.

POLLUTION ABSTRACTS
1970–present
Provides access to the technical literature on the environment as contained in over 2,500 domestic and foreign primary sources.

PSYCHOLOGICAL ABSTRACTS

PTS
U.S. and international manufacturing, marketing, industrial forecasts.

SCISEARCH
1974–present
Multidisciplinary index which, by covering core journals, provides access to 90 percent of the world's significant scientific and technical literature. This data base contains references from both SCIENCE CITATION INDEX and CURRENT CONTENTS.

SSCI (Social Science Citation Index)

SSIE (Smithsonian Science Information Exchange)
Includes last two years, revised monthly
Contains reports of both government and privately funded science and social science research projects either in progress or initiated and completed during the past two years. Collects data from funding organizations at the inception of a research project and provides a source of information on current research long before progress reports appear in the published literature. Provides name of project investigator, funding agency, summary, and detailed subject descriptors.

SOCIOLOGICAL ABSTRACTS

CONCLUSION

Many advances are underway. Not only are data bases that cover fresh subject areas proliferating, but current data bases are constantly expanding. On-line computerized information-retrieval facilities are available at more libraries each year. Data base producers are developing nontextual data bases. Numerical and statistical data will be presented graphically. A chemistry data base will display structural molecular formulae. In short, the field is rapidly expanding in scope, availability, and ease of use. Policymakers and their research staff will want to keep abreast of these innovations.

PART III

Predicting the Future

CHAPTER 11

Simulation

Simulation tries to show how an innovation or a change in policy might turn out without actually implementing the change. Such an approach can be essential if it is not feasible to try out the policy change just to decide which policy to implement. In spirit, simulation in the policy context resembles the use of simulators to train pilots and astronauts or the Environmental Protection Agency's laboratory procedure for measuring the gasoline mileage of automobiles. The techniques differ, however, relying on a combination of data and mathematical models rather than on a physical analog of a system. Physical models—small replicas of dams and waterways, say—still play an important role in policy decisions. Within the overall framework of simulation, mathematical models and data can be combined in many ways. The examples in the next section show both the variety of settings and the variety of techniques.

EXAMPLES

To illustrate applications of simulation, we present three examples: combustion engineering, welfare reform, and medical-facilities planning. The first of these models a fire in a bedroom, based on a complex description using the appropriate laws of physics. The second draws upon an extensive body of data to estimate the impact of about twenty welfare reform plans. The third uses a mathematical model of chance events to determine the relative need for intensive care beds for coronary and surgical patients.

Fire in a Bedroom

A fire in an enclosed space, such as a bedroom, develops by a complex process. Good scientific data on it are hard to come by, even though thousands of home fires occur each year in the United States. After a fire has been extinguished, investigators can often determine where it started and how it spread, but these facts do not tell precisely how rapidly the fire spread or how various combinations of materials in the room influenced it.

Igniting a fire in a model bedroom under laboratory conditions and monitoring its development by means of sensors and video cameras yield the desired kind of information. Unfortunately, the laboratory facilities are expensive, and an experiment takes time to set up (and to clean up afterward). Also, many factors affect the development of the fire and need to be manipulated in a program of research.

Even though a fire is complex, engineers understand many of its components and can describe them by using the laws and equations of physics. They also know the important interactions among the component processes, but a tidy solution for the overall system lies beyond today's theory. To gain an understanding of this process, Howard W. Emmons and his coworkers at Harvard University are using a computer to simulate the development of fires, performing the component calculations, coupling their results, and stepping the whole system along through time in small increments. They verify the results of the computer work by checking key measurements against laboratory data from actual test fires.

If we understand, at this level of detail, how fires develop, we can take several policy actions. For example, if some combinations of building or furnishing materials are more flammable or produce a larger quantity of toxic gases than the individual materials alone, then building codes for residences and hotels might prohibit their combined use. Or simulation experiments may provide better information on the length of time that people would have to escape safely. This knowledge would be useful to the public, as well as to furniture manufacturers and home builders. The indicated changes in furnishing materials and in construction would lengthen the time for safe escape. Eventually, fire simulation programs might be able to test the fire safety of the plan for a whole apartment building or hotel, before construction begins. Local governments might require such tests before approving the plans.

Emmons, Mitler, and Trefethen (1978) have developed a large-scale computer program, Computer Fire Code III, which simulates a fire in a single room. Their deterministic approach uses direct calculations based on physical laws and introduces no random elements. The following description gives an idea of the physical processes involved:

If we watch a fire in a large building, we see at first some small ignition process on some individual fuel element. It might be a lighted cigarette on an overstuffed chair or an extension cord under a rug. Eventually the smoking fuel begins to smolder and then breaks into flames. The flames feed heat back to the fuel to spread the fire and draw air in to produce a hot rising plume. At the ceiling the plume spreads out as a hot gas layer and thus heats the ceiling and by radiation further increases the fire and heats other fuels. The hot layer depth soon reaches the top of the door and/or open windows, and hot gas begins to flow out. Soon other fuel items in the room are heated to their ignition temperature, and the fire spreads rapidly to flashover.

As soon as the fire starts, the rapid expansion of the air begins to move air throughout the building. When hot gas begins to flow through a door into another room, the smoke and soot begin the process of value destruction by the soot deposited on delicate finishes. Furthermore, the toxic gases begin to permeate the building, endangering the lives of the occupants. (Emmons, Mitler, and Trefethen 1978, pp. 2–3)

These processes and events govern the components of the simulation program:

√ The fire.

√ The plume of smoke rising from the fire.

√ The hot layer of gases at the ceiling.

√ The vent (that is, the window or door).

√ The room (as a whole, involving overall conservation of mass and energy).

√ Heat transfer by radiation.

√ Heat transfer by convection.

√ Heating of the walls and the target.

At its present stage of development, this simulation program does a successful job of simulating the course of a fire, as these investigators have confirmed by comparing simulation results with the measurements obtained from some eight test fires carried out in a laboratory. Advances in computational techniques should enable them to make

"WAIT, CHIEF! WE'LL NEVER KNOW HOW THESE FIRES SPREAD UNLESS WE HAVE SOME CAREFULLY CONTROLLED OBSERVATIONS."

further progress, and the compartmentalized structure of the computer program will make it feasible to extend these simulations to buildings composed of many rooms, interconnected in various ways.

Welfare Reform

In recent years the number of people eligible for assistance under the various welfare programs has grown substantially, and the escalating costs of these programs make an important claim on federal, state, and local budgets. As a result, welfare reform—aimed at controlling these costs while still providing assistance in an equitable fashion to those who are eligible for it—is a persistent issue.

Among the goals of any income maintenance system are:

√ *Equity*—persons having the same resources and circumstances should receive the same assistance.

√ *Responsiveness*—the amount of assistance should adjust promptly to changes in need.

√ *Work incentives*—the system should make it attractive for recipients to work if they are able to do so.

√ *Cost-effectiveness*—the system should allocate the available money to the people who are most in need.

In evaluating possible welfare reforms, a key feature is the system's treatment of income (especially earned income) that beneficiaries receive. Operationally, an assistance program's income accounting system affects both eligibility and the amounts of ongoing payments, and thus it has major policy consequences.

Many existing welfare programs have grown gradually over the years and have not had to deal with the question of income accounting in a systematic way. To cope with a wide range of individual situations, however, an income accounting system must be complex. Its elements include the accounting period, the reporting period, the payment period, and the method of income reporting (prospective or retrospective). Various specifications of these elements have been the subject of welfare reform proposals and some limited experiments. For example, the Colorado Monthly Reporting Experiment and Pre-Test (Mathematica Policy Research 1979) has indicated some of the effects of using monthly retrospective reporting for the Aid to Families with Dependent Children (AFDC) program in Denver and Boulder.

Because such an experiment involves major changes in the procedures of a welfare agency, it is clearly not feasible or desirable to test many of the alternative income accounting systems in this way. In fact, the decision to test monthly retrospective reporting was preceded by substantial analysis of alternative systems. Simulation provides an effective means of directly comparing a considerable variety of income accounting systems—more than could be tested in the field, even with the best of experimental designs.

Allen (1973) discusses in some detail the problems of income accounting in income maintenance programs and illustrates important difficulties and alternatives by calculating the benefit payments corresponding to the income streams of hypothetical families. To see how alternative accounting systems affect costs, responsiveness, and caseloads, Allen applies simulation. The data for these simulations include the annual income histories (month by month) of 5522 families drawn from the income maintenance experiments sponsored by the Department of Health, Education, and Welfare in Seattle and Denver and the experiments sponsored by the Office of Economic Opportunity in New Jersey, Pennsylvania, North Carolina, and Iowa. For each family, the computerized model determines the annual total of benefit payments under each of seventeen alternative systems, using the income guarantee and tax rate parameters embodied in the Nixon administration's proposed Family Assistance Plan.

The characteristics of these systems indicate the variety of elements that Allen explored. Her aim was to aid Congress in assessing the trade-offs among possible welfare plans, such as balancing responsiveness to recipients' changing income and need against the equity and costs of the plans. We can summarize the characteristics in four groups: reporting system, forecasting accuracy and administrative response, carryover, and recapture.

One feature of a system is how often (monthly, annually, or quarterly) a family reports its income so that the amount of its payment can be (re)calculated. If the reporting method is *retrospective*, the family's payment is based on its income for the previous period (month or quarter). The annual entitlement plan uses the income for the last year, while the monthly entitlement plan works with the income for the current month (to show the result of matching benefits to need as promptly and closely as possible). The *prospective* method of reporting uses an estimate of the family's income during the next period (a quarter in these simulations, although a month might now be feasible). Because the simulation is based on previously collected income streams, "future" values are available, and Allen's simulation used these in estimating future income.

A realistic treatment of prospective systems required an additional component of the model to represent four features:

1. The likelihood that a family with a highly irregular income pattern will foresee a change in its income.
2. The common requirement that a family make an interim (intraquarter) report if its income changes substantially.
3. The probability that a family will submit such an intraquarter report.
4. The lags that tend to occur between the time when the agency receives an intraquarter report and the first assistance payment based on this new information. (Two patterns of administrative lags, "likely" and "pessimistic," were used.)

A *carryover* feature is part of many of these plans. By "remembering" the income (especially earnings) that a family received in prior periods and applying these resources to meet that family's need in the current period, the system seeks to smooth out substantial fluctuations in the family's income. Equity is the consideration underlying the carryover provision. Suppose that two families had identical situations, except that the earned income of one was constant for all twelve months of the year, while the earnings of the other added up to the same total amount but came in only six months of the year. Thus, both families have the same annual amount of earned income, but in the absence of any carryover, the second family would be eligible for a full assistance payment in each of the months when it had no earnings and hence would have a larger total income (earnings plus assistance) for the year. In these plans the carryover mechanism handles prior income amounts in two ways: first-in, first-out (FIFO) and last-in, first-out (LIFO). That is, in using prior income to offset current need, FIFO begins with the earliest period in the memory record (twelve months or four quarters), while LIFO begins with the most recent period.

Finally, because income forecasting cannot be perfectly accurate, a prospective system may include a provision for *recapture.* The idea is to reconcile projected income against actual income at the end of each accounting period and thereby ensure that the benefits a family has received are equal to its entitlement.

For policy purposes, the important comparisons among these systems are in terms of national estimates of caseloads and costs. Because the 5522 families in the data base did not have the same distribution on family size, race, sex of family head, and income as the U.S. population, it was necessary to weight the simulation results. (This is a natural consequence of the stratifications used in selecting the samples for the various experiments.) Using a straightforward adjustment procedure, Allen simultaneously took into account race, family size, sex of family head, and income class and obtained a set of weights that would make the results for the experimental population in urban areas comparable to those for the U.S. urban population. She applied a similar procedure using coarser categories to the data of the 296 rural experimental families.

Among the results of this simulation, perhaps the easiest to consider is the total cost. Table 11-1 lists the seventeen plans and shows two cost figures for each—one for the population inside standard metropolitan statistical areas (SMSAs) and the other combining this with the rural population. The benchmark plans, Plan 1 and Plan 2, were included to establish the (minimum) cost of an annual entitlement and the responsiveness of a monthly entitlement, respectively. For the inside-SMSA population, the cost difference between these plans was estimated at about $350 million. The retrospective plans (Plans 3 through 9) have estimated costs between these two extremes. Some would be only slightly more costly than Plan 1, and these offer varying degrees of responsiveness. As a group, the prospective systems (Plans 10 through 17) would be more expensive, and four had even higher estimated costs than Plan 2. While the whole set of plans simulated does not provide separate estimates of the costs (or savings) of the various features (such as quarterly versus monthly, prospective versus retrospective, and the carryover), a more detailed examination of the simulation results does indicate the approximate costs. Other outputs from the simulations included caseload size and a measure of

TABLE 11-1 *Seventeen assistance plans and their simulated costs (in billions of dollars)*

Plan		Cost for Inside-SMSA Population	Cost for Inside-SMSA Plus Rural Population
Benchmark			
1	Annual entitlement	2.59	3.74
2	Monthly entitlement	2.94	6.35
Retrospective			
3	Monthly, no carryover	2.94	6.35
4	Monthly, 12-month FIFO	2.61	3.76
5	Monthly, 6-month FIFO	2.63	3.94
6	Monthly, 12-month LIFO	2.61	3.76
7	Monthly, 6-month LIFO	2.65	4.04
8	Quarterly, no carryover	2.83	4.73
9	Quarterly, 12-month LIFO	2.61	3.79
Prospective (all quarterly)			
10	Pure	3.02	6.97
11	"Likely" forecast lag	3.02	7.36
12	Intraquarter reporting, "likely" admin. lag	3.03	6.97
13	Intraquarter reporting, "pessimistic" admin. lag	3.09	6.80
14	Intraquarter reporting, "likely" lags, LIFO	2.77	4.24
15	Intraquarter reporting, "likely" lags, FIFO	2.76	4.23
16	Intraquarter reporting, "likely" lags, recapture	2.88	4.83
17	Intraquarter reporting, "likely" lags, LIFO, recapture	2.66	3.98

From J. T. Allen, Designing Income Maintenance Systems: The Income Accounting Problem, *Studies in Public Welfare,* Paper No. 5, Part 3, Joint Economic Committee, Congress of the United States, 1973, Tables 9 and 13.

responsiveness (relative to Plan 2). A thorough comparative analysis of the plans from a policy point of view would consider all of these factors and the trade-offs among them.

In summary, as Allen points out, the choice of income accounting system has a substantial effect on the equity, costs, caseload size, and responsiveness of an income maintenance program. On the basis of more detailed analysis, she recommends a monthly retrospective accounting system with 12-month carryover as offering a good balance among these objectives.

New Specialized-Care Facility in a Hospital

Schruben and Margolin (1978) describe a study aimed at determining the best configuration for a new specialized-care facility in a hospital. The facility will contain coronary-care beds, surgical intensive-care beds, and intermediate-care beds for patients who have recovered sufficiently to leave the coronary-care unit or the intensive-care unit but who are not yet ready to be transferred to regular hospital care or perhaps discharged. The cardiologists and the surgeons on the hospital staff cannot determine how many beds of each type the new facility should have. It should have enough coronary-care and intensive-care beds to accommodate all patients requiring them, but these beds are more expensive than intermediate-care beds, which could be used to relieve some congestion.

For a given allocation of beds to the three types, which we call a configuration, the simulation produces synthetic data on the flow of patients through the facility over a period of several months. The failure rate, the number of patients per month for whom the proper bed is not available, measures the adequacy of a configuration. Previous experience may give the length of time between the arrivals of patients and their length of stay in each type of bed.* Thus, one can rapidly accumulate synthetic data on "failures," as well as other measures of the facility's operation.

In this example, because previous detailed data that would be appropriate to the operation of the new unit are not available, the mathematical model must incorporate probabilistic descriptions of all the chance events. These include three random elements: the time between successive patient arrivals, a patient's length of stay, and the chance that a patient will either be moved from a coronary-care or intensive-care bed to an intermediate-care bed or be discharged from the facility. This probabilistic component relies on available data to determine the statistical distribution governing each chance event and then uses random numbers drawn from those distributions to produce the synthetic outcomes for the chance events that mark a patient's progress through the unit. Thus, even without detailed data from previous experience, there should be no serious difficulty as long as the distribution of time between patient arrivals at the facility and the distribution of length of stay in a particular type of bed are well established. (By varying the properties of these distributions, we could

---

*In organizing the previous experience for use in such a simulation, it may be necessary to draw on information that has been recorded as part of the routine operation of the hospital. Chapter 8 on management records discusses the use of this data-gathering method on a larger scale.

check how results would vary. Such calculations, called sensitivity analyses, tell how sensitive the model is to various assumptions.)

Once the simulation has yielded failure rates for a reasonable variety of possible configurations for the specialized-care facility, the cardiologists, surgeons, and hospital administrators would have to agree on a final design configuration, taking into account failure rate, overall cost, and any other relevant aspects of the hospital's operation.

FEATURES OF SIMULATION

Simulation is the process of using a mathematical model, together with (input) data, to probe the response of a system to changes that have not actually been carried out. Often the system has not even been created in real life. The changes that people have in mind may be costly or far-reaching or may involve many alternatives. It is unrealistic to make all these changes or to construct the system solely for the purpose of measuring the consequences.

The examples previously discussed illustrate the role of a mathematical model. One can construct a full-scale laboratory model of a single room and study a fire in this setting, but this laboratory method could not be applied to a large building.

Actually implementing welfare reform for the entire United States could cost billions of dollars, and it would certainly disrupt operations in all the states as the policies and procedures were altered.

No hospital would be willing to purchase additional equipment and train new staff simply to determine what configuration a new facility should have; and constructing a new wing to house the facility requires architectural decisions that preclude certain alternatives. Furthermore, the hospital could face ethical questions if such an experimental approach put patients at risk. If, however, the hospital simply made choices without careful study, no ethical issues would come up. That would be policy, not experimentation.

The decision maker also benefits because simulation can often keep other influences equal when this would be impossible in the practical or political situation.

A simulation study has three main features: input data, a mathematical model, and output data. We describe these and draw on the previous examples to illustrate them. Then we discuss how simulation differs from other methods that have these same three components.

Input Data

The input data form the empirical base for the mathematical model. At one extreme, input data may be records on many individuals, as in the welfare reform example. At the other extreme, the place of the input data may be occupied by another mathematical model, which uses random numbers to generate the input. The properties of this data generator can come from careful empirical work or from the experimenter's accumulated experience, and often they involve only a few numerical constants, such as average length of stay and average time between patient arrivals in the hospital facility example. The fire example falls between these two extremes: it has neither a large data base nor a random data generator. Instead, it incorporates empirical information on the combustion properties of the components of the room (for example, the mattress on the bed).

Sometimes it is useful to distinguish between a *stochastic simulation*, which involves a random data generator, and a *deterministic simulation*, which does not.

Mathematical Model

An essential ingredient of a simulation study is a mathematical or computer model—a set of equations that describe the behavior of the system for any set of initial conditions or input data. Without such a description, it would be difficult to carry out a simulation.

Usually we create the model for the whole system by constructing good mathematical models for each of the subsystems. These are assembled according to their interconnections and interactions. Each of our earlier examples has this structure. In the bedroom fire simulation the subsystems are the fire, the plume of smoke, the hot layer, and the vent, as well as the components for heat transfer and for conservation of mass and energy. The welfare reform simulation has its carryover, lags, and recapture. And the hospital facility model uses information about the three types of beds, as well as the arrival of new patients.

The interactions among subsystems are often less well understood than the behavior of the subsystems themselves. Simulation models may therefore go through a phase of experimentation and tuning to make the whole model an adequate representation of the real world. Among the three examples, the bedroom fire best illustrates this, with its many complex physical processes. Separate laboratory experiments provide the data which, together with the principles of physics, yield mathematical descriptions of many of the component processes. Further experimentation helps to make these models more comprehensive and realistic.

In the hospital example, in contrast, the interconnections are straightforward and readily understood, as shown in Figure 11-1.

These two examples illustrate another distinction among simulation models: *continuous simulation* versus *discrete-event simulation*. The fire develops continuously as time advances, and the model handles this by stepping forward in small time increments. In the hospital care unit the model need only keep track of the specific events that produce changes (such as assigning patients to a coronary-care bed or transferring a patient from an intensive-care bed to an intermediate-care bed), and elapsed time between changes leaves no detailed record. This distinction between continuous and discrete simulations determines the nature of the mathematical model, as well as the computer language used to program the simulation.

FIGURE 11-1   *Patient paths in the hospital unit simulation.*[a]

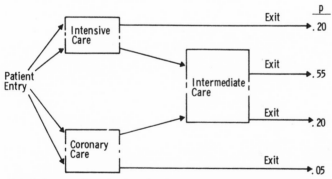

[a] Arrival rate and service time distributions in days are as follows: Patient arrival, Poisson (3.3/day); Intensive care stay, lognormal, $\mu = 3.4$, $\sigma = 3.5$; Coronary care stay, lognormal, $\mu = 3.8$, $\sigma = 1.6$; Intermediate care stay for intensive care patients, lognormal, $\mu = 15.0$, $\sigma = 7.0$; Intermediate care stay for coronary care patients, lognormal, $\mu = 17.0$, $\sigma = 3.0$. Finally, the column of p values at the extreme right of the figure indicates the probability of an arrival following the corresponding path.

From L. W. Schruben and B. H. Margolin, Pseudorandom Number Assignment in Statistically Designed Simulation and Distribution Sampling Experiments, *Journal of the American Statistical Association* 73: 504–520, 1978, p. 505. Reprinted with permission.

Output Data

The output data reflect the various conditions and changes in the system. Using these data, the policymaker must reach a conclusion. These results of the simulation may directly form the basis for the policymaker's decision. For example, the policymaker must choose a welfare plan by balancing equity and responsiveness against the cost figures listed in Table 11-1. The process is similar in deciding on the numbers of intensive-care and coronary-care beds, relative to the failure rate, for the hospital care facility.

Generally, the output data from a simulation should be treated like data collected by any other method—they must be explored, summarized, and analyzed. This stage of a study may trigger refinements in the model aimed at making its behavior more realistic.

WHAT SIMULATION IS NOT

Other techniques, and even much of data analysis, can be viewed as involving the same three components—input data, mathematical model, and output data. Forecasting focuses primarily on what will happen at some time in the future. The input data contribute to building a model for the behavior of a system (say, an industry or a sector of the economy) over time, and the model uses hypothetical or randomly generated data to forecast a few time periods ahead. Simulation treats its inputs as data to be acted upon by the model, rather than as information on which to base the model. That information may be data also, but it will already have been embodied in the model before the simulation begins. We explore forecasting in Chapter 12.

Sometimes we develop a mathematical model and study its properties to deduce how a system would behave. This process of modeling is discussed in Chapter 13.

Management records studies often involve substantial data bases, and their questions and analyses focus directly on the data.

STRENGTHENING SIMULATION

Broadly speaking, any step that strengthens one of the three components—input data, mathematical model, and output data—will improve the whole simulation. We give some possible strategies for improving each.

Input Data

The closer the input data come to mimicking the actual situation, the more confidence we can have in the results. When the simulation uses a substantial data base, a random sample from the target population constitutes the ideal input data. Often, however, no such sample is readily available, and we have to use what is on hand. In the welfare reform example, Allen applied weights so that the adjusted sample matched the U.S. population on several key characteristics.

Another valuable step is to perform some analysis on the input data. We can check plausibility and ensure that the data base is clean by detecting and removing impossible and anomalous cases.

In setting up a stochastic simulation, we can analyze some real-life data and use them to make the random data generator more realistic. For example, for the hospital simulation, we might observe the existing facilities and record the lengths of time between patient arrivals and the lengths of stay. Analyzing these data would keep the simulation in close touch with reality.

Sometimes, for technical reasons, the basic source of random numbers matters considerably. Unfortunately, difficulties have been discovered in the random-number generators built into several simulation packages and simulation languages for digital computers. Thus, it is worthwhile to find out, from someone who has studied the computational details of simulation, whether the basic random-number generator satisfies a criterion known as the spectral test (Knuth 1981, Section 3.3.4). This mathematical measure reveals whether the random numbers are too coarse in ways that have often caused trouble and otherwise might easily escape notice. Substantial evidence indicates that good generators pass the spectral test and poor ones do not.

Mathematical Model

In constructing the mathematical model, we strive for as much realism as possible (or as much as we can afford). In the previous section we mentioned that models sometimes go through a phase of experimentation and tuning. Often we pursue this systematically to check whether the model responds as it should. If some configurations of the model correspond to actual situations on which we have data, we can ask how closely the model reproduces the behavior in the data. Emmons, Mitler, and Trefethen (1978) did this in calibrating their fire model.

Output Data

Because we simulate to learn about behavior, the output data deserve the same extensive and careful analysis that should be carried out for an experiment. Even when we know a lot about the model and its behavior, by carefully analyzing the output data, we can discover behavior not adequately captured by routine summaries. Graphic displays and other techniques of modern data analysis can contribute to this process (see, for example, Mosteller and Tukey 1977).

One Overall Consideration

In a simulation involving time, we must allow for initial conditions or start-up phenomena. If the policy questions concern a steady-state situation, the simulation should continue long enough to minimize any transient effects of the initial conditions. For example, if we started a simulation of the specialized-care facility with no patients already being cared for, this unlikely situation would have a low failure rate compared with the actual operation of the unit; that is, the number of patients (per month) for whom the proper bed is not available would be too low. To remedy this, we would extend the time covered by the simulation and consider discarding some initial portion of the output data. In contrast, a bedroom fire is inherently a transient phenomenon, and the details of its growth are the desired output data.

MERITS OF SIMULATION

As a means of gathering information for policymaking, simulation offers several advantages. These arise mainly from its management of time, alternatives, and operational details and from its relatively low costs.

Many simulations provide substantial time compression, so that months or years of operation of the actual system are replaced by only a few minutes of computer calculation. In the welfare reform simulation, for example, only a few simple calculations serve to determine the payments that each household in the data base would receive during a year. Also, in the hospital example, the simulation quickly produces data for many months of simulated operation because the waiting time between discrete events is squeezed out.

The fire simulation could turn out differently. Each short time step requires substantial calculation, so that it would be important to use a reasonably fast computer. In simulating a fire in a large building, the simulation program might take more time than the actual fire; but time compression is hardly the main reason for applying simulation to this problem.

One difficulty in observing several systems and comparing their behavior is that the results reflect differences in the circumstances, as well as differences among the systems themselves. Simulation provides enough control to show how the systems perform under the same set(s) of conditions. The welfare reform example uses the same data base in evaluating each plan, and the hospital example uses the same stream of patient arrivals. Aside from the value of simulation in simplifying comparisons, its ability to hold conditions fixed has important benefits when one is improving the model or correcting an error in it.

Finally, simulation does not risk the data problems and operational mishaps of a real-life experiment. In an extreme situation, when we cannot do an experiment or a demonstration, we may still be able to use simulation.

WEAKNESSES OF SIMULATION

A simulation is only as strong as its components, and both the input data and the mathematical model may present difficulties.

If the important responses cannot be described adequately by a mathematical model, simulation cannot take hold of the problem. We have in mind mainly the forms of simulation that involve substantial computer work, rather than physical scale models of such systems as dams and waterways, but some fairly mathematical engineering work usually goes into determining the characteristics of scale models. To return to one of our examples, if the welfare reform to be simulated was a new way for recipients to report their household composition and their income, rather than alternative ways of determining entitlements and payments, no model for the accuracy of reports produced by the new method would be available. As another example, we may want to know whether a program such as "Scared Straight," which arranges discussions between groups of juvenile criminal offenders and groups of prison inmates, reduces recidivism among the juvenile offenders. Today, no one can quantitatively describe how such a program affects individual behavior, and this difficulty would rule out a simulation that makes a reassuring connection with the process. (A well-controlled experiment, on the other hand, could be very valuable.)

If the input data do not contain the proper information, it may be difficult to fill the gap in the mathematical model and so produce a useful simulation. The information may be missing, or it may have been collected in a form incompatible with the model. For example, a welfare plan could require monthly data when only quarterly data have been collected in the past.

QUALITY CHECKLIST

The characteristics in this checklist are factors that a policymaker should consider when evaluating a simulation study. Not all the questions apply to all simulation studies, but a reassuring answer to any question that does apply will contribute to the relevance or reliability of the results.

1. *Are the input data, the mathematical model, and the computing environment described in careful detail?* Solid information on the input data and the mathematical model is essential in judging the value of a simulation study for any policy question, including the question that motivated it. A policymaker will seldom want to reconstruct a data base and replicate the simulation, but nearly as much detail is needed in judging the strengths and weaknesses of the study. And the quality of the reporting often indicates the care taken with the study itself. Did the investigators develop their own computer program or use an established simulation language or package? Reporting what computer was used conveys (at least to specialists) valuable information about the properties of its arithmetic calculations and the general quality of its software.

2. *Are the input data, as a whole, an adequate facsimile of the target situation?* When the input data are not clearly relevant, the whole simulation falters. If, for example, the data for the welfare reform simulation had been collected in a setting with only a limited number and variety of chronically low-income households, the study could yield serious underestimates of total costs.

3. *Have the input data been analyzed and explored for possible outliers and gross errors?* Even when a data base has been "cleaned" to eliminate data items whose values lie outside the range of possible values (through coding or keypunch errors), anomalous or outlying cases may remain. Without excluding these cases, the modeler cannot guarantee that they have not distorted the results.

QUALITY CHECKLIST

1.	Descriptions of components?
2.	Relevance of input data?
3.	Analysis of input data?
4.	Defects of mathematical model?
5.	Does model still apply?
6.	Analysis of output data?
7.	Are results reasonable?
8.	Systematic program testing?
9.	Good random numbers?

4. *What important features have been omitted from the model?* How closely do the simulation and its results match the situation that the policymaker must handle? An important aspect may simply not have been included in the simulation, so that the results have little to say in this new setting. If, for example, the welfare simulation included only prospective accounting plans, it would be difficult to use its results in predicting the costs of retrospective plans. The policymaker has the responsibility to make sure that the modeler has built in the features that may affect the decision. The modeler does not always know what is on the decision maker's agenda.

5. *What simulated changes in the system will move it into new situations where the model does not apply?* Models often stray from the circumstances associated with the input data. When model and data no longer fit together, simulation results may be questionable. The welfare simulation uses household income data reported monthly. A quarterly reporting plan could easily add up the three monthly amounts in each quarter, but this makes the dubious assumption that a household's quarterly income report equals the sum of the three monthly amounts that the household would have given if it had been asked to report monthly. Lapses of memory or record keeping could easily lead to different reported income totals, and the difference could be large (say, whole paychecks omitted).

6. *Have the output data been analyzed in detail?* Anomalies and outliers afflict output data as well as input data, and a thorough analysis of the output data is always desirable.

7. *Are the results reasonable?* Generally, the most convincing results mesh with existing knowledge, but surprises can bring fresh insight. Any unreasonable result should be challenged—to learn whether it represents an error or what aspects of the model or input data may be responsible for it. We may have discovered a law counter to the prevailing wisdom.

8. *If a computer program is involved, is there evidence that it has been systematically tested to reduce the chance of errors?* Especially when the simulation requires whole new programs, it is essential to test them piecemeal to ensure that they work correctly, as well as to conduct some preliminary checks on the whole simulation program before starting the final runs. This testing process becomes complex, and an ambitious schedule with no time allowed for testing should arouse great suspicion. Using a suitable simulation language, rather than developing whole programs from scratch, eliminates the need for some (but not all) of this testing.

9. *Are the sources of random numbers known to be adequately free of defects?* This aspect of a stochastic simulation is rather technical. A policymaker would probably want to seek expert advice, especially if the results of the simulation seem at all unreasonable. The important defects of random-number generators have become well enough known that poor generators should now be seldom used, but a bad generator could still creep in to undermine the entire simulation.

POLICY IMPLICATIONS

In planning to use simulation, the policymaker faces several practical advantages and limitations. A decision to simulate should be based on careful consideration of all of them.

Time

Because a simulation can proceed more quickly than most other approaches, it may be very valuable when time is limited. When time pressure is not so great, the results of an initial round of simulation may suggest changes as a basis for a second round.

On the other hand, building a very complicated model from scratch may take years. Overambition and irresponsible optimism keep computer modelers going; their results may be slow in coming, and slow can be never. When the user asks, "Can you add this?" the answer is usually "Yes," but the price in time and money may be huge.

We advise getting the best time estimate for modeling a brand new problem and then considering the consequences if the estimate were multiplied by five.

Risk

By avoiding fieldwork with experimental subjects, simulation does not expose them to any risks, nor does the policymaker risk substantial political criticism for trying to carry out the study. Also, it may be relatively, though not absolutely, inexpensive.

Assumptions

The results of a simulation depend on the mathematical model and on accompanying assumptions, and both must be clearly stated. Because these may be open to criticism, the policymaker must maintain close contact with the simulation effort to ensure its realism and to be prepared to defend any assumptions, especially if minor changes in assumptions lead to markedly different outcomes. For this reason, sensitivity tests should be made to alert everyone to the consequences of changes in assumptions.

In preparation for carrying out a controlled experiment, simulation studies can narrow the choice among a set of alternatives. Of all the programs that could be tried, only a few can be tested. Sometimes several kinds of programs could be considered, and we would like to compare the best of each kind in a field trial. Sometimes a simulation can help in choosing nearly the best program of each kind for the field comparison. For example, many alternative centralized and decentralized programs might be possible. A simulation might help us choose a very good program of each kind for the comparison. (Probably no one program is the best from every point of view.)

Organization

No extensive field staff is required to construct a simulation study, but it is important to have available the proper expertise in building mathematical models, implementing them on a computer, and analyzing the related data (both input and output). In many instances adequate computing capability must already be on hand. For some important and complex problems, such as simulating the behavior of the atmosphere of North America in order to understand and predict the weather, the required kinds of expertise can add up to a large staff and an ongoing research program. A simulation on this scale would represent a continuing resource for addressing a variety of policy questions, rather than a study conducted to answer one timely question.

CONCLUSION

When the behavior of a system can be described adequately and economically by a mathematical model, simulation offers an attractive method for investigating the effects of changes in the system. This method of acquiring information often makes very efficient use of time and of financial resources. Because simulation involves a mathematical model and (usually) some existing data, however, it is not likely to be the first data-gathering method used in a field.

Simulation can be a valuable aid to policy in many areas, and its results will be most reliable when the policymaker helps keep the mathematical model well calibrated to reality. The analysts can strengthen the simulation by tuning the model and giving careful scrutiny to both input and output data.

REFERENCES

Allen, J. T. 1973. Designing Income Maintenance Systems: The Income Accounting Problem. *Studies in Public Welfare,* Paper No. 5 (Part 3), Joint Economic Committee, Congress of the United States. Washington, D. C.: U.S. Government Printing Office.

Emmons, H. W.; Mitler, H. E.; and Trefethen, L. N. 1978. Computer Fire Code III. Home Fire Project Technical Report No. 25. Cambridge, Mass.: Harvard University, Division of Applied Sciences.

Knuth, D. E. 1981. *The Art of Computer Programming,* Volume 2 (*Seminumerical Algorithms*), 2nd ed. Reading, Mass.: Addison-Wesley.

Mathematica Policy Research. 1979. *Colorado Monthly Reporting Experiment and Pretest: First Year Research Results.* Project Report 79–06. Denver: Mathematica Policy Research, Inc.

Mosteller, F., and Tukey, J. W. 1977. *Data Analysis and Regression.* Reading, Mass.: Addison-Wesley.

Schruben, L. W., and Margolin, B. H. 1978. Pseudorandom Number Assignment in Statistically Designed Simulation and Distribution Sampling Experiments. *Journal of the American Statistical Association* 73:504–520.

FURTHER READING

Chorafas, D.N. 1965. *Systems and Simulation.* New York: Academic Press.

Emshoff, J.R., and Sisson, R.L. 1970. *Design and Use of Computer Simulation Models.* New York: Macmillan.

Fishman, G.S. 1973. *Concepts and Methods in Discrete Event Digital Simulation.* New York: John Wiley.

Frenkiel, F.N., and Goodall, D.W., eds. 1978. *Simulation Modelling of Environmental Problems.* New York: John Wiley (on behalf of the Scientific Committee on Problems of the Environment, International Council of Scientific Unions).

Lehman, R.S. 1977. *Computer Simulation and Modeling: An Introduction.* Hillsdale, N.J.: Lawrence Erlbaum Associates.

Martin, F.F. 1968. *Computer Modeling and Simulation.* New York: John Wiley.

CHAPTER 12

Forecasting

Being able to foretell the future would certainly make policymakers' jobs easier. They would know whether to implement an expensive program to soften the effect of a feared but formerly uncertain outcome. They would know in advance the cost of a program that has an uncertain participation rate and unknown eligible populations. Comparing two or more policies would be easier if the effects of each, after they were implemented, were well known.

"Prediction, according to the delicate Chinese proverb, is very difficult—especially with regard to the future." (Wade 1980) But sometimes history can lead us to some insights. Certain future events may be ruled out by past or current events, or may appear to be more or less likely. Trends sometimes persist. Theoretical and empirical models predict the future effect of current policies.

This chapter deals with the use of forecasts. After considering two examples, we examine the available types of forecasts and projections, their appropriate uses, and their strengths and weaknesses.

EXAMPLES

We provide two illustrations of forecasts that have helped to guide policy decisions. The first example concerns future demands on the U.S. Social Security system. It illustrates a situation in which future outcomes depend strongly on present facts. The second example examines energy forecasts. In this area, policymakers take guidance from a multitude of forecasts about all aspects of energy policy. Here the future depends less obviously on the past. In practice, we often encounter forecasts with a wider range of dependence than suggested by these two examples.

Population Projections and Social Security

The U.S. Social Security system is a mechanism for providing income for disabled and retired workers and their dependents. Contrary to popular conception, workers do not build a reserve during their working lifetime from which they draw in old age. Instead, current workers contribute via a payroll tax to a fund that is disbursed to retired and disabled workers. The solvency of the system and the burden to current workers obviously depend on the relative numbers of working and retired people.

The government faces two important policy decisions. In the short run, Congress must plan the benefits to be paid out and the payments to be collected from workers so that they balance. For the long run, Congress must consider alternative funding schemes. For instance, the Social Security account could become part of the general U.S. Treasury operating budget, or a separate investment fund could be set up so that each generation of workers is supported in old age by the returns of investments made throughout their lives. Changing the retirement age could also alter the balance.

Both short- and long-range decisions depend upon the relative number of active and retired workers. To estimate these numbers, demographers make population projections based on certain assumptions. Beginning with a count of the present population, grouped by age, demographers estimate the proportion of each group expected to die each year and use these proportions to calculate the population one year hence. In addition, they estimate the number of births by calculating fertility rates, the proportion of women of each age expected to bear children, and coupling these with the number of women in each age group. Based on estimates of mortality and fertility rates for the future, the entire calculation is carried out year by year for as many years as necessary.

Of the three inputs, demographers know best the base year population, especially if the projection begins in a census year. They can easily calculate mortality rates for the current year using vital statistics, but they need estimates for future years for the projection. Mortality rates have fallen slowly and regularly for many years, so an extrapolation of this trend probably provides reasonable future estimates, barring catastrophes and fabulous discoveries. Yearly fertility rates for the future are the hardest part of the input data to estimate. They change rapidly and sometimes unpredictably. Furthermore, natural fluctuations in fertility rates affect the size and age distribution more seriously than similar mortality fluctuations.

Table 12-1 (Pitts 1978) gives the results of four population projections made by Social Security administrators in their 1973 to 1976 annual reports. The table gives the estimated population aged 65 and over as a percentage of the population aged 20 to 64. This proportion, called the "dependency ratio," roughly indicates the relative burden on the working-age population of supporting the retired population. Differences in estimates arise primarily from different assumptions each year about the future course of fertility rates. The fertility assumptions in these projections vary from 2.6 to 1.9 births per woman.

The projections begin with population data for 1975, so only the projections of the population under 20 in 1995 depend on the fertility assumptions. Since the dependency ratio depends only on population aged 20 or older, the various fertility assumptions do not affect the ratios for 1985 and 1995. The small differences in the columns of the table are the result of mildly varying mortality assumptions. The population 65 and older from 2005 through 2035 depends only on mortality assumptions and is relatively easy to predict. Beginning in 2005,

TABLE 12-1　*Projections of the old-age dependency ratio under various fertility assumptions*

	Year Projection Was Made			
Projection for Calendar Year	*1973*	*1974*	*1975*	*1976*
1975	19.9	19.1	19.1	19.1
1985	18.7	19.2	18.9	19.0
1995	19.0	20.2	19.7	19.8
2005	16.2	18.9	18.8	18.9
2015	17.3	21.7	21.9	22.3
2025	21.8	27.7	28.7	29.8
2035	22.4	29.3	31.2	33.3
2045	22.4	27.7	28.6	31.8
Fertility Assumption (number of children per woman)	2.6	2.1	2.1	1.9

From A. M. Pitts, Social Security and Aging Populations, In *The Economic Consequences of Slowing Population Growth*, T. J. Espenshade and W. J. Serow, eds., New York: Academic Press, 1978, p. 170. Reprinted with permission.

the working-age population increasingly includes people born after 1975; therefore, these projections are more sensitive to the fertility assumptions. For 2045 (and later years) both the numerator and the denominator of the dependency ratio are less stable than for the preceding years because of fertility assumptions. But regardless of the assumptions, the effect is clear: the dependency ratio will be substantially higher after the turn of the century.

One way or another, the Social Security system must react to the facts of demography. If we make fertility assumptions somewhat like those of the latest three projections, 2.1 to 1.9 births per woman, we see that the dependency burden will remain relatively constant through 2005. But after that it will increase dramatically. Only if fertility rates increase to over 2.6 births per woman (1978 rates implied only 1.8) will the dependency ratio be nearly similar to today's.

In the short term, perhaps the present payroll tax system can continue in some form. After 2015, however, the dependency ratio is likely to be large enough to force some sort of change. Demographic factors are only one set among many considerations in this policy issue. Population projections offer a means of extending our present knowledge to analyze future prospects and evaluate alternative policies. They alert us to a serious problem with the Social Security system and help us to plan rationally for the future.

Energy Forecasts

Energy policymakers face an almost unlimited variety of possible future supplies and demands. Furthermore, the outcomes of policy decisions are highly uncertain. To provide objective and credible analytic frameworks for decision makers, Congress created the Energy Information Administration (EIA). One of its mandates is to develop and maintain a capability for forecasting and analyzing short- and long-term relationships between energy supply and consumption and other appropriate variables (Energy Information Administration 1979).

The EIA's many forecasts reflect the variety of issues involved in energy policy. At the highest level, we must consider projected world energy consumption. Figure 12-1 illustrates historical trends and a range of projections through 1995 for consumption by non-Communist countries. According to these projections, production is always close to consumption.

The projections in Figure 12-1 are the result of a "market equilibrium" economic model, which begins by considering all of the factors

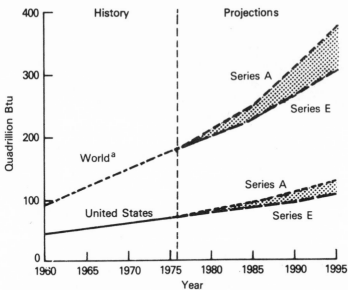

^a Excludes communist countries.

FIGURE 12-1 *World Energy Consumption: History and Projections, 1960–1965*[b]

[b]From Energy Information Administration, *Annual Report to Congress, 1978,* Volume 3, 1979, p. 17.

influencing the desire to buy or sell energy. The factors influencing demand are:

√ The product's own price.

√ The prices of other products, including those that substitute for or complement energy and those that embody energy as a constituent factor of production.

√ The level and content of economic activity.

√ The nature and composition of energy-consuming facilities.

√ Government regulations.

The factors influencing supply are:

√ The product's own price.

√ Other prices, including the various costs of finding, extracting, and converting energy, and delivering it to the ultimate user.

√ Energy resource availability.

√ The nature and composition of energy-producing facilities.

√ Government regulations.

Given these inputs, mathematical procedures find "equilibrium" energy prices and quantities: those prices and quantities at which the desires of buyers and sellers balance.

The uncertainty in the projection arises from uncertainty in two key factors for supply and demand: economic growth and the availability of non-OPEC energy resources. The EIA prepares five series of projections employing combinations of high, low, and medium assumptions for these two factors. Only the extreme projections appear in the figure.

The EIA prepares similar projections for national and regional areas, and separate projections for energy source and type of consumption. The information provided may include quantities, prices, and other factors related to exploration and development; production; power generation; refining; transportation; distribution; and consumption. These projections provide important information for energy policymakers, alerting them to future problem areas and potentials.

The EIA also conducts special studies to analyze a particular forecast or issue, or to compare and analyze alternative forecasts. Examples of these studies are:

√ Analysis of the effects on the economy of various types of petroleum supply interruptions and alternative government responses.

√ Determination of potential financial and related impacts of horizontal divestiture within the oil industry.

√ Assessment of the potential for importing differing types and quantities of energy supplies from foreign countries.

√ Assessment of the potential economic impact of installing 2.5 million solar residential units in the United States by 1985.

√ Inventory of past and current government interventions in U.S. energy markets and analysis of how such interventions have affected the functioning of those markets.

√ Estimates of incremental energy savings, unemployment, and other possible effects of various kinds and levels of tax credits for individuals or businesses initiating conservation and renewable resource measures.

The EIA develops and maintains several different types of computer models to make its many projections and analyses. The type of analysis to be performed and the character of the available data dictate the choice of model. Sometimes more than one model is appropriate for a situation, and comparing their results sheds some light on the inherent uncertainty of the projections.

FEATURES OF FORECASTS

All scientific forecasts depend in some way on historical experience extrapolated into the future. We make both formal and informal forecasts. This chapter deals more with formal extrapolations because only in this type of analysis can we evaluate the assumptions on which the forecast is based. Where few or no data are available, informal forecasts are frequently useful and may be the only appropriate method at our disposal.

For our purposes, it is important to distinguish between projections and predictions or forecasts. A *projection* or conditional forecast consists of: (1) specifying a model for what remains constant and how things change, (2) specifying particular parameter values (original levels, growth rates, and so on) and (3) calculating the future implications of these trends.

A *prediction* or *forecast* is a projection or set of projections for which the model(s) and parameter(s) are chosen to reflect the most likely future course or a range of possibilities for the future.

A projection is a mathematical exercise, and a forecast makes a judgment about future possibilities. Forecasts use projections as tools to extend trends, but judgments about what trends to use and how likely they are to continue are part of the forecasting process.

The key step in making a forecast is to identify what has remained constant in the past. For instance, we may discover that although population has been growing, the yearly increase, in percentage terms, has remained nearly constant over the past ten years. This pattern is known as "exponential growth." Frequently, only a decomposition of the historical data will reveal regularities. For example, the Social Security projections were "age-specific": fertility and mortality rates for each age group were calculated and projected. These individual rates are more stable and easier to understand and predict than the growth rate of the population as a whole.

Forecasts frequently rely on mathematical models to summarize relevant aspects of the past and extend trends into the future. These models are mathematical descriptions of a real world process. They are similar in many ways to physical models, such as model planes in wind tunnels, except that the language of mathematics instead of hardware describes the component parts of the process, their interrelations, and behavior.

The components of a mathematical model are called *state variables.* The values of one or more state variables for an instant in time convey all the information in the model about the state of the world at that time. For instance, in a mathematical model of population growth, the state variables may be the number of men and women alive at the end of each year. For more complex models, these figures must be broken down by age and race. State variables in an energy model may be quantities and prices for a set of energy sources.

The *dynamics* of a model is a set of mathematical relationships that describes the way the state variables progress in time. A wide variety of forms is possible. For instance, exponential growth is one of the simpler ways to model population growth. More complex relationships take into account the age of the individuals. In the Social Security example, the age distribution of future populations was important to know. This called for the introduction of mortality and fertility rates for each age group. In the energy example, the procedure to balance supply and demand desires provides the dynamics of the forecasts.

Parameters tailor the general form of the mathematical relationship to a specific situation. For instance, the choice of an annual growth rate makes the concept of exponential growth specific. "Elasticities" indicate the extent to which energy demand follows economic growth.

We can distinguish two types of parameters: policy variables and background variables. Policy variables are parameters over which the decision maker has some control. In the population example, family planning programs may influence the birth rate but not the death rate. Energy policy analysts study the effects of changes in tax rates, which the government controls. Background variables are parameters over which the policymaker has no control, such as the death rate or projections of energy reserves available at various prices. Nevertheless, these must be included in the model to obtain realistic results.

WHAT FORECASTING IS NOT

In the statistical literature, the term "prediction" often refers to determining the likely outcome for an individual. For instance, a college admissions committee predicts the freshman-year grade average for all potential students as a screening device to identify those who are academically capable. An insurance company predicts the accident rate of a new policyholder to determine his or her annual premium.

The statistical issue underlying these problems is how to predict the behavior of an individual with certain characteristics based on the experience of other individuals with similar characteristics. This chapter concerns the projection and prediction of aggregate variables. Here the emphasis is on the historical analysis of trends and dynamic relations.

STRENGTHENING FORECASTS

A number of techniques are available to strengthen the policy relevance of predictions. Some are used in data collection and analysis to improve the technical quality of the estimates. Other techniques explore potential mathematical models to find the most appropriate model or to estimate the range of uncertainty.

A Clear Statement of Assumptions

Forecasts are no more than the logical consequence of a set of assumptions about appropriate models and parameter values. If these are not clearly stated, a policymaker cannot determine the relevance of the forecast to the problem at hand. Many forecast reports describe controversial assumptions and general methodology in a prominent place and relegate other assumptions to an appendix. Not infrequently, the "noncontroversial" assumptions and choice of model are as important to the final results as those the forecaster chooses to highlight. Clear documentation of all assumptions is necessary for us to evaluate forecasting results.

Leading Indicators

In fields where forecasting has been common for some time, certain variables have distinguished themselves as precursors of change. For example, many measures of economic activity—such as manufacturers' new orders, building permits for private housing, and orders for factory equipment—have been found to foreshadow general economic activity. The Department of Commerce publishes a monthly index of twelve of these measures to forecast the direction of business activity and employment. The index has won general acceptance because of its record in correctly forecasting economic declines. (The index tends to be more accurate in predicting the times of recessions than their severity.)

Time Series Analysis

Statisticians have recently developed a set of techniques to analyze the way a series of observations evolves in time. By understanding the structure and random variation of historical observations, the forecaster can predict future values and establish the limits of possible variation.

Parameter Estimation

Where possible, statistical studies of historical data provide better estimates of model parameters than educated guesses. Forecasters sometimes feel that minor parameters buried deep in a complicated model do not seriously affect the projection results, but this is not always so.

Level of Aggregation

Both simple and complex models have their place. If the total U.S. population must be forecast, a simple extrapolation of total population trends may yield the best results. But policy decisions frequently require a further breakdown: the Social Security Administration needs projections of the elderly population, and highway planners need population projections for local areas. The level of aggregation of a forecasting model, the degree to which it consists of summary or detailed state variables, strongly influences the type of policy question the model can address.

The Delphi Technique

When parameter values must be guessed, it is sometimes helpful to obtain estimates from a group of experts. The Delphi technique, one way to achieve a consensus in such a group, involves the repeated use of an anonymous questionnaire. The anonymity in the process prevents strong personalities from dominating the group. The repeated revisions and feedback encourage panel members to reconsider extreme estimates in the light of more moderate estimates. For a detailed discussion, see Chapter 14 on introspection and advice.

Sensitivity Analysis

Complex models require estimates of many background variables. Sensitivity analysis is a systematic exploration of the way that forecast results depend on assumptions about background variables. Since these parameters are frequently not easy to estimate, we prefer forecasts that are not overly sensitive to assumptions about them. Failing that, we want to know which variables to keep an eye on.

Exploration of Models

Choosing a model to extrapolate past observations to the future is often crucial. In general, sensitivity of the results to the choice of model increases as the forecaster attempts to look further into the future. For example, extrapolations from exponential and linear models of population growth look similar in the short run, but they diverge as time goes on. One way to explore sensitivity to the choice of model is to compare results obtained from different models. The EIA often does this for energy forecasts. If diverse models using different assumptions yield similar results, we can be more confident of their reliability.

Independent Forecasts

Even when forecasters make an honest effort to consider a wide variety of possible projection models and parameters, "assumption drag" (Ascher 1978) occasionally sets in. It is difficult to foresee changes from the patterns of the past, or even to believe they are possible. Thus, what seems like a wide range of possibilities to an individual forecaster often turns out to have been too narrow.

One way to reduce assumption drag is to compare multiple forecasts from diverse sources. But because many simultaneous forecasts make similar assumptions, even this approach may not convey the true range of uncertainty. Amory Lovins, a proponent of energy conservation through efficiency changes, put together a table illustrating the change in the range of predicted U.S. energy demand at the second millenium. What in 1972 was "beyond the pale" (predictions by low-growth advocates, such as Lovins) in 1978 became "superstition" (predictions by high-growth advocates, such as utility companies).

TABLE 12–2 *Evolution of approximate estimates of U.S. primary energy demand in the year 2000 (units are "quads per year," i.e. 10^{15} BTU/year: the 1978 rate was about 78 quads/year)*

	Source of Forecast			
Year of Forecast	Beyond the Pale	Heresy	Conventional Wisdom	Superstition
1972	125[a]	140[b]	160[c]	190[s]
1974	100[e]	124[f]	140[g]	160[h]
1976	75[a]	89[i]–95[j]	124[g]	140[h]
1978	33[k]	63[m]–77[m]	95[n]–96[m]–101[p]	123[q]–124[r]

Origin of Estimates:

a Lovins speeches
b Sierra Club
c U.S. Atomic Energy Commission
d other federal agencies
e Energy Policy Project "ZEG"
f Energy Policy Project "TF"
g U.S. Energy R&D Admin. (ERDA)
h Edison Electric Institute

i von Hippel & Williams (Princeton)
j Lovins, *Foreign Affairs*, 9/76
k Steinhart (U. Wisc.) (for 2050)
m CONAES I–III (for 2010)
n USDOE, 9/79, $32/bbl (1977 $)
p Weinberg (IEA-Oak Ridge) "low"
q USDOE, 9/79, $18 & $25/bbl av.
r Lapp (believes E/GNP fixed)

From Amory B. Lovins, "Economically Efficient Energy Futures," in W. Bach, J. Pankrath, and J. Williams, editors, *Interactions of Energy and Climate*, Dordrecht, Holland: D. Reidel Publishing Company, 1980, p. 8. Reprinted with permission.

Model Validation

The last and best test of a prediction model is to let it perform and to evaluate the results. To do this, forecasters sometimes put aside the last few years of data and model only the earlier data; then they try to predict the set-aside data. If the prediction and actual results are not far apart, policymakers can be more confident about current predictions. Final projections are then calculated from the entire data base.

While always helpful, this technique can sometimes be misleading. Basically, no forecaster can really set aside a batch of recent data. Even if the recent data do not enter into the estimation of model parameters, the forecaster will not choose a model that does not reflect the pattern of the recent data. Since recent data cannot truly be ignored, validity tests based on set-aside data will tend to overestimate a forecast's accuracy.

A better, but harder to implement, technique is to examine a forecaster's historical record. If a group of forecasters or a set of techniques has been around for some time, we can examine projections made, say, ten years ago, and see how they compare to this year's actuality.

MERITS OF FORECASTS

Forecasts have several merits, which vary according to the particular situation.

What Is Most Likely?

For planning purposes, ideally we would like to know one outcome, the one judged most likely to occur. How many rush-hour riders will the subway have to serve ten years from now? When will the new nuclear generating station start producing power? Answering these questions requires setting up a realistic model, making the best estimate of present values and future trends, and calculating the most likely scenario. "Most likely" here implies the scenario based on the assumptions regarded as the best guess of what is and will be the case.

What Are the Likely Possibilities?

Realistic planners understand that the future cannot be forecast with certainty, so they want to know the range of likely possibilities. The number of subway riders ten years from now will depend on the subway fare, the price of gasoline in the future, the number of downtown office workers, and many other factors. The starting date of the new generating system depends, among other things, on weather conditions, delivery of materials on schedule, the timeliness of licensing procedure, and possibly the amount of political opposition. None of the determining factors is known with certainty, but alternative projections for low and high assumptions about the determining factors give a range of likely values for the eventual outcome. Using these figures, planners can prepare both for likely and for worst cases. Although, say, 500 subway cars are likely to be sufficient, the possible need for 750 must be taken into account.

THE WASHINGTON POST   Sunday, March 23, 1952

"How 1952 Looked to 26 American 'Seers' in 1941"
by Alfred Friendly

October 27, 1941

"Dear _____:

"I have what may strike you as rather a crazy idea, but one which I should like to have you help me follow through . . .

"It occurred to me that it might be of interest to some of us 10 years from now to look back on our nebulous predictions and square them with the state of the world in 1952.

"I am wondering, therefore, if, sometime when you have a minute or two to daydream, you could write out in a page or two your general predictions of how things will turn out within the next 10 years. . ."

The author of the above letter was Dr. Hadley Cantril, director of the Office of Public Opinion Research of Princeton University's Psychology Department. He sent it to 72 persons, nearly all of whom had earned some reputation in public or professional life. The time was barely six weeks before Pearl Harbor.

Of Cantril's friends and acquaintances, 40 were brave enough to return their predictions, under a promise of anonymity. He took 26 replies as being typical and published them in the clinical supplement of the Journal of Abnormal and Social Psychology—doubtless the appropriate repository for the comments of anyone foolhardy enough to commit to writing a forecast of things to come 10 years hence.

The predictions make fascinating reading. Three or four are uncannily correct (and if you think it would have been easy to be right, pose yourself the problem of forecasting the situation in 1962 and figure how much money you would bet on your accuracy). Three or four are frightfully wrong, particularly those done by a then Communist and one by a pro-Fascist.

Most were partly right and partly wrong. Short of a detailed analysis of the sort Cantril may prepare in the future, it is difficult to say why people were correct about some things and mistaken about others.

A few common tendencies are, however, clearly apparent. Of the 26 whose replies are published, 3 wrote what amounted to philosophical dissertations, ducking the problem of making firm predictions.

Considering only the 23 remaining replies, then:

1. Nineteen correctly called the turn of the Axis defeat. The great majority of these figured the war to end more or less when it did; the guesses ranged from 1944 to 1946. Two saw a much longer war; two thought it would peter out without any clear decision.

2. Eight foresaw the creation of what we know as the United Nations. Seven mentioned American efforts at postwar reconstruction of Europe and aid to it. (These figures doubtless underestimate prescience on these points, for many of the forecasters may have anticipated those events but framed their replies in such form that their implications were not likely to be mentioned.)

3. About 10 made reference to American impoverishment and exhaustion after the war. Only two forecast high prosperity for this country. Six, however, specifically referred to the thought that the United States would emerge as the most powerful country in the world, and this notion was implicit in the statements of many others.

4. Nine made the prediction that either the United States would come close to a civil war or would be gravely threatened by indigenous American Fascist movements. The preoccupation with a Fascist coup in this country—something that seems to us now as so remote—is one of the most interesting points to emerge from the compilation.

5. Many of the replies indicate a belief that Russia would emerge from the war as a politically and militarily powerful force. But—and this is the single most striking phenomenon in the whole affair—only 3 of the 23 forecasters predicted the central dominant and overriding circumstance of our world today—the clash between East and West.

From A. Friendly, "How 1952 Looked to 26 American 'Seers' in 1941," *The Washington Post*, March 23, 1952. Reprinted with permission.

What Are the Feasible Possibilities?

Certain constraints on the future are already implicit in the present. If central city parking lots are already full and no reduction in the downtown work force is foreseen, the number of subway riders in the short run cannot decrease. The number of 65-year-olds ready to retire 10 years from now cannot exceed the number of 55-year-olds today plus immigrants during the period. If all logistical, bureaucratic, and political impediments to construction of the new power plant are removed, the minimum construction time will still depend on the time it takes to draft designs, get contracts, create structural steel, and test equipment. An accurate forecast of the range of feasible possibilities helps a planner set attainable goals for an entire project.

Warnings

Many projections warn about the consequences of current trends. At the present worldwide population growth rate, an estimate of the number of years before every man, woman, and child has one square meter of land area is clearly not intended as a realistic view of the future. Instead, it serves to enlighten us dramatically about how fast the world is currently growing. Projections of the future shortfall of petroleum resources if present trends of consumption and production continue are similar. No one will ever be able to measure the amount of oil that would have been used if it had been produced. Yet the concept of a shortfall is a salient indicator of the danger of continuing current production and consumption trends.

Conditional Forecasts (what would happen if . . .)

Instead of making claims about what the future will be like, conditional forecasts state what the future could be like if certain decisions were made or certain events took place. Our original Social Security example could be extended by calculating expected yearly costs in the future. These costs depend not only on the number of retired people, but also on the amounts they receive. Congress sets the amounts, and conditional forecasts estimate the future cost of such a policy decision. Energy forecasting models could be used to compare the effects of a new gasoline tax and mileage regulations for automobile manufacturers. Thus, conditional forecasts allow us to compare the effect of a new policy to an established benchmark or to evaluate several competing alternatives.

WEAKNESSES OF FORECASTS

All forecasts are extensions, in one way or another, of past trends into the future. Therefore, their major weakness is that the world sometimes changes in unexpected ways. No energy forecast made before

1973 could have foreseen the vast changes in energy consumption patterns since OPEC's disruption of the oil market in the winter of 1973–74. Forecasters try to circumvent unexpected trend deviations by seeking deeper, more consistent trends. Until recently, the number of automobiles on the road in the United States had grown almost exponentially at about 4 percent per year. But by 1978, there were 117 million cars and only 141 million licensed drivers (U.S. Bureau of the Census 1979). The population is growing at a rate of less than 1 percent per year, so future growth in the number of automobiles is probably better predicted by considering population trends than by extrapolating from the automobile growth pattern. Although seeking deeper trends may lead to more accurate forecasts, no trend, no matter how basic, is immune to change. In the early 1960s the Port Authority of New York and New Jersey predicted a large enough increase of air traffic in the New York area to require a fourth major airport. These projections proved too high—"Nobody anticipated the wide-body planes" (Carroll 1981).

Sometimes forecasters continue to use trends that have already shown signs of change but write off recent deviations as random fluctuations. In general, there is no good standard for detecting real turning points in trends.

Many complex forecasts use more basic predictions as input data. For example, energy models frequently rely on independent projections of the GNP. The use of outdated input projections obviously leads to outdated forecasts.

Complex forecasting methodologies do not always yield the most accurate forecasts. Makridakis and Hibon (1979) studied forecasts for a group of 111 economic time series and found that a very naive method—simply taking the last observed value as a prediction—often performs better than more complex mathematical extrapolation formulas. When used blindly without the analyst's judgment, complex methods tend to overfit the data and follow random deviations; simpler methods tend to follow a safer middle range of possibilities.

Projections can be self-fulfilling or self-defeating. If highways are built to connect major cities and nearby rural places that are projected to grow in population, the presence of the roads will increase the likelihood that the area grows. On the other hand, prophecies of world overpopulation are already helping to lower the birth rate. Considering accuracy alone, self-fulfilling prophecies are a big success, and self-defeating prophecies a failure. But the benefits to society may be the reverse. Proponents of zero population growth regard their doomsday projections as a success if they turn out not to be true. Projections that led to the growth of rural areas through the construction of highways would be regarded as failures by someone opposed to suburban growth.

Forecasts sometimes provide us with a false sense of security. Predictions are worth no more than the assumptions on which they are based. But the mathematical and computer trappings, and sometimes "official" status, may mislead policymakers. Narrow-mindedness about possible models, parameter values, and changes in trends tends to reduce the range of possibilities suggested by the forecast.

We must be careful not to interpret projections as predictions. The U.S. Bureau of the Census regularly publishes "illustrative projections" of the U.S. population, based on three assumptions about future fertility rates. The Bureau says that these are merely extrapolations; the user must decide which fertility assumption to believe and use the corresponding projection. In practice, many users have no valid basis for deciding which fertility assumption is most likely. They may decide the central assumption is most likely, and take the outer two to represent the range of credible values. Or users may decide which of the final results is more desirable from their point of view, and convince themselves of the validity of its underlying fertility assumptions.

QUALITY CHECKLIST

1. *How adequate are the data on which the forecasting model is based?* Forecasts are no better than their input data. Is there an adequate historical record? Are model parameters estimated from the data, or are they educated guesses? Are the data properly documented?

2. *How valid are the a priori assumptions?* Are values reasonable? Are all important factors included in the model? Are educated guesses discussed and documented?

3. *Are the components and level of aggregation of the model appropriate to the problem at hand?* Energy models can tell us nothing about the effect of a new tax on oil production in Texas unless taxes and some details of Texas production are features of the model. Analysis by components sometimes reveals simpler, more basic trends. The drawbacks of a more detailed model are added complexity and more parameters to estimate.

4. *Is the scope of the forecasting model too wide or narrow?* Comprehensive forecasts (the systems analysis approach) attempt to project a set of interactive trends simultaneously. Proponents of comprehensive forecasting reason that a study of all of the important factors is necessary to anticipate changes in trends. Because individual projections have the benefit of simplicity, they are easier to understand and appraise.

5. *How does this forecast compare with other related work?* A consensus forecast is not necessarily more accurate, but is more believable, than a result that stands alone.

6. *How remote is the target date of the forecast?* In general, the closer the date, the more accuracy we can expect.

7. *How stable are the trends?* Longer, more stable trends in the past strengthen the validity of forecasts based upon them.

8. *Is the forecaster biased?* What individual or institutional biases are likely? Forecasts can reflect the optimism or pessimism of their authors; perhaps they reflect subconscious or deliberate biases. Does the forecaster's institution have access to a reliable data base?

9. *What is the forecaster's training?* Some kinds of training may provide forecasters with greater insight than other kinds. Different academic disciplines have their own standard approaches to problems, and particular types of forecasting models are often associated with academic disciplines.

10. *What is the forecaster's or the institution's track record?* The accuracy of previous forecasts may suggest whether the forecaster is likely to be accurate in making further predictions.

POLICY IMPLICATIONS

With many current issues competing for their attention, policymakers usually find it difficult to concentrate on problems of the future. Yet future difficulties are often apparent in today's trends and are easier to alleviate if work is done now. Forecasts bring tomorrow's troubles to the current agenda by stressing the future implications of today's trends, policies, or actions.

Forecasts appear in the policy process for planning purposes. They can inform, warn, or influence decision makers, or they can set expectations for the future.

QUALITY CHECKLIST

1. Adequacy of data base?
2. Validity of assumptions?
3. Level of aggregation?
4. Scope of model?
5. Relation to other forecasts?
6. Remoteness of target date?
7. Stability of trends?
8. Forecaster's bias?
9. Forecaster's training?
10. Forecaster's track record?

Planning

The most neutral use of projection models is in planning. For instance, the school board has decided to close a school, and planners use forecasts of neighborhood populations to help determine which school should be closed. A city council uses conditional forecasts to evaluate the merits of competing zoning plans. Forecasting models are often built or commissioned by planners, and so are responsive to their needs.

Advocacy

Forecasts are often the tools of advocates. Environmentalists present forecasts of an imminent collapse in the world's ecosystem as ammunition in the battle to start the clean-up now. Oil companies give pessimistic projections of future crude oil production in the hope of reducing taxes and government regulation. The wide latitude in choosing projection models and assuming parameters often allows advocates to produce any outcome they please. Divergence among the projections of competing parties does not necessarily mean that the projections are inaccurate or misleading, but it does indicate the importance of assumptions and may indicate the variety of possible results of policy decisions. A careful examination and sensitivity analysis of a forecast's assumptions may separate important policy decisions from wishful thinking.

Setting Expectations

Forecasts can set realistic or unrealistic expectations for the future. Projections of continued high gasoline prices and possible intermittent shortages encourage drivers to buy more fuel-efficient cars. On the other hand, a President's unwarranted predictions of a severe recession may lessen the negative political impact of an eventual mild recession.

To be effective, the development and presentation of forecasts need to be appropriate to their audiences. Forecasts comparing various futures will help policymakers more if the variables leading to the differing outcomes are under the policymakers' control. Legislators write laws and make appropriations, whereas administrators decide how to deploy resources. Thus, forecasts based on differing legal approaches to crime might well be addressed to legislators, but those involving management of police should be addressed to police commissioners and police unions.

CONCLUSION

Many aspects of the future are important to policymakers and are implicit, to some degree, in present trends and decisions. Forecasts shed light on connections between the present and the future and bring future considerations to today's agenda.

But the future cannot be known with certainty. Forecasts are inaccurate for two reasons: first, their models and assumptions do not exactly represent the real world; and, second, some aspects are intrinsically unknowable. Good forecasts relay uncertainty as well as likely values.

A projection is no more than a mathematical extrapolation of the past, conditional on assumptions about the future. Taking the projection as a forecast or prediction implies some belief about the validity of the assumptions. Sometimes seemingly unimportant assumptions have large effects, and so advocates can devise forecasts to illustrate almost any point. A careful examination of the assumptions may bring out the true message of a forecast.

REFERENCES

Ascher, W. 1978. *Forecasting: An Appraisal for Policy-Makers and Planners.* Baltimore: The Johns Hopkins University Press.

Carroll, M. 1981. Cost of Expanding 3 Airports Estimated at $1 Billion. *New York Times*, January 11.

Energy Information Administration. 1979. *Annual Report to Congress, 1978*, Volume 3.

Lovins, A. B. 1980. Economically Efficient Energy Futures. In *Interactions of Energy and Climate*, W. Bach; J. Pankrath; and J. Williams, eds. Dordrecht, Holland: D. Reidel Publishing Co.

Makridakis, S., and Hibon, M. 1979. Accuracy of Forecasting: An Empirical Investigation. *Journal of the Royal Statistical Society, Series A* 142:97–145.

Pitts, A. M. 1978. Social Security and Aging Populations. In *The Economic Consequences of Slowing Population Growth*, T. J. Espenshade and W. J. Serow, eds. New York: Academic Press.

U.S. Bureau of the Census. 1979. *Statistical Abstract of the United States: 1979*, 10th ed. Washington, D.C.: U.S. Government Printing Office, 003-024-02129-3.

Wade, N. 1980. For the 1980's, Beware All Expert Predictions. *Science* 207 (January 18): 287–288.

FURTHER READING

Encel, S.; Marstrand, P. K.; and Page, W., eds. 1975. *The Art of Anticipation: Values and Methods in Forecasting.* New York: Pica Press.

Greenberger, M.; Crenson, M. A.; and Crissey, B. L. 1976. *Models in the Policy Process: Public Decision Making in the Computer Era.* New York: Russell Sage Foundation.

CHAPTER 13

Mathematical Modeling

Man tries to make for himself in the fashion that suits him best a simplified and intelligible picture of the world; he then tries to some extent to substitute this cosmos of his for the world of experience, and thus to overcome it.

Albert Einstein, *Ideas and Opinions*

A key concept in simulation and forecasting (see Chapters 11 and 12) is what we call a mathematical model. Such models mathematically represent some aspects of the real world, just as a child's model airplane shares some physical features with a commercial passenger jet. Edith Stokey and others have noted that making a model involves a deliberate and systematic loss of information; we ignore some facts we hope are not essential and explore and experiment with a simplified, and perhaps abstract, version of the world. The child's model plane need not represent the age, sex, or even the number of passengers to illustrate the ideas of aerodynamics. Similarly, models of intensive-care hospital beds or the Social Security system need not reflect every fact known about hospital intensive-care systems or the rules of the Social Security Administration. A model complex enough to represent all that we know about a system is probably too unwieldy to be useful.

Lest you suppose that mathematical models are used only by academics, consider the conversation one of the authors had with a Manhattan taxi driver:

"I'd like to go to 633 Third Avenue. I think it's near 41st Street."

After a pause, the driver said, "That's about right."

MANHATTAN ADDRESS LOCATOR

To locate avenue addresses, take the address, cancel the last figure, divide by 2, add or subtract the key number below. The answer is the nearest numbered cross street, approximately.

To find addresses on numbered cross streets, remember—numbers increase east or west from 5th Ave., which runs north-south.

Ave. A	Add 3	Amsterdam Ave	Add 60
Ave. B	Add 3	Audubon Ave	Add 165
Ave. C	Add 3	Broadway (23 to 192 Sts.)	Subt. 30
Ave. D	Add 3	Columbus Ave	Add 60
1st Ave	Add 3	Convent Ave	Add 127
2nd Ave	Add 3	Edgecombe Ave	Add 134
3rd Ave	Add 10	Ft. Washington Ave	Add 158
4th Ave	Add 8	Lenox Ave	Add 110
5th Ave.		Lexington Ave	Add 22
Up to 200	Add 13	Madison Ave	Add 26
Up to 400	Add 16	Manhattan Ave	Add 100
Up to 600	Add 18	Park Ave	Add 35
Up to 775	Add 20	Pleasant Ave	Add 101
From 775 to 1286	Cancel	St. Nicholas Ave	Add 110
last figure and subtract 18		Wadsworth Ave	Add 173
Up to 1500	Add 45	West End Ave	Add 60
Above 2000	Add 24	Central Park West	Divide
Ave. of the Americas	Subt. 12	house number by 10 and add 60	
7th Ave	Add 12	Riverside Drive	Divide
Above 110th St	Add 20	house number by 10 and add 72 up	
8th Ave	Add 10	to 165th Street	
9th Ave	Add 13		
10th Ave	Add 14		

Source: New York Telephone Company, *Manhattan Telephone Directory,* 1979. Reprinted with permission.

"You have them all memorized?"

"No, I use the code, you know."

"What's that?"

"Well, drop the last number makes 63, divide by 2 makes 31, and add 10 makes 41, like you said. It works pretty well."

"You always add 10?"

"Oh, no, it's different for each avenue, like for Broadway you subtract 30, and Fifth Avenue is a little crazy. I have a little card, but now I remember them all and don't need it."

The Manhattan telephone book gives this rule for finding near what numbered street an address on a north-south avenue falls.

The previous chapters did not discuss the mathematical character of models and the process of building them. This chapter does so through three examples from among many kinds of mathematical models.

MODEL OF A PANEL OF EXPERTS

For those who are unfamiliar with mathematical modeling, a modest example may make the idea more concrete. In preparing Chapter 14 on introspection and advice, the authors discussed among themselves the use of a panel of experts. Someone asked how large the panel should be. Someone else conjectured: the bigger, the better. Another pointed out that costs would surely grow and the number should be limited. This discussion led us to formulate a model whose first version, which can be readily criticized, would give us a way to show how such a model might evolve, ultimately, into something of practical value. We do not intend the model for practical use as it stands.

The Problem

An organization plans to market a new product or to carry out some task. To aid the effort, the manager plans to invite a panel of experts to submit new ideas separately by mail; in principle, each idea can make a contribution of value. How many experts should be invited? To get started, we need some assumptions.

Initial Assumptions

1. *Overhead.* Forming the panel costs some fixed amount, independent of its size; call this amount A.

2. *Fees.* Members of the panel are paid; if there are r members, each being paid w, the panel costs rw.

3. *Processing.* Each suggestion submitted has to be reviewed. They can be thought of as falling into two categories:
   a. Ideas previously submitted, each of which, on the average, costs a small amount, c, to process.
   b. New ideas, which on the average cost a substantial amount, C, to explore for feasibility.

4. *Number of ideas.* Each panel member is to submit exactly k ideas (say, 3). (We could equally well suppose that the *average* number submitted is k; the model and analysis do not distinguish between these assumptions.)

5. *Value.* A new idea has value V (or on the average has value V). An old idea is assigned a value of zero; it had value V when first submitted. One could give a resubmitted idea some value as a verification, but we shall not complicate the model in this manner.

6. *Chances of a new idea.* Because the home office already has a few ideas of its own, even the first idea submitted by the first panel member is not certain to be new. Furthermore, as each panel member's suggestions are processed, more new ideas will have been received, so those processed later are less likely to be new.

We assume that the k ideas sent in by a panel member will be different and that each of them has the same chance of being a new idea. We need a formula that tells us how the probability of a new idea decays as more and more panel members' submissions are processed.

We shall assume that α, a number less than 1, is the proportion of items in the first panel member's submissions that are new, on the average. For the second panel member, we assume α^2 applies to each idea, and so on. Then each of the rth set of ideas processed has on the average the proportion

$$P_r = \alpha^r$$

of new ideas. Thus, if the first panel member's ideas have a 0.9 chance of being new, the second member's have 0.81 chance, the third 0.729, and so on.

Although we are not trying to justify this decay function, if we believe that there is a large but finite pool of ideas (say 10,000) and that panel members sample from these randomly and independently, then this decay function, α^r, might be a reasonable approximation. As r increases, P_r tends to zero.

Analysis

With these assumptions, we now want to balance costs and values received. We ask what the net value of the rth panel member's submission of k ideas is expected to be. If it would be positive, we should try to get it; if negative, not. There should be an indifference point when the cost just balances the value, because the proportion of new ideas tends to zero.

Let us first compute the expected value of the k ideas produced by the rth panel member. Because $k\alpha^r$ is the expected number of new ideas and each is worth V, their value is

$$k\alpha^r V. \tag{1}$$

The marginal costs (excluding overhead, which we consider later) of the rth panel member's contributions are the member's fee, plus the average cost of processing the new ideas, plus the average cost of processing old ideas, giving

$$w + k\alpha^r C + k(1 - \alpha^r)c. \tag{2}$$

Now we search for the indifference point by equating expressions (1) and (2), and we get

$$k\alpha^r V = w + k\alpha^r C + k(1 - \alpha^r)c. \tag{3}$$

Since we want to solve for r, it is well to bring all terms involving r together, so we have

$$k\alpha^r(V - C + c) = w + kc,$$

and dividing by $k(V - C + c)$ gives

$$\alpha^r = \frac{w + kc}{k(V - C + c)}$$

If we take logarithms and then divide through by $\log \alpha$, we get the optimum value of r:

$$r_{\text{opt}} = \frac{1}{\log \alpha}\left[\log\left(\frac{w + kc}{k(V - C + c)}\right)\right]. \tag{4}$$

Then, except for choosing the smaller of the two surrounding integers, r_{opt} is the most profitable size of the panel, if we have one.

Let us try this out for a set of values. Suppose that we ask each panelist to submit 3 ideas, that the fee given each panelist is \$500, and that it costs \$5 to process an old idea and \$200 to process a new one. Suppose also that a new idea is worth \$1,000 and that the initial proportion of new ideas is 0.95. Then we are choosing $k = 3$, $w = 500$, $c = 5$, $C = 200$, $V = 1,000$, and $\alpha = 0.95$. We plug these numbers into formula (4) and get

$$r_{\text{opt}} = \frac{1}{\log 0.95}\left[\log \frac{500 + 15}{3(1000 - 200 + 5)}\right]$$

$$= 30.1.$$

Thus, we would have 30 panel members if we decided to launch the panel. Using this model, we would need to know the overhead amount, A, and then see whether the total positive contributions from the program would exceed A. We do not carry out this calculation, though it is not difficult with this model. Finally, we need to decide whether other investments of personnel and facilities would be likely to benefit the organization more than this panel would.

The precise values (V, c, C, and so on) and the details may not be correct or appropriate, but the model forces us to recognize how r_{opt} changes with changes in the values of the variables. For example, Table 13-1 shows how the panel size would change if the fee, w, were raised by increments of \$500. It suggests that the organization could pay its idea people too much—believe it or not. All told, then, this model illustrates a mathematical approach to an optimization problem. The model, or an improved version of it, might be useful for considering a situation in which all new ideas can be used.

Revision

Forming a tentative model gives us an opportunity to think about how to improve it. For example, the proportion of new ideas need not go to zero. We could have $P_r = \alpha^r + \beta$, where $0 < \beta < 1 - \alpha$, so that after many panel members' submissions had been processed, a small proportion of new ideas would persist. Or, again, we might think that c and C would change as r increased. Perhaps c gets smaller and C increases. The overhead might depend on r. The decay function α^r might be replaced by a function based on experience with similar problems in the past. Thus, the model can be made more realistic through modification.

An important tension in building a mathematical model arises from determining the necessary amount of complexity. Models must have

TABLE 13–1 *Optimum size of panel for various sizes of fee, w*

w	r_{opt}
\$ 500	30
1,000	17
1,500	9
2,000	4
2,500	0

enough features of the real world to give an informative representation, but they must also be simple enough to express in equations and to interpret easily. Different versions of a model, or even entirely different models, may be appropriate for analyzing different aspects of a policy. Balancing realism (complexity) and ease of interpretation (simplicity) makes modeling an art as much as a science.

Policymakers, even those with little or no mathematical background, may find playing with simple models profitable. Putting pencil to paper can help clarify how a process or system is likely to work. The most insight often comes from very simple models.

If a decision maker must take action based on information that is foreign to his or her training, the question is how to use that information. We discuss this in Chapter 14 on introspection and advice. Here we focus directly on models. Suppose that a mathematical model has been prepared, and, as often happens, someone challenges it. Suppose further that the policymaker cannot master the model—lack of time or previous preparation prevents it. We discuss this with the aid of a convenient model produced by Sørensen and Hallinan (1977), a criticism by Hauser (1978), and a reply by Sørensen (1978).

MODEL OF THE LEARNING PROCESS

The model developers began by expecting that ability, effort, and opportunity produce variations in learning. They made the fundamental assumption that the amount learned depends linearly on the amount of new material presented to a student. This and a few more mathematical assumptions lead to a differential equation, which the authors solved. The mathematical model has some constants in it whose numerical values had to be supplied.

In casting about for information that would bear on the model, the modelers found that the data neither strongly supported nor strongly challenged belief in the model.

If we accept the model and the estimates of constants that the authors provide, two types of school effects emerge. First, opportunities for learning provided by the schools interact with the student's background and abilities. Second, compensating effects produced by the school environment act on the student's ability and effort. The model sees the effect of opportunities as increasing the inequality among students, whereas the effect of environment acts to reduce inequality.

Three statements by Sørensen and Hallinan (1977) cover the main points:

It has been shown further that schools that provide many opportunities will be schools where differences among students in academic achievement—or inequality of achievement—are large. In poor schools where no opportunities are provided, no one will learn, whether dull or gifted. (p. 288)

There are thus two types of school effects: (1) opportunity effects that determine the effect of a student's ability and effort on learning and that produce inequality in achievement resulting from differences among students in ability and effort, and (2) additive effects that directly influence ability and effort, and that may be compensatory, and reduce inequality. Only the latter effects can be identified directly from the linear additive models applied to cross-sectional data so common in research on school effects. Direct estimation of the level of opportunities for learning provided by schools is not possible using linear models on cross-sectional data. (p. 288)

Only new data collection can establish more conclusively the validity of the conception of the learning process and its mathematical specification presented in this paper. As it stands, however, the model does provide a number of qualitative implications that cast doubt on the prevailing belief among sociologists of education regarding the importance of schools. (p. 289)

An emphasis on the possibility that schools might make students more unequal has never been greeted with enthusiasm by educators or policymakers. Much of the argument for the universal school system comes from the idea of increasing equality, not decreasing it. In the old days, equality meant equality of opportunity, not equality of achievement, but today many think of these as identical.

In an evaluation of "Sesame Street," Cook et al. (1975) complained that, though the television program improved the academic performance of all children who watched it, since more advantaged children might watch it more and thus gain more than disadvantaged children, the program could lead to inequality:

Any policy decisions about "Sesame Street" have to deal with one paramount issue: To what extent should the program be selective and thus compensatory? To say it should not be selective and that it should be equally available to all would increase the preschool knowledge level of millions of children to an as yet unknown extent over their viewing career, but it might also increase the achievement gap since resources that are equally available to all children are not necessarily equally used. To what extent, and in what ways, should "Sesame Street" be a selective social service? We ask this question again because it is the most important single policy issue that this report raises. (p. 372)

Sørensen and Hallinan generalized their model to a set of simultaneous equations and discussed both shortcomings and difficulties.

Hauser criticizes the model on the grounds that it is "neither novel nor plausible." The novelty need not detain us, because policymakers will not be panting for mathematical innovations. Instead they will find that Hauser offers a translation of the outcome of the model into a new form called simultaneous structural equations. However enthusiastic policymakers are about models, and even if they are equipped to follow two rather different forms of mathematical descriptions, they scarcely have time to verify the detailed connections and will rarely be on firm ground in such a discussion. Thus, they usually have to be guided by instruction or advice.

Plausibility is something that policymakers can perk up about. Hauser argues that the model and its outcome depend on the scale of measurement, the metric of performance. Hauser asks, "How does one know that a theory is confirmed by the shape of a relationship between variables when the metrics of these variables may be stretched or compressed at will in any segment of their range?" (1978, p. 70). This sort of change does not just move the zero point and change the scale, such as the change from Fahrenheit temperature to Celsius; it rumples the numbers.

"Again," Hauser says, "the history of data analysis is filled with instances in which functional forms may be altered by transformations of metric . . ." (1978, p. 70), and he offers the individual earnings function from economics and sociology as an example.

Hauser also says that the outcome that good schools may increase inequality is enough to make one suspicious. (Since Cook et al. [1975] regarded this as a serious outcome of viewing "Sesame Street," we might not find it so suspicious.) Hauser also notes the difficulty of verification and criticizes some quantitative analysis. He ends on the friendly note that, when the model passes certain empirical tests that he believes can ultimately be applied, he will be happy to accept it.

Sørensen responds by amplifying the discussion and thanking Hauser for some constructive suggestions. He also accepts the complaint about the metric more readily than most authors would. He emphasizes the need to develop and verify the model.

What should the policymaker make of this? Except for the temperate character of the debate, the situation described is a common one. The researchers have developed a potentially valuable model of the learning process that has serious implications, but little has been verified. Both the originators and their critic agree that current data are inadequate to assess the model. Thus, the model should not be used as the basis for immediate action. However, it might prove important if more information could be obtained. Therefore, the policymaker might consider encouraging some group to gather appropriate data.

Unlike Longfellow's Wattawamat, who was not born of woman but sprang forth fully armed from an oak tree riven by lightning, mathematical models in the physical sciences evolve from endless years of checking assumptions and details, and making forecasts together with special investigations to check them. The part that the elementary science student rarely hears about is the continuing revision of actual definitions of physical quantities so that the formulas work better.

In the social sciences we have no models that have been checked in this way except a few that are almost automatic—queuing theory comes to mind and inventory control in business, perhaps double-entry bookkeeping. Fire department policies and ambulance strategies can be made to match their models fairly well because (1) both the model and the system are available for change; (2) many models will give nearly the same result; and (3) their purpose is to help choose among many alternatives, not predict exactly what will happen.

The basic difficulty with models of social processes is not only that their details must be checked, but that human behavior changes with the years and with the changing social system. A model that may be rather helpful at one time will fall on its face at another.

Therefore, the policymaker cannot count on using social models in the short run unless they have been tested for the range of circumstances under which they will be used. And they cannot be counted on in the long run unless they partake only of simple accounting features, such as "input minus output is total change of inventory."

Yet models are worth creating. They can suggest dominant effects. They can locate instabilities in systems, but usually not pinpoint the time when the system will actually blow up. This is similar to earthquake forecasting: we are told it is highly probable that an earthquake will occur within a few decades. Models do have the merit of forcing attention on variables. They create thoughtful arguments (as in our example of Sørensen/Hallinan and Hauser) and encourage new lines of research and measurement. They focus attention on unexpected outcomes.

The process of building the model, as opposed to using its results, can also be helpful to the policymaker. The necessary careful thought about definitions and dynamics, as well as the gathering of data, strengthens one's understanding and intuition about the system being studied.

How might a policymaker profit from the Sørensen-Hallinan model?

1. Recognize that many years of study would be required to verify and modify the model.
2. Consider the outcome suggested by the model that good schools, at the same time that they elevate the educational achievement of the whole population, may also be creating additional inequality in educational achievement among students. Think of it as a hypothesis and ask how, as a fact, it might benefit or hinder the nation and what other consequences it would have.
3. Consider whether these hypothetical consequences suggest the wisdom of encouraging schools to be poorer, which seems to be easy, or to be better, which is hard. In other words, the model should be treated in the same way as a speculative book written by a good scholar, a book admittedly not well founded in fact. Use it as a mind stretcher.

One special brand of model is the causal model, which can be a structural-equation, simultaneous-equation, or path-coefficient model. In the 1980s the causal model has become especially popular in economics, political science, sociology, and psychology. Indeed, Hauser translated the outcome of Sørensen and Hallinan's model into a structural-equation model. Such models describe inputs from several variables, interactions among them, and their effects on the output variables. Often a picture goes along with the model, indicating the flow of effects from variable to variable.

MODELING LAND AVAILABILITY AND FERTILITY IN BRAZIL

Population policy in developing countries is greatly concerned with the determinants of fertility. Excessive population growth aggravates the difficult process of economic development, so policymakers must examine current practices and proposed policies with regard to their effect on fertility.

Thomas Merrick (1978) uses a technique called path analysis to study the effect of land availability on fertility in rural Brazil. In earlier work, Easterlin (1976a, 1976b) argued that the availability of land on the American frontier in the nineteenth century was the most important determinant of fertility rates. But Merrick claims that the American settlers were more homogeneous than are present-day rural Brazilians in terms of such socioeconomic characteristics as child mortality, literacy, and access of the poor to land. Because the socioeconomic factors themselves affect fertility, all influences must be considered simultaneously to assess their individual and joint effects. Merrick's goal is to assess "the prospects for rural fertility decline given that (a) quality agricultural land is becoming increasingly scarce (and rising in cost) and (b) large segments of the rural population have a very limited opportunity for ever owning land and thus, being exposed to the economic forces that decreasing land supply might bring to bear on rural reproductive behavior" (1978, p. 322).

To study the joint effects of land availability and socioeconomic factors on fertility, Merrick developed the path-analysis model illustrated in Figure 13-1. He constructed three independent indices of land availability. The first, $F1$, depends primarily on the amount of usable land in 155 "microregions" in 6 frontier states of Brazil. (The Brazilian Census Bureau defines a microregion as a group of homogeneous

FIGURE 13–1. *Path Analysis of Fertility Rates for Married Women Aged 30 to 34*

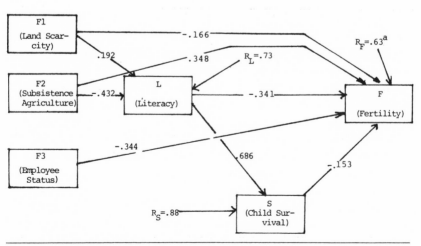

Note: a) Residual $= \sqrt{1 - R^2}$

From T. W. Merrick, Fertility and Land Availability in Rural Brazil, *Demography* 15, no. 3:321–336, 1978, p. 332. Reprinted with permission.

municipalities.) Positive values of $F1$ indicate scarcity of land. The second index, $F2$, identifies regions with a high level of subsistence farming and a low level of land use—regions that have largely been bypassed by the development process. The third index, $F3$, is basically the employment level of the microregion.

The path-analysis model assumes that fertility is directly affected by each of the land variables, $F1$, $F2$, and $F3$. In Figure 13-1 the lines between each land box on the left and the fertility box on the right indicate these direct relationships. The numbers $-.166$ on the $F1$ line, $.348$ on the $F2$ line, and $-.344$ on the $F3$ line indicate the strength and direction of these relationships. Thus, land scarcity, $F1$, correlates with lower fertility, and high levels of subsistence agriculture, $F2$, lead to higher fertility. Furthermore, the second relation is twice as strong as the first.

Literacy of women is often a strong negative correlate of fertility, both as a direct determinant and as a proxy for other socioeconomic factors. The line from the literacy box to the fertility box in Figure 13-1 indicates a strong negative effect on fertility, $-.341$. Furthermore, literacy partly depends in turn on $F1$ and $F2$. In particular, high levels of subsistence agriculture, $F2$, are associated with low literacy values.

Child survival is another traditional determinant of fertility; a high child mortality rate means that more births are required to achieve the desired number of adult offspring. Child survival appears in Merrick's model both as a determinant of fertility and as a function of literacy.

Path analysis helps break a complicated process, such as the determination of fertility, into its components. This type of analysis has two basic strengths. First, it provides a way of analyzing and displaying each of the links in the process. For instance, Merrick found no link between employment level, $F3$, and either literacy or child survival. Second, path analysis allows the investigator to decompose the variation in fertility among regions into direct effects of the primary variables (the land variables in the present model) and indirect effects of the same variables mediated through secondary variables (here literacy and child survival). Table 13-2 gives such a breakdown. For instance, two-thirds of the effect of land scarcity on fertility, $-.166$, is direct, and the other one-third, $-.086$, is mediated through literacy.

Path analysis thus brings Merrick to the following conclusions:

The statistical analysis in the previous section indicates that differentials in land availability play a significant, though not exclusive, role in rural

TABLE 13–2 *Decomposition of path analysis of regressions for women aged 30 to 34*

| Variables | Total Effect | Indirect Effect Via | | Direct Effect |
		Literacy (L)	Child Survival (S)	
Land scarcity (F1)	−.252	−.086	.000	−.166
Subsistence farming (F2)	.544	.193	.003	.348
Rural employment (F3)	−.305	.036	.003	−.344
Literacy (L)	−.445	×	−.104	−.341
Child survival (S)	−.153	×	×	−.153

From T. W. Merrick, Fertility and Land Availability in Rural Brazil, *Demography* 15, no. 3:321–336, 1978, p. 334. Reprinted with permission.

fertility differences in the center-south of Brazil. While consistent with Easterlin's study of the United States, the findings also reveal important differences in the role of other factors. (p. 334)

The opportunities for Brazilian frontier settlers are constrained by land tenure structure and by the shifting of rural workers to employee status. This combination of institutional factors on the frontier with rapid urbanization and the persistence of traditional subsistence farming in the more settled regions implies that the ability of most rural Brazilians to transmit the fruits of their labors to their offspring through the acquisition of land is more limited than that of their American pioneer counterparts. (p. 334)

The prospects for further decline in rural fertility in Brazil may well depend more on the course of public policy affecting access of the rural population to land than on its actual scarcity or abundance. (p. 335)

Investigators use a combination of theory and empiricism to construct such models. By now a very complicated literature advises the student how to construct them, and several graduate courses may be required to understand the technology, avoid the pitfalls, and use the shortcuts. One might well think of these models as complicated regression models intended to use ideas of causation both to analyze a system and to make predictions as to what will happen when variables in the system change their values.

Since most of the analysis must be based on static information—cross-sectional information—and on observational studies, rather than on deliberately introduced changes in the system, we have few checks on the outputs of these models. What is needed to check them usually is not available, because the experiments usually are infeasible. Thus, it is hard to get good checks in the manner mentioned earlier for physical science models.

This does not mean the models are not instructive, but it does mean that they cannot be regarded as a solid foundation for understanding causes and for forecasting the outcomes of policy moves.

Beyond this, of course, we have large-scale economic models that take ten or fifteen years of effort by many researchers to develop, test, and revise. Usually the workers know a great deal about the model: what features they believe are still missing, what kinds of questions it is good or poor at answering. They have views about how to proceed when the model disagrees with other forecasts. Such a large-scale model, in the hands of seasoned researchers, can make contributions to policy, because the researchers understand the model's strengths and weaknesses. This is different from the situation with a newly invented model.

These three examples complete our exemplification of mathematical approaches to modeling.

REFERENCES

Cook, T.D. et al. 1975. *"Sesame Street" Revisited.* New York: Russell Sage Foundation.

Easterlin, R.A. 1976a. Population Change and Farm Settlement in the Northern United States. *Journal of Economic History* 36:45–75.

———. 1976b. Factors in the Decline of Farm Family Fertility in the United States: Some Preliminary Results. *Journal of American History* 43:600–614.

Hauser, R.M. 1978. On "A Reconceptualization of School Effects." *Sociology of Education* 51:68–73.*

Longfellow, H.W. 1910. *The Courtship of Miles Standish and Other Poems.* New York: Grosset and Dunlap.

Merrick, T.W. 1978. Fertility and Land Availability in Rural Brazil. *Demography* 15, no. 3: 321–336.

New York Telephone Company. 1979. *Manhattan Telephone Directory.*

Sørensen, A.B. 1978. Reconceptualizing School Effects. *Sociology of Education* 51:230–233.*

Sørensen, A.B., and Hallinan, M.T. 1977. A Reconceptualization of School Effects. *Sociology of Education* 50:273–289.*

*Hauser 1978, Sørensen 1978, and Sørensen and Hallinan 1978 appear together in Reprint 336, 1979, Institute for Research on Poverty, University of Wisconsin, Madison, Wisconsin 53706.

FURTHER READING

Drake, A.W.; Keeney, R.L.; and Morse, P.M. 1972. *Analysis of Public Systems.* Cambridge, Mass.: MIT Press.

Greenberger, M.; Crenson, M.A.; and Crissey, B.L. 1976. *Models in the Policy Process: Public Decision Making in the Computer Era.* New York: Russell Sage Foundation.

CHAPTER 14

Introspection and Advice

Policymakers solve most of their problems by introspection: a problem arises, the policymaker thinks briefly about the pros and cons, perhaps asks a question or two to clarify facts, and makes a decision. Defining the problem, marshalling pros and cons, and clarifying facts form a time-honored information-gathering method, as the letter below from Benjamin Franklin to Sir Joseph Priestley illustrates. In many situations the activity seems so fast and so tied to the decision process that we think of it as part of deciding or policymaking, rather than as a method of gathering information for policy.

EXAMPLES

Moral or Prudential Algebra

Letter from Benjamin Franklin (1772) to Joseph Priestley:

London, Sept. 19,1772

Dear Sir:

In the affair of so much importance to you, wherein you ask my advice, I cannot, for want of sufficient premises, advise you what to determine, but if you please I will tell you how. When those difficult cases occur, they are difficult, chiefly because while we have them under consideration, all the reasons pro and con are not present to the mind at the same time; but sometimes one set present themselves, and at other times another, the first being out of sight. Hence the various purposes or inclinations that alternately prevail, and the uncertainty that perplexes us.

To get over this, my way is to divide half a sheet of paper by a line into two columns; writing over the one Pro, and over the other Con. Then, during three or four days consideration, I put down under the different heads short hints of the different motives that at different times occur to me, for or against the measure. When I have thus got them all together in one view, I endeavor to estimate their respective weights; and where I find two, one on each side, that seem equal, I strike them both out. If I find a reason Pro equal to some two reasons Con, I strike out the three. If I judge some two reasons Con, equal to some three reasons Pro, I strike out the five; and thus proceeding I find at length where the balance lies; and if, after a day or two of further consideration, nothing new that is of importance occurs on either side, I come to a determination accordingly. And, though the weight of reasons cannot be taken with a precision of algebraic quantities, yet when each is thus considered, separately and comparatively, and the whole lies before me, I think I can judge better, and am less liable to make a rash step, and in fact I have found great advantage from this kind of equation, in what may be called moral or prudential algebra.

Wishing sincerely that you may determine for the best, I am ever, my dear friend, yours most affectionately.

B. Franklin

Note here that Benjamin Franklin is giving advice to his friend Sir Joseph Priestley on how Priestley can most efficiently use introspection.

Sometimes, rather than turning inward to ourselves or consulting a single adviser, we seek the advice of a group.

Systematic Advice: An Atomic Attack on the United States?

In the early 1950s, U.S. strategic policy planners wanted information to help estimate the number of atom bombs required to reduce American munitions output by various amounts and to estimate those U.S. industrial targets likely to be chosen by strategic bombing planners from the Soviet Union (Dalkey and Helmer 1963).

The Rand Corporation set up a panel of seven experts to consider (1) which U.S. industrial targets would be selected, and (2) how many atom bombs would be required to reduce U.S. industrial production to a quarter of wartime capacity. Four experts were economists, one was an electronics engineer, one was a systems analyst, and one was a bomb damage expert. Several questionnaires were used in an iterative fashion, interspersed with controlled feedback of the group's responses to previous questionnaires.

Between successive queries, the panel received additional information, such as data previously requested by one of the experts (for instance, industrial production figures for a specific industry) or factors suggested as potentially relevant by a panel member (such as how much energy production could be reallocated after a bombing attack). The panel was instructed:

Assume that a war between the U.S. and the S.U. breaks out on 1 July, 1953. Now, further assume that the enemy during the first month of the war (and only during that period) carries out a strategic A-bombing campaign against U.S. industrial targets, employing 20-KT bombs. Within each industry selected for bombardment, assume that the bombs delivered on targets succeed in hitting always the most important targets in that industry. What is the least number of bombs that will have to be delivered on target for . . . the chances to be even that the cumulative munitions output . . . would be held to no more than one quarter of what it would otherwise have been?

In successive questionnaires each expert stated the number of bombs required by specific industries and laid out some of the reasoning leading to the estimate. The expert gave 10 percent and 90 percent subjective probability limits and suggested data that would be helpful in arriving at a better estimate. The second round of questionnaires dealt with the vulnerability of various industries, their ability to recover after attack, the effect of initial stockpiles, and interrelationships among target industries. Later questionnaires asked for a reconsideration of original estimates in the light of new information, such as the experience with 20-KT bombs in the bombing of Japan in World War II. If one expert requested some available data, the information was given to each of the others as well. Through a repetitive process, the range of successive estimates of bomb requirements was narrowed. The smallest estimate increased from 50 to 167 A-bombs, while the largest decreased from 5,000 to 360 bombs. The median advanced from 200 to 276. Although the initial response showed a hundredfold range between the smallest and largest, by the response to the fifth questionnaire, this range was under threefold.

FEATURES OF INTROSPECTION AND ADVICE

Introspection

Introspection is an important information-gathering method in widespread use, yet in other respects it is different from those we have considered. At some point, most problems profit from thoughtful consideration of available data, of potential policy possibilities, and of a possible formulation or modeling of the process at hand. Almost any problem, policy or otherwise, undergoes this process eventually.

By introspection, we mean organizing one's own knowledge and experience preparatory to applying it to the problem at hand. By advice, we mean asking others for their opinions or knowledge and, in turn, organizing them into the policymaker's introspective process. Thus, introspection could be regarded as getting advice from oneself.

Introspection is most likely to occur when we find the data unsuitable. For example, current data are inadequate and cannot be improved, or they are adequate but do not bear directly on the question, though they may be partially relevant, or data could be had but would be too expensive or take too long to gather.

By and large, policy decisions taken at one moment do not represent the final word on a subject of importance to a nation, so lack of data for a decision now would not be a good excuse for failing to gather data for a better informed decision later.

Circumstances usually force policymakers to reach decisions and to set programs in motion on the basis of less than adequate information. A policymaker may well decide that the available information or some portion of it is inadequate to form a basis for policy. Yet, occasionally, action is required and, as many observers like to point out, failure to act becomes a policy response in itself. Policymakers must make the best of what is available, and they can also ensure that what will be available is best.

What we are discussing, then, is a process of organizing information, knowledge, experience, and expertise in the mind of the policymaker. As an important step in attacking such problems, we first carefully consider what we know and how certain we are of that knowledge, as well as how the process works. We are all acquainted with Franklin's pen-and-paper technique of sitting down and making a list of the pluses and the minuses associated with a potential move. We all recognize the advantage of seeking the advice of others. We have all had the experience of discovering that the simple process of laying out the problem in written or verbal form for another person has led to some new insight. Even without any formal structure, the marshaling of ideas that occurs in a thoughtful conversation (or in written notes) frequently produces unexpected solutions.

Advice

We all have others to whom we turn for advice, people who bring to problems a different set of experiences or thought processes than we have ourselves. Some are thoughtful generalists; some we regard as experts. Occasionally, we seek academicians, well known in a special field of study; other times we ask people with a lifetime of experience in a profession or field.

We have considered introspection as an activity involving one or two people: the individual seeks information through self-examination or by consulting an adviser. The contact may be face-to-face, by telephone, or even by mail. Frequently, we study problems by asking a group for advice. This permits us to consult people with varied backgrounds, and to benefit from several people hearing and reacting to a formulation of the problem, as well as to one another's thoughts. Sometimes group advice will be sought through a conference telephone call, so that the group can interact even though its members are spread around the globe. More frequently, the members of a committee gather in a face-to-face encounter, taking full advantage of new information brought by each member and of fresh insights provided through this process of cross-fertilization and discussion.

Committee meetings may be small or moderately large. They may be free-flowing and informal or tightly controlled from the chair. As it gets larger, a committee meeting becomes a seminar or formal conference or even a congress. The easy give-and-take of a smaller meeting gives way to formal presentations or reading of position papers with few interactions and limited opportunity for discussion and comment. The large conference may transfer information from the speaker to listeners efficiently, but the relatively few opportunities for listeners to contribute considerably hampers the interchange of ideas.

Most groups from whom we seek advice are relatively small. The difficulty in getting large numbers of people together and the drag of size, as we have observed, interfere with the give-and-take of group discussion. Large groups often produce large volumes of information, thus adding to the policymaker's woes.

Perhaps meetings to develop a consensus form an exception to these general rules. Policymakers bring together a substantial number of experts from relevant fields to seek a consensus; that is, they identify those facts or aspects of the problem that the experts agree about. Such a process may help shape policy and identify those areas that require further specific research.

An example of a consensus panel is the Consensus-Development Conference on Adjuvant Chemotherapy of Breast Cancer, sponsored by the U.S. National Cancer Institute (NIH Consensus-Development Panel 1980). A group of expert physicians, cancer research specialists, and others concerned with the treatment of breast cancer tried to reach general agreement on the results of adjuvant chemotherapy trials in cancer of the breast and the message these trials hold for medical practice. Adjuvant, or auxiliary, chemotherapy uses drugs after primary therapy (usually surgery) for cancer. It may eradicate hidden remaining disease that would otherwise be fatal. Chemotherapeutic agents are cellular poisons that have a variety of more or less unpleasant side effects. The assessment of adjuvant chemotherapy must balance therapeutic effectiveness against toxicity. The net benefit measures an increase in the patient's survival against a decrease in quality of life due to toxic side effects of the drugs. Primary breast cancer has both varying potential for recurrence and varying response to chemotherapeutic drugs.

The ten-member panel met and reviewed the results of previous trials for chemotherapy in patients who had had local surgical therapy, such as radical mastectomy. They listed five major issues of concern and attempted to provide the best general agreement on the state of knowledge in each area. They tried to identify the best current therapy for patients with cancer of the breast and to specify areas needing research.

For example, the panel said that chemotherapy using a combination of several agents had been shown to be more effective than chemotherapy with a single agent. They said that adjuvant chemotherapy appeared to be particularly indicated for premenopausal patients with evidence of lymph-node spread who have undergone local therapy by mastectomy, although the optimum dose of drugs had not yet been determined. The survival benefits in premenopausal patients with lymph-node spread appeared to outweigh the disadvantages of early toxicity. The panel felt that no hormonal manipulation could be recommended as standard therapy, although clinical trials should continue. The panel agreed that patients without evidence of lymph-node spread should not routinely be given adjuvant chemotherapy. Furthermore, they felt that postmenopausal patients should receive chemotherapy and hormonal therapy only in the setting of well-controlled trials.

WHAT INTROSPECTION AND ADVICE ARE NOT

Do not confuse introspection with decision making. We consider introspection and advice additional means of gathering information about a policy problem, not a substitute for deciding. Panels, committees, and advisers serve a variety of functions. They can operate to make decisions, to formulate a policy, to execute or delay a policy, to coordinate an action, to transmit information, or to diffuse responsibility. We deal here with the issue of giving advice or formulating judgments concerning information.

We get different things from advisers. Sometimes we call an expert on the telephone and ask for a fact. We get an answer, an answer we could have found for ourselves by simply doing some digging. By consulting an expert, we short-circuit the process of investigation. Where we might have spent an hour or a morning in the research library looking for the answer, the expert has it at hand and can tell us what we need to know at once.

As an example of what may happen when one calls on an expert, we report an experience of one of the authors. He wondered whether there were terms that could be used to describe words or statements that are self-illustrating, such as "wee" or "polysyllabic," or words that defy their meanings, such as "monosyllabic" or a statement like, "Don't use contractions in writing, or you're sure to offend." Having had some good experiences with William Kruskal in such wordy problems, he wrote asking whether Kruskal knew of such terms.

He soon received a sheaf of pages in response. Kruskal had already corresponded on this very question with the Harvard philosopher and logician W. V. Quine, who had replied that "autological" and "heterological" might be good terms for these usages. Heterological was illustrated by "long" and "German." He said that Grelling's Paradox is asking whether "heterological" is autological or heterological. The terms do not appear in the *Oxford English Dictionary* or in *Webster's New International Dictionary*, second edition.

Later Kruskal found a long poem (Lerner 1975) devoted to this question and containing a dialogue between a computer named Arthur and its master.

Using introspection, we ask ourselves or our advisers for an *opinion* about current or historical data not accurately known or now available. We ask for an opinion about the significance of an event, or we ask for an opinion that requires some understanding of a process so complex or so poorly understood as to make more formal (for example, mathematical) modeling or simulation impossible.

For example, in June 1940, just after the evacuation and fall of Dunkirk, Prime Minister Winston Churchill asked his close adviser, Professor Frederick Lindemann:

While we are hastening our preparations . . . the Germans will be organizing the whole industries of the captured countries. . . . What sorts of relative outputs must be faced next year unless we are able to bomb the newly acquired German plants? Germany also, being relieved from the need of keeping a gigantic army in constant contact with the French army, must have spare capacity for the air and other methods of attacking us. Must we not expect this will be very great? How soon can it come into play? Hitherto, I have been looking at the next three months because of the emergency, but what about 1941? (Churchill 1949, p. 171)

Churchill wrote of Lindemann after the war: "He had two qualifications of vital consequence to me. First, as these pages have shown, he was my trusted friend and confidant of twenty years. . . . But Lindemann could decipher the signals from the experts . . . and explain to me in lucid, homely terms what the issues were" (Churchill 1949, p. 382).

STRENGTHENING INTROSPECTION AND ADVICE

To get the best from introspection and advice, one must consider four aspects: (1) selecting advisers, (2) getting the best from each adviser, (3) using several advisers, and (4) the Delphi technique.

Selecting Advisers

We select advisers who we think will provide good advice, possibly choosing on the basis of their having provided good advice in the past. There are two steps. First, we decide what types of advisers are needed. Next, we decide who, among those available, is the best in each category.

It is not always easy to tell what kind of advice we need. Do we need a generalist, an expert, or both? Of course, it depends on the problem. If we need help formulating the problem, balancing the pluses and minuses of potential policy options, constructing a cost/risk/benefit analysis, we seek a careful, thoughtful, experienced friend. Some people have an intuitive feel for human motivations, for political nuances, for how the public, allied forces, or potential adversaries might react.

If the issue turns on questions requiring special expertise, we seek an adviser who is knowledgeable or experienced in a profession or discipline. To what fields do we turn? Again, it depends on the problem. Usually it is clear that a specialist in, say, Argentine banking or U.S. labor law is needed. Sometimes it may not be so clear, and the policymaker must seek advice on potential advisers. Some first-rate specialists may not be good at taking a sufficiently general view, although they may be quite impressive in their own field of expertise. Some individuals may not be good at helping recognize that expertise from a different field is required. Such specialists may see the world only from the view of their own narrow specialty. Conversely, others may take an unduly narrow view of their expertise and say that they have nothing to offer on the problem.

Where appropriate, it is probably a good idea to seek the advice of both specialists and generalists, and to seek the advice of specialists from several relevant fields. This way, one gets expert advice less constrained by a narrow outlook. Also, later, when decisions based on the advice must be defended, those aggrieved by the decision may find it less easy to attack.

In 1980 the Food and Nutrition Board of the National Research Council issued a report on the efficacy of the dietary control of cholesterol as a means of reducing arteriosclerosis and heart disease (Food and Nutrition Board 1980). This report has been widely attacked by those who believe strongly in the efficacy of diet. The attack on this policy statement has been enhanced by the opponents' ability to criticize the report on the grounds that no experts were consulted from the field of epidemiology. Thus, not only must the process of selecting a panel of advisers be broad, but also in retrospect, its breadth needs to be evident.

Once we have determined the areas where we need advice, we must select individual advisers. Here, one must look at the track record of each individual: which advisers have proven themselves in the past? This question is difficult to answer. Some policymakers have consulted advisers frequently in the past and can rely on their own experience. Frequently, the policymaker must turn to others and consult colleagues about the reliability and accuracy of individual advisers. Some advisers may be expert in special fields, yet have difficulty communicating their knowledge to policy people. Aside from looking at the track record of an adviser, one can, of course, consider his or her qualifications, such as years of professional experience, offices held, research reputation, and publications. Unfortunately, such factors may be poor indicators of the adviser's ability to perform in a helpful way on a specific problem at a specific time. The adviser's past record of performance is a sounder guide.

Getting the Best from Advisers

How can we help our advisers to help us? Three issues come to mind: (1) are we asking the right question, (2) are we giving the advisers the help they need, (3) are we rewarding them adequately?

We ask an adviser for an opinion. Perhaps we ask for substantive, factual information or for a prediction. Although expert advisers have deep knowledge of a special field, we cannot count on their understanding problems from the standpoint of the policymaker. It is important that we clearly lay out the issue. Experts frequently feel they are being asked the wrong question, and frequently they are right. Sometimes, policymakers rush to seek expert advice before carefully thinking about the issues, before really identifying the problem.

Before seeking expert advice, the policymaker should try to construct a model or scheme of the process at hand. Even—no, especially—a tentative, oversimplified model may serve to focus ideas and aid thinking about the problem. (Our model for panel size in Chapter 13 illustrates this.) When experts are consulted, communication of the problem may be enhanced by the existence of a model. The policymaker will make sure that his or her advisers understand that the model and problem formulation are tentative and will seek their advice on how to modify them. Once the problem and the process are identified, the work of the expert adviser can begin. Policymakers can help advisers by supplying additional information as the advisers require it.

Sometimes the expert also needs assistance, such as library work, computing, secretarial support, or relief from current obligations. The opportunity to interact with other advisers may give the expert fresh insight on the problem or may suppress originality.

Often advisers are asked to supply free labor. Sometimes this occurs when the adviser is a member of one's own organization. If the committee or panel assignment is added to many other responsibilities, if the issue is not of special interest to the adviser, or if the adviser comes from a different branch of the organization, we may get less than a best effort.

Outside advisers or experts are also frequently called on and frequently not compensated for their work. As long as this makes only a brief intrusion into the adviser's or expert's time, this may not prove much of a problem. Many people like to be helpful. Most people are flattered at having their opinion sought, and most recognize the give-and-take in life. We are asking for the adviser's help this week; next week our roles may be reversed. However, we all know friends and acquaintances, to say nothing of strangers, who abuse this process. It is one thing to ask for one hour once, another to ask for one hour many times or several days at other times.

If we do not compensate people for their efforts, we almost ensure that we get only a small fraction of their attention. Admittedly, we each have had the experience of paying people and still getting small return. Nevertheless, if a problem is serious enough to involve our time, it may well be serious enough to get the best advice we can and to offer something in return for it.

We compensate people in many ways. Honor is one. The advisers may think that the policy issue is so important that it demands their best efforts. The adviser may see that only a small group has been selected for a panel and therefore feel that the contribution of each member counts for a lot. Washington uses this mechanism a great deal. As a committee or panel gets larger, it becomes more likely that individual members may devote less of themselves to the project than they would if the panel were smaller. For one thing, a large panel may tend to dilute in the member's eyes the importance of each one's contribution. Second, it makes interactions with the policymakers less obvious, and they are perhaps less able to acknowledge the efforts and importance of each panel member, whether economically or in other ways. One is always flattered to be asked to help, but the degree of pleasure one gets may be inversely proportional to the number of others similarly honored. Washington also uses the enormous panel, perhaps to excess.

Using Groups of Advisers

The traditional way to seek advice is by face-to-face discussion. It may be a solitary discussion, although there is some social stigma attached to being observed or overheard talking to oneself. (We understand, but cannot verify, that recent research gives approval to talking to oneself.) The policymaker may have a conversation with a single adviser, a series of conversations with individual advisers, face-to-face small-group discussions, or meetings of larger and larger committees.

Presenting a specific position to a small group and following up with a critical discussion can be most helpful.

When the advice of several people is to be asked, they may be contacted separately, the problem laid out individually, and the advice of each sought. While this makes sure that one gets the views of each adviser, it sacrifices the give-and-take of group interaction, the cross-fertilization of questions and answers, the chance that one adviser will gain insight from an idea or a new formulation offered by another adviser. In spite of repetition, working with several individuals may be speedier by far than convening a group.

Each of us has had the experience of having experts with apparently equivalent credentials give quite different advice on the same issue. (Multiple solutions may make conflicting advice perfectly reasonable.) In seeking advice from a panel or committee, we sometimes hope to replace this diversity by some convergence of opinion as the various advisers offer suggestions, ask questions, or share insights based on their varying backgrounds and perspectives. For equal costs, one ought to get greater reliability as the number in the panel or committee increases. Of course, we never find equal costs, and the problems of cumbersomeness, attention span, and quality control always arise as a group gets larger.

In addition, as we increase the size of a committee or a panel of advisers, we face the problem of handling the extra information produced. At some point, the advice must be reviewed by the policymaker. Policymakers want to receive as much input as they can, because information from additional people may be new and contain fresh insights. On the other hand, receiving and processing information have their own costs. Time is a cost, too. The optimum size of an advisory panel may depend on the value of new ideas, how frequently they occur to each additional panel member, and the cost of identifying an idea as a new one. For example, what is expressed as a new idea may, after examination, be revealed as simply an old, previously considered idea. (See the example of determining panel size in Chapter 13 on mathematical modeling.)

In groups face-to-face discussions can be hampered by (1) the influence of dominant individuals, (2) group pressure for conformity, or (3) confusion.

A committee can be highly influenced by rhetorical skill, and we all know from political debates the low correlation between rhetoric and knowledge. A group may be highly influenced by the opinion of a senior or powerful figure. People may be reluctant to disagree with Professor Famous, the most influential and distinguished authority in the field, or with old Mr. Longterm, who has dealt with these problems for thirty years. Whatever the reason, dominant figures greatly influence group opinion. Sometimes this is good, sometimes not.

The problem of dominant individuals can be somewhat reduced if the advisers communicate by mail. However, this process sacrifices a great deal of the ferment and the stimulation that occur when each member of a group can hear and immediately react to every other member's contributions, unless unusual care is taken to provide this feedback by methods we discuss later. Mail has the tremendous advantage of savings in time on the scene, because irrelevancies are reduced and one person can process the contradictions and disagreements for the policymaker. Polling a panel of advisers by mail is more like consulting each adviser individually than convening a panel or group meeting.

A second difficulty with group interaction is the group pressure for conformity. When most members of a group are convinced that a given answer is correct, it is hard for a small minority to defend a contrary view. This pressure for conformity may silence individual judgment and decrease the number of options produced for the policymaker. It also reduces the perception of uncertainty. Of course, one benefit frequently sought from a committee or panel of experts is some convergence on a corporate view.

A final disadvantage is unhelpful confusion. Much of the conversation in a committee or panel meeting is related not to problem-solving, or at least not to solving the policymaker's problem, but to other individual or group interests. Although it may appear to be oriented to the stated problem, much of this conversation is actually irrelevant and time-consuming, and may appear in the report in such a way that its irrelevance is not evident. It confuses us and diverts us from those thoughts that are sharply focused on the problem.

The Delphi Technique

The Delphi technique was developed in the early 1950s by Olaf Helmer and Norman Dalkey at the Rand Corporation. In the strategic bombing study (Dalkey and Helmer 1963) given as an example earlier in this chapter, Rand had been asked to estimate the number of Soviet atomic bombs required to produce specific levels of damage and to identify likely U.S. industrial targets. (This was not a question U.S. policymakers desired to put to an experiment or even to a less well-controlled observational study.) It seemed to be a matter particularly appropriate for solution by a panel of expert advisers.

The designers of the technique sought to avoid some of the drawbacks we have already discussed in face-to-face meetings of advisory panels. They used several questionnaires in an iterative fashion. The panel did not meet as a group. Between successive questionnaires, the individual panel members received continual feedback on the opinions stated by others. This controlled feedback of the group's responses to previous questionnaires did not reveal the authorship of particular opinions.

The experts estimated the numbers of atom bombs and their allocations among primary U.S. industrial targets. Questions were also posed to uncover the reasoning behind the estimates, the factors considered relevant to the problem, and the experts' assessment of these factors, as well as the kind of data that, if available, might result in a better appraisal of relevant factors and more confident estimates.

Highly respected or rhetorically skilled participants could not give undue influence to their own opinions. Each idea stood on its own. The artful use of continual feedback preserved much of the stimulating give-and-take of conventional debate.

At the same time, the Delphi process requires a great deal from its organizers. They must design an initial questionnaire to send to the panel. After that questionnaire is returned, they must summarize the results, provide feedback, and develop a second questionnaire. Ordinarily, the panel has at least one opportunity to revise its original answer or estimate, based on an examination of the anonymous responses of the group.

The success of a Delphi program clearly depends on the behavior of the organizers, who must be skillful and dispassionate at summarizing the responses of the panel. Otherwise, the questionnaires and the feedback can be subtly contaminated by the prejudices of the organizers. Individual advisers participating in a Delphi panel have the same needs that other advisers have. Because Delphi is frequently conducted by means of a mailed questionnaire, the organizers may not properly express their appreciation to panel members.

The panel members, as well as the organizers, must appreciate the demanding nature of Delphi work. Dropout rates can be high. The ease of approaching relative strangers by mail may entice Delphi organizers into sending many invitations in the hope of organizing a large panel. The panel actually recruited may consist of advisers who have not thought carefully enough about what they have undertaken and the time required to deliver. As the weary drop out, the panel gets smaller and may not be a good sample from the population that the organizers wanted to use. If the organizers are not conscious of this and if they are not careful in their appreciation and exploration of minority views, the dissenters will join the weary and thus generate an artificial consensus. They may later attack the findings.

As with any new technique, both good and bad results have emerged. Delphi is certainly most effective when the organizers are skillful, and it probably works better when the panel is modest rather than enormous. It has been used most often in forecasting (Linstone and Turoff 1975).

MERITS OF INTROSPECTION AND ADVICE

What kinds of problems respond well to the strategy of introspection? We need it when relevant data are not now available or cannot be acquired or accurately known even with appropriate effort. We find it particularly appropriate when the problem is obscure or complex, perhaps involving unknown variables or the interplay of known variables in ways not clearly understood. We seek its benefits when an important step is the outlining and balancing of pros and cons associated with potential policy options. It may be vital for understanding human motivations or clarifying the priorities of personal values.

By organizing a committee or panel of advisers, the policymaker can seek the opinions of experts from a variety of different fields and can include as members both generalists and specialists. Few would include incompetent advisers on a committee if they could be identified beforehand. Indeed, issues about the competence of experts or the relevance of their fields always arise, particularly in retrospect, from those who are aggrieved by the committee's advice.

Despite our jokes about committees, they are ingrained in our lives. We have a saying: "Two heads are better than one." If one asks for an estimate of a number by a panel or a committee, the median response of the committee should be at least no worse than half of the estimates by individual committee members and may, of course, be considerably better. For example, Knight (1921) asked students to estimate the temperature in a classroom. Although the individual estimates were highly inaccurate, ranging from 60 to 80 degrees, the mean rating of 72.4 degrees closely approximated the temperature of 72.0 degrees indicated by a thermometer (Epstein 1980, Stroop 1932).

Practically all important decisions, whether they affect large institutions or our own families, ultimately involve at least some issues that cannot be decided on the basis of solid information. We all know this and learn to live with it. Although such issues arise, *most* problems are readily solved on the basis of experience or superstition. Others are solved merely by the need for decision; the result may have no value, but the lack of decision would entail loss. Yet some problems do turn on issues we cannot resolve with available data, however excellent. Introspection then becomes our primary tool.

WEAKNESSES OF INTROSPECTION AND ADVICE

Introspection and advice are usually poor substitutes for solid information and should be used in those circumstances where data are inadequate for policymaking. Even then, too much use of introspection may discourage the search for relevant empirical data.

The major weakness of introspection and advice is that we humans are too sure of our guesses, too certain of our beliefs.

To examine the relation between empirical frequency and subjective belief about the range of an unknown number, Alpert and Raiffa (1969) questioned graduate students studying business or arts and sciences at Harvard University about their beliefs concerning various numerical values. For example, students were asked to guess the number of physicians listed in the Boston telephone directory by listing the median, the quartiles, and the 1 percent point and 99 percent point of their beliefs. In all, 100 students responded in this manner to 10 questions. The upshot was that 16 percent of the time the actual number was smaller than their 1 percent point, and 27 percent of the time the actual number was larger than their 99 percent point. To put it another way, if their subjective intervals agreed with empirical frequencies, the interval from the 1 percent point to the 99 percent point should have included the true number 98 percent of the time. Instead, it was correct only 57 percent of the time. Put the other way around, events that the students believed would occur about 2 percent of the time actually occurred 43 percent of the time.

What this means is that the students were too sure of their guesses. Their guesses were *less reliable* than they believed or reported them to be. When a forecasted event with a 2 percent chance of occurring happens, the forecaster should be surprised. The students would have been surprised nearly half the time.

Their centering was not as far off as their estimates of uncertainty. Instead of 50 percent, 44 percent of the true values were smaller than the guessed median.

Shapiro (1977) gives examples of wide variation among physicians' estimates of probabilities in therapeutic situations. This information is also relevant to our discussion but different from that of Alpert and Raiffa. Shapiro shows that physicians differ a good deal in their estimates; the Alpert-Raiffa study shows that people are much further off than they expect to be. Spetzler and Staël von Holstein (1975) give a good review of techniques for eliciting expert information on probabilities that avoid these and other forms of bias.

If accurate, reliable information can be found with an appropriate amount of effort, seek it. Introspection will rarely be better than good, relevant data.

QUALITY CHECKLIST

1. *Is this issue an empirical question, or does it turn on value judgments?*

2. *Is there time to do the research needed to obtain better data?*

3. *Do the costs of acquiring empirical data outweigh the expected benefits?*

4. *Do we need general or expert advice?*

5. *Is this an issue on which an expert can be expected to know something an ordinary person (I or my staff) does not?*

6. *Does asking for the advice commit us to follow it?*

7. *What are the advisers' personal interests or biases?*

8. *Is the advice sought within the advisers' field of expertise? Should advisers from other fields be consulted?*

9. *Are the advisers being adequately compensated for their advice?*

10. *Are we asking the right questions? Do the advisers understand the issues and appreciate our needs?*

11. *Can the advisers suggest appropriate research efforts?*

12. *Do the advisers agree? Is there a minority view?*

13. *How will the process look later? Will the decision appear well advised?*

14. *Should we get advice from additional people, perhaps if only to make the process look better?*

1. Empirical issue?
2. Research takes too long?
3. Research too costly?
4. Advice: general or expert?
5. Experts know better?
6. Advice commits us?
7. Advisers' biases?
8. Problem within advisers' fields?
9. Advisers compensated?
10. Problem understood?
11. Advisers suggest research?
12. Advisers agree?
13. Process look good?
14. Additional advisers?

POLICY IMPLICATIONS

Marjorie Olson has reviewed articles on the topic of science advising by seven scientific advisers to the President of the United States (Golden 1980). She has distilled the main points on the matter of advising from these articles, and these appear in the box on p. 270. Although advising the President on science is a very special job, many people in high places need advice, and similar considerations would apply. Although science is a special field, the features about advising associated with it seem to parallel those in other fields. The President's science adviser has a full-time job, staff assistants, and a program to develop, whereas advisers generally may not.

For advisers and policymakers who hold less imposing positions, we have translated this advice into the following points:

1. The adviser must relate well personally with the policymaker and meet often enough and know the situation well enough so that the advice is relevant, acceptable, and implementable.

2. The policymaker may be helped by the weight of the adviser's reputation.

*MARJORIE OLSON'S SUMMARY OF SCIENCE ADVISERS' VIEWS
ON PRESIDENTIAL ADVISING*

1. The relationship between President and adviser is all-important. Frequent direct contact is essential, and advice should be given with consideration for the President's interests, priorities, and assimilative capacity, and with broad political considerations, but not advocacy, in mind.

2. The science adviser should be a person of prominence and a generalist, backed up by a committee or group of advisers who are also generalists, with specialists brought in from time to time to give specific advice on narrow issues. The number of advisers and staff should be big enough so it is not dependent on one view, but not so big that it is unmanageable.

3. Advisers should exist to serve the Presidency, though they should still speak for science and the scientific community. The adviser must aid the President to appreciate the importance of science and to utilize the fundamental strength of scientific prestige. The President's advisers should not be expected to serve Congress.

4. The science adviser should not deal only with crises, but should be orderly, think ahead, and anticipate Presidential needs.

5. Advisers need full access to information and to all parts of the executive branch, including the Departments of Defense and State and the National Security Council.

6. The science adviser must work well with the Office of Management and Budget. The budget process is an important channel for influencing the massive events in which science and technology are involved.

7. Advice in private is desirable.

8. Advice is difficult, problems are complex, and not all are solvable.

Based on articles by former Presidential science advisers Edward E. David, Jr., Lee A. DuBridge, Donald F. Hornig, James R. Killian, Jr., Frank Press, I.I. Rabi, H. Guyford Stever, and Jerome B. Wiesner, in William T. Golden, ed., *Science Advice to the President*, New York: Pergamon Press Ltd., 1980.

3. As an adviser, one's prime loyalty must go to the policymaker. One cannot also serve the policymaker's potential antagonists.

4. A regular adviser has a program as well as a trouble-shooting role.

5. Advisers need access to information from all parts of the organization.

6. Regular advisers must work well with the financial side of the organization.

7. Although the policymaker may flaunt the adviser's advice to gain political support, the adviser should first advise in private.

8. The policymaker must understand that the adviser cannot solve all problems and that, if they were easy, no adviser would be needed.

CONCLUSION

If we do not have reliable data or if we do not understand the process sufficiently well, we first seek to remedy these defects. Introspection is generally second-best. However, in those cases where, for whatever reason, something better is not going to be found, we turn to ourselves and our advisers. We order what we know and assess the various factors, pro and con. We try to synthesize the relevant lessons from our past experiences and observations. We try to extrapolate from our past knowledge to the present problem.

The policymaker's approach to seeking advice will largely determine its value. Careful attention to selecting advisers and structuring their interaction with the policymaker and with one another will do the most to strengthen the results. The Delphi technique represents one novel approach to using a panel of advisers.

REFERENCES

Alpert, M., and Raiffa, H. 1969. A Progress Report on the Training of Probability Assessors. Unpublished paper. Cambridge, Mass.: Harvard University.

Churchill, W.S. 1949. *Their Finest Hour.* Book Two of *The Second World War.* Boston: Houghton Mifflin.

Dalkey, N., and Helmer, O. 1963. An Experimental Application of the Delphi Method to the Use of Experts. *Management Science* 9: 458.

Epstein, S. 1980. Stability of Behavior. *The American Psychologist* 35: 790–805.

Food and Nutrition Board. 1980. *Toward Healthful Diets.* Washington, D.C.: National Academy of Sciences.

Franklin, B. 1772. Letter to Joseph Priestley. In *The Benjamin Franklin Sampler.* New York: Fawcett, 1956.

Golden, W.T., ed. 1980. *Science Advice to the President.* New York: Pergamon Press.

Knight, H.C. 1921. A Comparison of the Reliability of Group and Individual Judgments. Unpublished master's thesis. New York: Columbia University.

Lerner, L. 1975. *A.R.T.H.U.R. The Life and Opinions of a Digital Computer.* Amherst, Mass.: University of Massachusetts Press. Also published in 1974 by Harvester Press, Hassocks near Brighton, England.

Linstone, H.A., and Turoff, M. 1975. *The Delphi Method—Techniques and Applications.* Reading, Mass.: Addison-Wesley.

NIH Consensus-Development Panel. 1980. Adjuvant Chemotherapy of Breast Cancer. *New England Journal of Medicine* 303: 831–832.

Shapiro, A.R. 1977. The Evaluation of Clinical Predictions. *New England Journal of Medicine* 296: 1509–1514.

Spetzler, C. S., and Staël von Holstein, C. S. 1975. Probability Encoding in Decision Analysis. *Management Science* 22: 340–358.

Stroop, J.R. 1932. Is the Judgment of the Group Better than That of the Average Member of the Group? *Journal of Experimental Psychology* 15: 550–562.

FURTHER READING

Golden, W.T., ed. 1980. *Science Advice to the President.* New York: Pergamon Press.

Linstone, H.A., and Turoff, M. 1975. *The Delphi Method—Techniques and Applications.* Reading, Mass.: Addison-Wesley.

PART IV

Special Issues

CHAPTER 15

Have Things Gone Awry?

We begin our treatment of errors with the more modest everyday difficulties and work up to deliberate frauds. No matter how careful a study, mistakes are likely to occur, and we must be careful not to be dazzled by the technologist's expertise or the reporter's assurances that all is well. Computers provide a steady source of difficulties because they do such complicated things and so many of them. The newspapers frequently remind us of these mistakes, such as the issuing of a million-dollar welfare check to an individual.

So many "impossible" events occur that we can almost believe in gremlins or, to use a more literary allusion, in the men from Porlock. A man from Porlock banged on the door and pulled the poet Samuel Taylor Coleridge out of his spell when he was creating the poem *Kubla Khan.* He never finished it. A science fiction writer (Jones 1947) memorialized this idea by suggesting that a superior culture has infiltrated ours with "men from Porlock," and whenever we are about to make a major breakthrough, a Porlockian deliberately causes a mistake that stops us. These men from Porlock assume important but unobtrusive roles—chief lab assistant, vice-president, deputy secretary—and are poised to spoil any advance. Their work explains why the error made is the one mistake that can spoil the whole study, or why the broken equipment is the only piece crucial for all major systems, or why the wrecked experiment in a series is the only one that cannot be reproduced for another decade. Although these fanciful ideas are humorous to practicing scientists and technologists, in daily work they often feel that nature harasses them nearly this severely. And so they have to be ever vigilant in checking for mistakes. We turn now to a variety of strategies for checking.

CHECKING FOR MAGNITUDE

If certain numbers are important findings in a study, it is wise to take a look at their magnitude and check them in some manner. Several approaches can be considered.

Find a Useful Number

Sometimes a known number can be located to compare with a dubious number.

Example: Welfare "Reform"

We are told that a program will reduce the number of persons on welfare by 100,000 in a small state. We might be impressed, but we should try to check the number. We could start by trying to find out how many people are on welfare currently. Such a figure, while "soft," is likely to be available in one or more forms. If it turns out that only 100,000 are now on welfare, however broadly defined, something has come unstuck. We may get this number from the appropriate government agency, from a reference library (see Chapter 9 on official statistics), or even from a special sample survey or some other original data-gathering method, if the matter is sufficiently important.

Bounds

Sometimes crude bounds on the probable value of a number may help locate errors.

Example: Cost of Education

If we wonder how much education costs us per pupil, we might try to set bounds. In 1978, for teacher, physical plant, and materials, it must cost at least $2/day per student, or around $400 for the year. For a class of 30, this would barely pay a starting teacher's salary. It does not seem likely that the annual cost is as much as $3000 per student, because expensive private universities charge on the order of $6000 for tuition. The bounds may not be close enough to be useful, but they can catch gross errors. (According to the 1979 *Statistical Abstract*, all but one city reported annual per-pupil costs under $3000.)

Triangulation

Getting at a number in several ways is comforting when the different approaches more or less agree. This method of checking is sometimes called "triangulation."

Example: Total Driving Miles*

How far did the American motorist drive in 1972? How one manipulates numbers may be rather personal, so the discussion is given partly in the first person singular to emphasize that others might work differently.

Approach 1. There are 93,000,000 cars registered in the United States, according to the 1972 *World Almanac.* They probably average between 6000 and 20,000 miles per year apiece. I use 6000 as the low figure because I average 6000 miles in my car, which all my friends tell me is very little; I use 20,000 as the high figure because those who drive this much are said to be driving a lot. As a compromise, let us

*From Fairley/Mosteller, *Statistics and Public Policy,* © 1977, Addison-Wesley Publishing Company, Inc., pages 175–176. Reprinted with permission.

use 11,000, the geometric mean between these limits. Then the total mileage for cars is $(9.3 \times 10^7) \times (1.1 \times 10^4) \approx 10 \times 10^{11} = 10^{12}$, which is about 1 trillion miles.

Approach 2. The U.S. gasoline use for 1970 was 2.2×10^6 thousand 42-gallon barrels (1972 *World Almanac*). If it were all used by cars and cars averaged 12 miles per gallon (perhaps an overestimate, as people tend to exaggerate their mileage), we would have 92×10^9 gallons all told. Since $92 \times 12 \approx 1100$, this gives us about 1.1 trillion miles.

Although the agreement between 1 and 1.1 is close, we cannot be satisfied, because perhaps a quarter of this fuel is used for trucks and other equipment. This would cut our estimate to about 825 billion miles. Modest changes in miles per gallon in Approach 2 and of miles per year in Approach 1 would put these numbers into agreement. The range based on these two approaches seems to be 800 to 1100 billion miles.

Approach 3. Look the number up in the *World Almanac*, remembering that the number is only an order-of-magnitude estimate. This approach is a version of Approach 2.

An Additional Example for Estimation of Magnitudes

In using willingness-to-pay methods to assess the value of a life lost by hazardous work, Bailey (1980) obtained a variety of estimates based on past research. Adjusting them to 1978 dollars and distinguishing between values for death and for permanent disablement, Bailey found that the values ranged from about \$170,000 to \$5,000,000. The values he had the most confidence in were centered around \$360,000. He wanted to assess the reasonableness of the larger figures. To do this, he asked what the insurance payment would need to be to reduce the average risk of death for all members of a family of 4 making \$18,500 per year from an annual risk of 6 per 1000 to 5.5 per 1000. This drop is what the United States achieved in the interval from 1970 to 1975. The difference is also about half that between the risk in the average job and that for jobs labeled hazardous. He found values running from \$300 to \$1400 per year for the values he thought more reliable. For a value of \$5,000,000, the insurance premium would be \$10,000, a value he regarded as unreasonable.

SMOOTHNESS

Plotting one variable against another sometimes suggests a possibility of error, as Figure 15-1 illustrates. The median height of boys is plotted for each age from 1 to 16 years. Note that the relationship is smooth

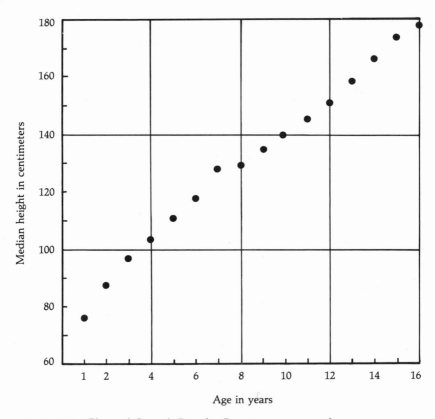

FIGURE 15-1   *Physical Growth Rate for Boys 1 to 16 years of age.*

except for the point at age 7, height 128.6, which we suspect is an error. We first check our plotting from the data in Table 15-1; it does show a height of 128.6 for age 7. We next check *Vital and Health Statistics,* Series 11, Number 165, *National Center for Health Statistics Growth Curves for Children, Birth–18 Years, United States* (U.S. Department of Health, Education, and Welfare, November 1977, p. 20), and find that we had copied the height incorrectly—it should have been 123.6 instead of 128.6. This correction would bring the point into line with the other points.

MODELING

A third method of checking is to try to create a model of the process leading to the number and, by using various pieces of information, get an estimate. (See Chapter 13 on modeling.)

TABLE 15-1   *Physical growth rate for boys from 1 to 16 years of age*

Age	Median Height (centimeters)	Age	Median Height (centimeters)	Age	Median Height (centimeters)	Age	Median Height (centimeters)
1	76.2	5	110.9	9	135.2	13	158.3
2	87.7	6	117.4	10	140.4	14	166.1
3	96.5	7	128.6	11	145.6	15	173.9
4	103.6	8	129.5	12	151.0	16	178.4

WARNING SIGNALS

Although it is valuable to check the sizes of numbers that seem important, sometimes the situation has symptoms that emit substantial warning signals. A few of these follow.

Premature Publicity

When a program promises publicly to solve problems society has been struggling with for millenia, it is time to worry. Newspaper claims of cures for cancer to be available in three years should be viewed with great skepticism. Perhaps an advance has been made in treating a special kind of cancer, but we can afford to doubt large claims.

Less spectacularly, a new method of teaching that improves reading of all children by 50 percent can use a lot of doubting—5 percent improvement maybe, 50 percent no. Small valuable improvements do sometimes occur when social innovations are introduced, but rarely huge ones.

Usually such large effects have been observed in a special group treated in an unusual way, and often with poor controls. (See Hugo Muench's laws in Chapter 2 on experiments.)

New Mechanism

A new engine is going to reduce fuel consumption by 75 percent while doing all the work of the old engine. Its brand new design makes this possible. Without knowing a thing about the matter, we can afford to doubt such a claim. By and large, new designs have many problems, and such claims will simmer down. If it turns out that seawater has been discovered as a cheap fuel, the surprise should be enough to warn us.

Lack of Reproducibility

When one investigator claims to get an important effect and other competent investigators cannot verify it, instead of taking sides, we should probably wait and see. If the successful investigator seems to be playing a martyr's role instead of explaining what the others are doing wrong, we have further reason for suspicion.

Self-Interest

Needless to say, if public acceptance of a claim or estimate would serve someone's own interest, especially when that person is the source of the claim or estimate, we should be suspicious. An economic forecasting method that has "hit it right on the nose" will need a lot of prospective rather than retrospective testing before we give it credence; and the forecasting rules need to be laid out publicly, hard and fast, in advance. Even a prospective study can be misleading if the forecaster is allowed to choose one from among many different forecasts. When a forecaster's "on the nose" method fails, claims that some standard adjustment was not made but would have made the forecast "on the nose" can be calmly set aside.

PROTECTION AGAINST HOAXES AND FRAUDS

In some instances, rather simple routine measures can do a lot of good. A case in the 1930s involving a drug company illustrates this. On paper the company had warehouses full of valuable products, but in fact these warehouses did not exist; the financial position of the company was misrepresented by its books. Apparently, routine auditing at that time did not include checking the existence of warehouses and their contents.

On the other hand, elaborate, carefully developed frauds usually yield only to bad luck on the side of the perpetrators or long-term investigation by experts. Sufficient prevention of fraud would probably halt the wheels of science and commerce.

Nevertheless, some measures can be taken if the issue is such that the danger of fraud seems great. Try to have more than one person involved in supplying data. One person may be dishonest, but the chances of two or three being dishonest are smaller. While elaborate conspiracies occasionally occur, they are rare. For the same reason, try to have more than one research team supply the data, and cross-check one team's material against the other's. Look for self-interest. Does one or another data source have a vested interest in the outcome? Set a good example. Never let a subordinate think you are interested in anything but the unvarnished data. Make sure your group does not become emotionally committed to one outcome. Occasionally, a worker, trying to be helpful, will tamper with the data to "make it come out the right way." Get rid of any data source you find is dishonest.

REFERENCES

Bailey, M.J. 1980. *Reducing Risks to Life: Measurement of the Benefits.* Washington D.C.: American Enterprise Institute for Public Policy Research.

Jones, R.F. 1947. The Person from Porlock. *Astounding Science Fiction* 47 (August): 96–115.

Mosteller, F. 1977. Assessing Unknown Numbers: Order of Magnitude Estimation. In *Statistics and Public Policy*, W. Fairley and F. Mosteller, eds. Reading, Mass.: Addison-Wesley.

FURTHER READING

Mosteller, F. 1977. Assessing Unknown Numbers: Order of Magnitude Estimation. In *Statistics and Public Policy*, W. Fairley and F. Mosteller, eds. Reading, Mass.: Addison-Wesley, pp. 163–184.

CHAPTER 16

Privacy and Confidentiality

The basic notion that information leads to better decisions and therefore benefits society conflicts with a deeply held belief in our right to privacy. The conflict is complex, both ethically and statistically, and is the subject of intensive study, debate, and legislation. This brief chapter gives an overview of the dimensions of the problem and the current state of resolution.

We must first define the terms "privacy" and "confidentiality," which might appear to refer to the same thing but actually have different meanings. *Privacy* is the right of individuals to determine what information about themselves they wish to share with others. The U.S. Privacy Act of 1974, among other things, prevents the invasion of personal privacy. The Act provides a means for individuals to learn what information about themselves the government has and how it is used. In addition, the Act gives an individual some control over the information he or she supplies to the federal government.

Confidentiality refers to the status of records maintained by the government or other organizations. Government agencies frequently collect information from individuals with the promise that it will be held confidentially—will not be further disseminated. Confidentiality can have different degrees, and an agency often specifies the degree when it collects the data. The agency may promise not to disclose the information in a way that would allow the identification of any individual. For instance, the collectors may promise to publish the data only as averages or proportions for groups of individuals. Sometimes agencies give specific guarantees, such as not to use the data for regulation, inspection, or investigation. For instance, in its attempt to learn about the causes of air traffic accidents, the Federal Aviation Administration (FAA) asks pilots, crew, and flight controllers to report on all "near-misses." To make this request credible, the FAA promises not to use the information in any way against the providers.

Three considerations govern society's approach to confidentiality of statistical records. First, the accuracy of some kinds of data depends strongly on assurances of confidentiality by the collector and on perceptions about these promises by the provider. Respondents consider the reputations of specific agencies, of the statistical profession, and of the government as a whole. During the 1980 census, assuring the public of the U.S. Census Bureau's unblemished record, especially in protecting information about illegal aliens, was an important aspect of the Bureau's public relations activities.

Second, we believe that democracy works best when the government's decision-making and administrative information is available to the public. This is the basis of the U.S. Freedom of Information Act of 1974, which provides for public access to government information. Thus, there must be provisions for disseminating data for analysis by others.

Third, the amount of effort and burden required of the respondent should be minimized. For many problems, it is simpler, less costly, and more accurate to obtain information already collected by another agency directly from that agency, rather than asking an individual to supply it again. The U.S. Federal Reports Act of 1942 and the work of the Commission on Federal Paperwork specify the conditions and procedures for government agencies to share information.

Agencies in the public sector use data in two very different ways, and the distinction affects the way we think about confidentiality. Often policy analysts need not identify the individual cases with which they deal. Familiar "statistical uses" involve taking averages, computing proportions, and making other more complex analyses of data, but these do not require individual identification in either the analysis or reporting phase of the work. Only processing and quality control require identification of records, and the identification can be removed before analysis takes place. The U.S. National Center for Health Statistics regards the individual records gathered for purposes of aggregate analysis as "protected data" and is required by law not to disclose them under any circumstances (Simmons 1980).

In contrast, other data refer to actions or decisions dealing with specific individuals or entities. These activities include licensing, inspection, regulation, reimbursing, and charging. The National Center for Health Statistics refers to these data as "case-action data." In addition to their primary purpose, aggregates of such data serve many useful statistical purposes, as we discuss in Chapter 8 on management records.

Because only statistical uses are intended or allowed, it is useful and proper to extend full guarantees of confidentiality to protected data. Case-action data present a more difficult problem. Sometimes an operations agency passes data to another agency for analysis. How much further the data can be disseminated, and for what purposes, should be clearly stated. Normally, we prohibit the use of the data for further case action, but we allow statistical uses that omit identification of individuals.

Different components of data required for some analyses are often collected and stored separately by different agencies. For instance, an investigation of the health effects of occupational exposure to a chemical requires information on both health status and previous work experience. The Health Care Financing Administration has protected medical records for large segments of the population covered by Medicare, and the Social Security Administration has employment records. *Data linkage* combines information from two such sources into one file for analysis. Researchers match information about each individual in the first source with other information about the same individual from the second source. The final statistical analysis does not identify individuals, yet matching requires that individuals be identified in each source file. Data linkage between agencies can help to reduce the paperwork burden and sometimes leads to more accurate figures. But the necessity of identifying individuals may conflict with promises of confidentiality.

The conflict between society's right to know and the individual's right of privacy is deep and not easily resolved. In the course of gathering data, policymakers must make choices about sources of data, how they are recorded and stored, and how the results are transmitted, and at each step they must balance the ethical and legal costs and benefits of alternative proposals.

REFERENCE

Simmons, W.R. 1980. *Issues Regarding Confidentiality of Data in the Cooperative Health Statistics Systems.* Vital and Health Statistics, Series 4, Number 22, Documents and Committee Reprints. Washington, D.C.: National Center for Health Statistics, DHEW publication no. (PHS) 80-1459.

FURTHER READING

Boruch, R.F., and Cecil, J.S. 1979. *Assuring the Confidentiality of Social Research Data*. Philadelphia: University of Pennsylvania Press.

National Academy of Sciences, Committee on Federal Statistics. 1979. *Report of the Panel on Privacy and Confidentiality as Factors in Survey Response*. Washington, D.C.: National Academy of Sciences.

Privacy Protection Study Commission. 1977. *Personal Privacy in an Information Society*. Washington, D.C.: U.S. Government Printing Office.

Simmons, W. R. 1980. *Issues Regarding Confidentiality of Data in the Cooperative Health Statistics Systems*. Vital and Health Statistics, Series 4, Number 22, Documents and Committee Reprints. Washington, D.C.: National Center for Health Statistics, DHEW publication no. (PHS) 80-1459

The journal *IRB, A Review of Human Subjects Research*, published by The Hastings Center (360 Broadway, Hastings-on-Hudson, New York 10706), deals regularly with ethical issues going beyond those treated in this chapter.

CHAPTER 17

Summary of General Questions and Issues

In discussing specific methods, we listed questions that a policymaker might profitably ask in gauging the strength of a study. Some questions, common to any study, raise general issues that deserve to be summarized, and we review these here, not as they impinge on single methods of data gathering, but as they suggest broad principles worth attention.

1. *Are the questions clearly stated and relevant to the policy issues?* Unfocused studies, while sometimes useful, generally waste time. Fishing expeditions sometimes get fish but rarely answer important policy questions. Policymakers who plan or evaluate a study usually should ask that a specific question, or questions, be stated. Generally, the best way to find something is to go out and look for it, to conduct a systematic search with an identified object in mind. If you have no object in mind, or only a vague one, this suggests the need for further planning before starting the investigation. As a policymaker, you have a special obligation to make sure that your data gatherers know what information you want.

If data gathering is to form the basis for a policy decision, any investigation should be aimed at the policy issue. Occasionally, information gathered for one purpose or to answer one question will bear on another, but most often answers obtained will apply to the questions asked, not to some other problem or question. It is always pleasant to discover that something done for one purpose is good for another, but the best route in policy-oriented investigations is likely to be straight and directed at the issue. Again, the policymaker must spend time with the data gatherers to make sure that they know what is required.

2. *Is the study practicable, timely, and affordable?* An investigation that is not feasible deserves no further consideration. Policymakers should require evidence at the start that proposed projects are feasible and can be done in an appropriate time span. When a policy decision is in the offing, the timing of an investigation is important. Late information, no matter how relevant, cannot influence a decision already made. Of course, good information coming to light after a decision will be useful when the question is reopened at a later date, as it almost surely will be. A policy decision at any one time rarely represents the final word on the subject. Nevertheless, we do place a high premium on having information available before the decision is made, and policymakers commissioning studies must keep this in mind.

If a study is viewed as an effort to inform a specific decision, the evaluator must choose between a data-gathering strategy to produce the needed data immediately, and thus inform the decision, and a strategy for generating knowledge that has consequences beyond the immediate decision. It is probably useful for the organizers of a study to be as explicit as possible when describing their choice of data collection procedures and to explain the possible trade-offs. If, for the sake of timeliness, procedures are chosen that are clearly second-best, a clear statement of that fact can go at least part way toward defusing arguments about its strengths and weaknesses.

Three items need special consideration: true calendar, time for appreciation, and hustled work. First, much policy work moves slowly because so many steps are necessary. It is probably fair to say that the true calendar usually offers much more time for study than the one posted in the policymaker's mind. In the first years of the work of the National Academy of Sciences' Institute of Medicine, its program committee decided that it was too late to begin a study of national health insurance, because the matter would be settled before the Institute could make a contribution. At the Institute's tenth anniversary, members of the program committee were wondering again whether it was not time to make a study of national health insurance. Often we have plenty of time for a good study.

Second, when a study has been completed, the policymaker needs a little time to let its implications marinate. First thoughts are not always the best.

Third, the choice sometimes seems to be between throwing something together in time for the policy discussion or leaving matters to take their course. To illustrate, an excellent doctoral student was writing a careful dissertation on certain financial issues concerning elections. Legislators, hearing of his work, asked him to come and testify and submit materials, even though the research was far from finished, "because we need your guidance now, and later will be too late." How flattering. Who could resist?

The student presented his half-developed research. The opponents cheerfully pointed out the weaknesses of the study because of the missing work, probably destroying the study for all time and damaging the student's reputation. The study was ultimately completed and well done. In the end, the proposed legislation was not taken forward at that time, and the student's contribution probably amounted to nothing, whereas the full study at later hearings might have had an impact had it not been prematurely tainted.

Half-baked studies produced under the excuse of timeliness invite disaster.

We are eager for all the information we can get, yet information has costs, and costs must bear some relationship to expected benefits and available resources. A feasible and timely study may cost more than you are willing to pay. Yet it is important to make sure you are paying enough. Sometimes research groups are so eager to supply information that they offer to do it for less than its cost. Often they do this after policymakers have driven a hard bargain on costs. We are all used to the marketplace and to cost negotiation. At the same time, remember it is you, the purchaser, who will want to use and depend on the information furnished. Cost containment and free-market bargaining have their place, but true bargains are rare. If a contract price is too low, you may receive shoddy merchandise rather than a bargain. Sometimes it is hard to be sure which you have purchased, and time constraints may make it hard to go back and get better-quality information later. It will certainly be expensive if you find this necessary.

3. *Are the assumptions implicit in the study valid?* We almost always make a series of simplifying assumptions, circumstances we must take as given for the study to proceed. Perhaps these are the values of input variables, perhaps a simulation or model of the way a process works, or perhaps an assumption about the comparability of groups. To the extent that these assumptions are confirmed by past experience, by well-verified theory, or by reliable data, our confidence in the investigation is advanced. If, on the other hand, the basic assumptions of the

study seem shaky, the results are likely to seem shaky as well. You need to review the assumptions before deciding what confidence you will have in the information derived from the study. Will you feel able to make policy on this basis?

4. *Does the track record of the investigators suggest that they will do a competent job?* Even the best-planned investigation can be wrecked by poor execution. You will want to look at the training and experience of the investigators. Are they up to the job? What have they done in the past? Have they any biases that may affect their work? Biases are curious things. Everybody has them, and in some studies they appear strongly to affect the work we do. Knowing the biases of the investigators may affect the confidence you have in their work. For example, if a scholar known to have a strong liberal bent seems to reach a conclusion favored by conservatives, a neutral observer may find the conclusion unusually convincing. The reputation of the investigators can make a study more compelling than an examination of the report alone would support.

5. *Are the data-gathering methods carefully documented? Do they appear solid?* If you intend to use the results of a study as a basis for policy, you must have confidence in the way the data were collected. You will be most confident if you know and understand exactly how information was gathered; if you can check that the specified measures were taken; and if, all things considered, the method seems valid and likely to produce solid, reliable information. If you lack confidence in the way the basic data were gathered, you will probably lack confidence in the results of the study, and rightly so.

Although policy analysts inevitably debate the methodological details of an evaluation, and distinguished scientists, social or natural, may have sharp disagreements on what the data show, they should not be debating how the data were gathered. That information should be well documented and available to everyone. Policy is politics. Documentation may not help win an argument about the origins of the numbers, but good documentation, however time-consuming, is fundamental to a well-conducted study. It focuses debate on findings and implications. These remarks about documentation apply also to data analysis.

6. *Does the study report outline and discuss difficulties encountered?* Almost any investigation will meet problems along the way. How well these problems are dealt with will influence your views about the study, the investigators, and the results obtained. If no difficulties are

mentioned, you should fear that some may have been concealed, unless the study is so simple as to present no problems, even for an idiot.
Always ask about difficulties encountered and insist on a careful discussion of them.

Although most of us fear or despise extensive footnotes and discussions of difficulties and departures from plan, these are the hallmarks of work by honest, responsible investigators. Unfortunately,
the opposition may try to take advantage of such honesty to discredit
good work. You must recognize that big studies always have some
flaws and that the question is whether the flaws are substantial enough
to undermine the conclusions. The serious critic—and, if the study has
been done for you, you should be a serious critic—asks how much difference the flaws can make and asks the analysts to prepare information on this issue. Irwin Bross (1960) regards this as the job of the responsible critic; still, the critic may not have the skill, information, or
inclination to make careful estimates, whereas the original investigators may have these traits.

7. *To whom or to what are the results generalizable?* We almost never
do a study for information only about the subjects examined. We usually hope to extrapolate information from the study, to generalize it to
a wider group of individuals or activities. The extent to which information derived from a study is generalizable to the population that the
policymaker cares about is a major factor in the usefulness of an investigation for policy purposes. The report should make clear the population to which it applies.

8. *Are the results reasonable?* This is a basic question. Do you believe
the results of the study? Do they require us to repeal the law of gravity
or the second law of thermodynamics? Do the results confirm or deny
your past experience, or what you have come to believe about human
nature? Some aspects of this issue are discussed in Chapter 15 ("Have
Things Gone Awry?"). If the results of a study seem unreasonable,
they ought to be checked, cross-checked, and rechecked. Unreasonable results frequently turn out to be wrong, and some explanation for
unusual findings should be supplied in the report. Of course, conventional wisdom occasionally turns out to be wrong. But, although the
race is not always to the swift, nor the battle to the strong, as Damon
Runyon said, that's the way to bet.

To sum up, a feasible, timely, well-baked study depends on practical assumptions and pointed questions posed by the policymaker. A
good report documents data gathering and analyzes its weaknesses as

well as strengths, confirms the study's reasonableness, and generalizes its findings to appropriate populations. The policymaker still has to decide how to apply the results.

REFERENCE

Bross, I.D.J. 1960. Statistical Criticism. *Cancer* 13:394–400. Reprinted 1970 in *The Quantitative Analysis of Social Problems*, E.R. Tufte, ed. Reading, Mass.: Addison-Wesley, pp. 97–108.

CHAPTER 18

Strengthening the System

Our tour through the ways of assembling information for policy has led from controlled experiments through introspection and advice. The diversity of these methods reflects the great range of situations where a policymaker may need to marshall data before making a decision. Each method has its strengths and weaknesses; each is powerful in some situations but useless in others. By bringing these strategies into sharper, more comparative focus, we hope to smooth the policymaker's path; but we cannot shift the responsibility. The choice of strategy still rests, as it must, on the policymaker's judgment and skill.

What enables us to choose strong information for policy is the broad existing information system. We have a relative luxury in that so many organizations in both the private and public sectors routinely collect, organize, and present information useful for policy. In this concluding chapter we argue that this system must be maintained and strengthened. Accomplishing this requires the public, as well as policymakers, to develop an appreciation for the process of using information to improve society. We turn now to five factors that tie information-gathering systems to the conduct of policy: the role of the public, issues for those who commission policy research, issues for those who supply information, issues for those who use it, and steps we feel will be important for the future.

THE ROLE OF THE PUBLIC

Since good information underlies much of good policy, an enlightened public must understand when and why information is needed, and why they are asked to supply it. This understanding is not sufficiently widespread.

First, the public needs to think about confidentiality and the trade-offs implied by wishing for as much of it as possible. For example, many influential people think, on the one hand, that our census should be voluntary and, on the other hand, express distress at an undercount.

We mentioned in Chapter 16 on privacy and confidentiality that we need personal identification of individual records in order to link one set of records with another for statistical purposes. But after the link is made, the names or identifiers are no longer needed; they can and should be erased. The public needs to appreciate this. For example, we have many records of exposure to environmental hazards and many records of diseases, but we have done little to link exposure and disease. Progress in prevention requires such linkage. If we want to know about exposure to environmental hazards, possibly through employment, we need to link health records with employment records, and we need to do so in a manner that will not be disadvantageous to the citizen whose data are linked. Citizens need to understand the benefits of allowing record linkage and to insist on the protection of confidentiality afforded by such agencies as the U.S. Bureau of the Census, which has an especially good record in the area of confidentiality. Its confidentiality regulations for employees have strong teeth; more important, the Bureau maintains a proud tradition and a policy of indoctrination to sustain protection of information. This branch of the government, then, offers one corps for organizing and linking statistical information for purposes of study.

The public has the choice, of course, of rejecting such investigations and paying for ineffectively designed, but expensive and weaker, programs of protection from environmental hazards. This is just one of many examples of data needs.

Second, if we are to have effective investigations in a democratic society, the people need to have faith in the good will of the investigators, in the potential value of the investigations, in the equity of the arrangements, and in the precautions being taken. It should be true that social, medical, and policy investigations are carried out for the benefit of the participants.

Without well-justified trust, we cannot expect people to consent to participate in experiments, surveys, or other investigations; to finance them; or to follow the indications of their results. To achieve such trust, people need to be informed about the importance of data gathering for their own well-being. They need to understand that, to know the effect of changing a system, we must change it. They need to know that things often do not work as expected—not just as a joke, but as a practical, everyday feature of life. Therefore, we should educate the public about the need for investigations and the citizen's essential part in them.

To show that cooperation and trust do pay off, we should publicize the successes of such data gathering ventures, explaining how all the components were necessary. We must also highlight the role of participating organizations, so that they receive appropriate credit for upholding the trust placed in them. Without a continuing effort to keep this meritorious but often unglamorous service before the public eye, it will generally go unnoticed and be little valued.

COMMISSIONING POLICY RESEARCH

A special responsibility falls to those who have the privilege of commissioning and organizing policy research. They have an opportunity to improve the quality of life for many citizens. Accomplishing this goal, whether through government or private organizations, will be helped by a firm appreciation of certain relationships between policy research and real societal change.

First, although the innocent may hope that the findings of a study will settle a policy matter, the sophisticated know that such a result is rare. They know too that political considerations weigh heavily in any large policy move. Other policies are usually already entrenched, and changes may mean loss of benefits for some groups. Yet the wise do not jump to the conclusion that data have little value; they know that data help policymakers see which options remain viable. We can pay $20,000,000 to save a life, or even a few lives, but we cannot afford this for each of a million lives. Thus, information sets boundaries and limitations, and sometimes opens up opportunities.

Second, our discussion in Chapter 2 suggests that, when carefully evaluated, only about half of our innovations provide improvements. Except for revolutionary discoveries, in such well-worked fields as medicine and education, our experience is that, even when present, improvements are modest—a few percent. Nevertheless, such gains are extremely valuable when applied to a large group; a 5 percent reduction in deaths is impressive. To detect these small improvements and retain them requires careful evaluation. This news says that it is hard to make large improvements in a society with substantial democratic constraints, especially where many solutions to problems have already been tried and have failed. It is also true of systems that are working rather well, for they are hard to improve.

SUPPLYING INFORMATION FOR POLICY

Throughout this book we have suggested both strengths and caveats for different ways of gathering information. Within cost limitations policy analysts should try to acquire the strongest and most informative data to answer their questions. In an imperfect world studies occasionally cannot be organized around the best kind of data. Sometimes even studies using an ideal design have flaws: measurement errors, dropouts, imperfect instruments, missing data, and the like. Our strong advice here is to make sure that flaws in the study are noted carefully by the investigators, not brought out as surprises by opponents. All investigators encounter obstacles and settle for some imperfections in study design and execution, but reports on results sometimes avoid mentioning these problems. Progress in overcoming imperfections would be more rapid if the important pitfalls and practical problems were more often reported, so that others could learn from them. If a report says nothing of the rough edges that everyone knows must be present, then the thoughtful, prudent reader will ask what else is being hidden.

Second, those who supply data as well as analysis should not be surprised if users with opposing purposes question the interpretation or meaning of a data set. How can the same data be used to support two conflicting sides of an argument? Opponents on an issue often have different conceptions of what this world is or should be like. Arguments about the fair profit of a business depend on what components are used as a base, capital investment or sales, for example. The worth of a public project may depend on the choice of the annual discount rate used to bring the future value to the present. Should it be 2 percent or 20 percent? We always have plenty of room for argument about the meaning of a study, even if we take the facts as firm.

USING POLICY RESEARCH

First, grave social problems have usually been worked on for decades, and we will continue to wrestle with them. Thus, the complaint about the time required for investigating particular treatments should not be as urgent a criticism as it often seems. It may be hard for short-term legislators and executives to develop enthusiasm for programs that cannot be carried out within their terms of office. We have not seen a good investigation of this question, however. Many bills in Congress and many executive programs require a long time to carry out—cancer programs, waterways systems, and highways, for example. The argument about short-sighted office holders has clear counterexamples. Many congressmen and senators serve more than one term and, despite election pressures, are more far-seeing than they are given credit for. The average number of terms already served by incumbent congressmen, including the current term, has run between 5 and 6 in recent years (Stigler 1981).

Second, research often has its greatest effect cumulatively over time. Rein and White (1977) and Lindblom and Cohen (1979) have argued that a single study, even when very well done, rarely leads to a major policy action if the result goes against the common wisdom. But an accumulation of evidence may eventually lead to action, as the results begin to sink in over time and change the prevailing climate of opinion. Accumulated evidence may also make its mark if it represents several studies, conducted by different research teams using different methods of gathering data and reaching similar conclusions. For example, evaluations of the first youth job training programs found that most of them were not particularly successful (National Research Council 1974). Critics pointed out that almost all of these studies were observational, not experimental. In the late 1970s several experiments were conducted, with similarly disappointing results. The consequence is that the diversity of data showing similar results convinced even the supporters of these programs that they were not working very well in their present form (Kemper and Moss 1978, Stromsdorfer and Farkas 1980).

A third point concerns disappointing findings. A policy analysis may require much money, time, and care, only to discover that an innovation is not working. When this happens, we unfortunately tend to complain about the messenger rather than the facts. One has to realize not only that carrying on ineffective programs is expensive in immediate costs, but also that these ineffective programs become roadblocks for future progress.

Fourth, proponents of a position often maintain that, although the data are not very good, they are all we have, and therefore something should be made of them. However, it is perfectly reasonable to make little or nothing of a bad set of data. Our checklists can help policymakers decide when the data are good enough to influence their actions. Sets of data vary widely in strength; when none are adequate, even after a new attempt to fill the gap, it is better to explain the deficiency rather than use inadequate information. Accepting poor data and blundering ahead may force us to repudiate the policy later, when better data come along, amid accusations that the data problems were well-known all along.

WHAT THE FUTURE SHOULD HOLD

A few further steps, although modest, would support information collection and policymaking.

When a study has gathered important data, their usefulness seldom ends with the conclusion of the study. We see substantial advantages in arrangements for assembling related data sets and placing them in an archive where they would be available for subsequent analyses. Such mechanisms would serve policy needs in several ways. For example, when a major policy is at stake, it is important to confirm the validity of initial analyses. Advances in analytic techniques may uncover information from the data that had not previously been suspected, even though they could undermine or give improved support to previous conclusions. Large-scale policy studies often have features that strain the analytic state of the art, so that the approach actually chosen represents only one possible line of analysis and not the one correct answer. An archive of data from collections of policy studies would encourage secondary analyses of collections of studies rather than simple reanalyses of single studies. Because the costs of secondary analyses are comparatively small, funds for such work should be more readily forthcoming. Another benefit of an archive is that a previously collected set of data (perhaps after minor supplementation or updating) may provide a satisfactory basis for answering new policy questions, thus saving time, money, and effort.

Looking forward to the future, we would stress the role that the flow and cost of information play in a democratic society. As citizens, each of us has a stake in being well-informed, and we expect at least as much of our government and institutions. In turn, this expectation creates a responsibility for us to participate in the system of gathering information for well-conceived purposes.

If information is expensive—that is, if we as individuals yield it only with great reluctance—then the basis for making rational decisions is weakened. Policymakers do not always make rational decisions, but they should at least have the opportunity to do so on the basis of an accurate presentation of the facts.

Ill-informed decisions can affect us in many ways. We feel the consequences

√ socially, when an educational system adopts an inferior program or a court system begins an unevaluated plan for pretrial release of criminal defendants;

√ personally, when we are given an inferior medical or surgical therapy; and

√ financially, when a costly but ineffective way of administering welfare or organizing job training continues in place.

What we don't know *can* hurt us.

REFERENCES

Kemper, P., and Moss, P. 1978. Economic Efficiency of Public Employment Programs. In *Creating Jobs: Public Employment Programs and Wage Subsidies*, J. L. Palmer, ed. Washington, D.C.: Brookings Institution.

Lindblom, C., and Cohen, D. K. 1979. *Usable Knowledge.* New Haven: Yale University Press.

National Research Council. 1974. *Final Report of the Panel on Manpower Training Evaluation: The Use of Social Security Earnings Data for Assessing the Impact of Manpower Training Programs.* Washington, D.C.,: Assembly of Behavioral and Social Sciences, National Research Council—National Academy of Sciences.

Rein, M., and White, S. H. 1977. Can Policy Research Help Policy? *The Public Interest* 52 (Fall): 119–136.

Stigler, G. J. 1981. Legislative Tenure with a supplement on The Tenure of Business Executives. Working Paper Series. Center for the Study of the Economy and the State, University of Chicago.

Stromsdorfer, E. W., and Farkas, G. 1980. *Evaluation Studies Review Annual,* Volume 5. Beverly Hills: Sage Publications. See especially Chapters 12, 13, 16, and 35.

FURTHER READING

Mosteller, F. 1981. Innovation and Evaluation. *Science* 211 (February 27): 881–886.

Index

Record systems
  comparability, 152
  uniformity, 150
Redundancy checking, in management
  records, 157
Reforms, and experiments, 32–33
Regression analysis, 28–31, 68
Rein, M., 297, 299
Reorganization experiments, 50–53
Representative sample, 86
Reproducibility of study, 280
Research Triangle Institute, 97
Responsiveness, and causation, 31
Retirement age, 215
Retrospective comparison, 57
Risk, in simulation, 211
Rivlin, Alice M., 47, 54
Roberts, Harry V., 176, 178
Robinson, John, 136
Roper Poll, 126
Rosenkrantz, Barbara G., 132, 146
Ruckelshaus, William, 1
Ruopp, Richard, 64, 74

Sabin polio vaccine, 128
Saint-Exupéry, Antoine de, 42, 46
Salk polio vaccine case study, 5, 128–129
Samaritans, 133
Samples, 20, 22
  biased, 110
  cluster, 94
  fortuitous, 86
  multistage, 95, 107
  one-shot, 107
  random, 92
  representative, 86
  stratified, 93
Sample surveys, 78–105
  background information collected
    with, 8–9
  call backs in, 96–97
  case studies and, 128–129, 130
  causal relationships in, 78, 90, 100,
    102
  causes of nonresponse in, 95–96
  census and, 102, 166
  clustering in, 94–95
  controlled experiments and, 25–26
  cost of censuses and, 8

data collection in, 90
design refinements in, 92–95
examples of, 2, 78–85
expert choice in, 86–88
in experiments, 20, 39
features of, 85–90
fortuitous samples in, 86
frame in, 90
inaccurate information from
  respondents in, 100
kind of samples in, 85–88
management records and, 155–156,
  161
merits of, 99–100
multistage samples in, 95
nonresponse in, 95–97
objectives of, 88
observational studies with, 56–57
policy implications of, 104–105
population used in, 88
in pre-election polls of 1948, 125
probability sampling in, 88
quality checklist for, 101–104
quality controls in, 104
rare events in, 102
replacing nonrespondents in, 97
results in, 101–102
sample techniques used in, 102–103
sampling organizations in, 97–99
sampling unit in, 90
statement of question in, 101
steps in organizing, 88–90
stratification in, 93–94
strengthening, 91–99
survey instrument description in,
  103
systematic, 156
weaknesses of, 100
Sampling
  in emission standards example, 2
  length-biased, 156
  and management records, 155–156
  physical, 156
  probability, 88
  random, 88
  systematic, 156
Sampling fluctuations, 90
Sargent, Frank, 135, 136
"Scared Straight", 207

ᴜᴇ